A WOMAN
OF INFLUENCE

A WOMAN OF INFLUENCE

The Spectacular Rise of Alice Spencer in Tudor England

VANESSA WILKIE

ATRIA BOOKS

New York   London   Toronto   Sydney   New Delhi

An Imprint of Simon & Schuster, Inc.
1230 Avenue of the Americas
New York, NY 10020

First Atria Books hardcover edition April 2023

ATRIA B O O K S and colophon are trademarks of Simon & Schuster, Inc.

For information about special discounts for bulk purchases, please contact Simon & Schuster Special Sales at 1-866-506-1949 or business@simonandschuster.com.

The Simon & Schuster Speakers Bureau can bring authors to your live event. For more information or to book an event, contact the Simon & Schuster Speakers Bureau at 1-866-248-3049 or visit our website at www.simonspeakers.com.

Interior design by Erika R. Genova

Manufactured in the United States of America

1 3 5 7 9 10 8 6 4 2

Library of Congress Cataloging-in-Publication Data

Names: Wilkie, Vanessa, author.
Title: A woman of influence : the spectacular rise of Alice Spencer in Tudor England / Vanessa Wilkie.
Other titles: Spectacular rise of Alice Spencer in Tudor England
Description: First hardcover edition. | New York : Atria Books, 2023. | Includes bibliographical references and index.
Identifiers: LCCN 2022036961 (print) | LCCN 2022036962 (ebook) | ISBN 9781982154288 | ISBN 9781982154301 (ebook)
Subjects: LCSH: Derby, Alice Egerton, Countess of, 1559–1637. | Nobility—Great Britain—Biography. | Great Britain—History—Elizabeth, 1558–1603. | Great Britain—History—Early Stuarts, 1603–1649.
Classification: LCC DA358.D35 W55 2023 (print) | LCC DA358.D35 (ebook) | DDC 942.05/5092—dc23/eng/20220803
LC record available at https://lccn.loc.gov/2022036961
LC ebook record available at https://lccn.loc.gov/2022036962

ISBN 978-1-9821-5428-8
ISBN 978-1-9821-5430-1 (ebook)

To Matt,
who has been there for every iteration of this

CONTENTS

THE STANLEY WOMEN

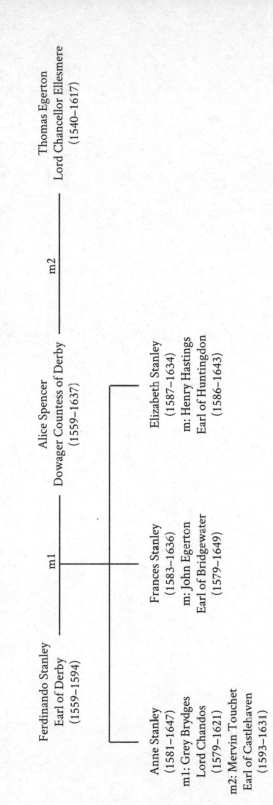

Ferdinando Stanley
Earl of Derby
(1559–1594)

m1

Alice Spencer
Dowager Countess of Derby
(1559–1637)

m2

Thomas Egerton
Lord Chancellor Ellesmere
(1540–1617)

Anne Stanley
(1581–1647)
m1: Grey Brydges
Lord Chandos
(1579–1621)
m2: Mervin Touchet
Earl of Castlehaven
(1593–1631)

Frances Stanley
(1583–1636)
m: John Egerton
Earl of Bridgewater
(1579–1649)

Elizabeth Stanley
(1587–1634)
m: Henry Hastings
Earl of Huntingdon
(1586–1643)

THE SPENCER FAMILY

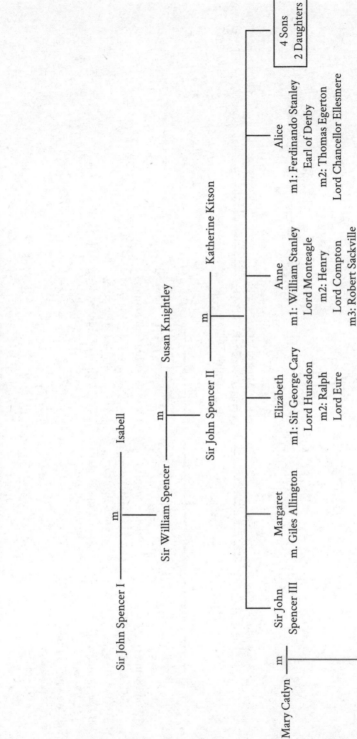

Sir John Spencer I — Isabell

m

Sir William Spencer — Susan Knightley

m

Sir John Spencer II — Katherine Kitson

Margaret
m. Giles Allington

Elizabeth
m1: Sir George Cary
Lord Hunsdon
m2: Ralph
Lord Eure

Anne
m1: William Stanley
Lord Monteagle
m2: Henry
Lord Compton
m3: Robert Sackville
Earl of Dorset

Alice
m1: Ferdinando Stanley
Earl of Derby
m2: Thomas Egerton
Lord Chancellor Ellesmere

Sir John
Spencer III — Mary Catlyn

m

Sir Robert Spencer
Lord Wormleighton

4 Sons
2 Daughters

TUDOR/STANLEY BLOODLINES

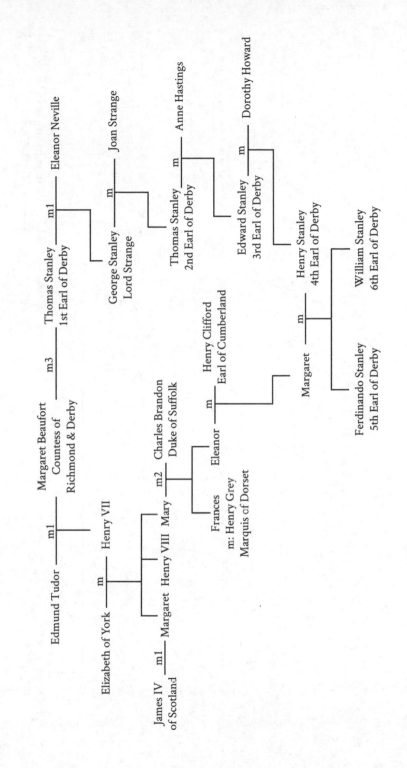

THE EGERTON FAMILY

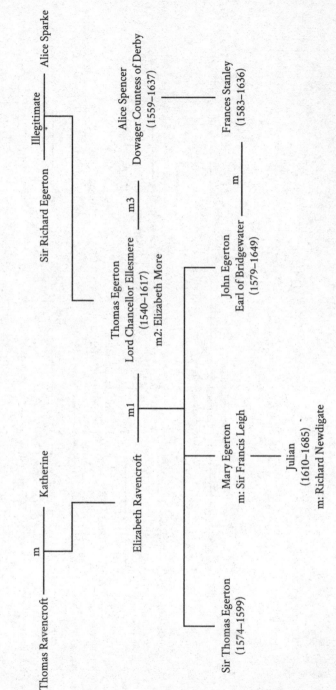

THE BRYDGES FAMILY

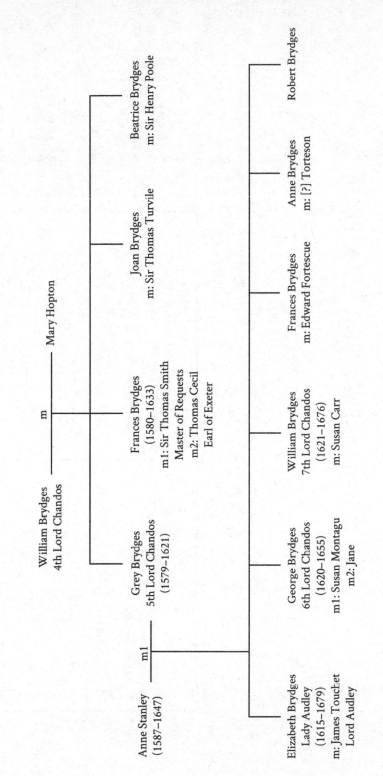

Anne Stanley (1587–1647) ── m1

William Brydges 4th Lord Chandos ── m ── Mary Hopton

Grey Brydges 5th Lord Chandos (1579–1621)

Frances Brydges (1580–1633) m1: Sir Thomas Smith Master of Requests m2: Thomas Cecil Earl of Exeter

Joan Brydges m: Sir Thomas Turvile

Beatrice Brydges m: Sir Henry Poole

Elizabeth Brydges Lady Audley (1615–1679) m: James Touchet Lord Audley

George Brydges 6th Lord Chandos (1620–1655) m1: Susan Montagu m2: Jane

William Brydges 7th Lord Chandos (1621–1676) m: Susan Carr

Frances Brydges m: Edward Fortescue

Anne Brydges m: [?] Torteson

Robert Brydges

THE BRIDGEWATER FAMILY

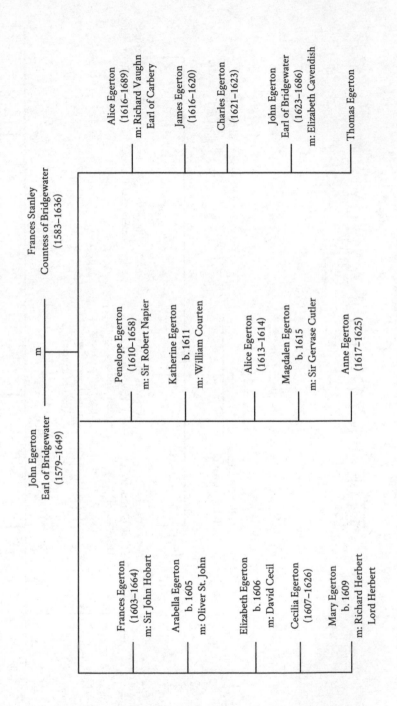

John Egerton
Earl of Bridgewater
(1579–1649)

m

Frances Stanley
Countess of Bridgewater
(1583–1636)

Frances Egerton
(1603–1664)
m: Sir John Hobart

Arabella Egerton
b. 1605
m: Oliver St. John

Elizabeth Egerton
b. 1606
m: David Cecil

Cecilia Egerton
(1607–1626)

Mary Egerton
b. 1609
m: Richard Herbert
Lord Herbert

Penelope Egerton
(1610–1658)
m: Sir Robert Napier

Katherine Egerton
b. 1611
m: William Courten

Alice Egerton
(1613–1614)

Magdalen Egerton
b. 1615
m: Sir Gervase Cutler

Anne Egerton
(1617–1625)

Alice Egerton
(1616–1689)
m: Richard Vaughn
Earl of Carbery

James Egerton
(1616–1620)

Charles Egerton
(1621–1623)

John Egerton
Earl of Bridgewater
(1623–1686)
m: Elizabeth Cavendish

Thomas Egerton

THE HASTINGS FAMILY

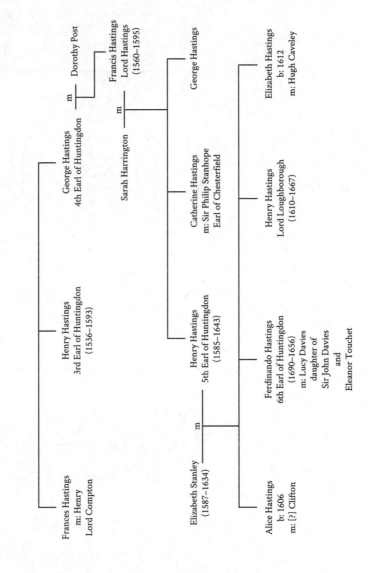

Frances Hastings
m: Henry
Lord Compton

Henry Hastings
3rd Earl of Huntingdon
(1536–1593)

George Hastings
4th Earl of Huntingdon
m Dorothy Post

Francis Hastings
Lord Hastings
(1560–1595)

Sarah Harrington

m

Elizabeth Stanley
(1587–1634)

m

Henry Hastings
5th Earl of Huntingdon
(1585–1643)

Catherine Hastings
m: Sir Philip Stanhope
Earl of Chesterfield

George Hastings

Alice Hastings
b: 1606
m: [?] Clifton

Ferdinando Hastings
6th Earl of Huntingdon
(1690–1656)
m: Lucy Davies
daughter of
Sir John Davies
and
Eleanor Touchet

Henry Hastings
Lord Loughborough
(1610–1667)

Elizabeth Hastings
b: 1612
m: Hugh Caveley

THE TOUCHET FAMILY

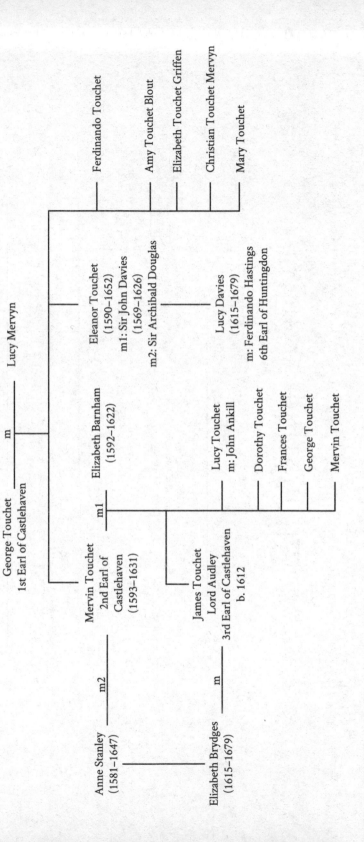

George Touchet
1st Earl of Castlehaven

— m —

Lucy Mervyn

Anne Stanley
(1581–1647)

— m2 —

Mervin Touchet
2nd Earl of
Castlehaven
(1593–1631)

Elizabeth Barnham
(1592–1622)

— m1 —

Ferdinando Touchet

Eleanor Touchet
(1590–1652)
m1: Sir John Davies
(1569–1626)

m2: Sir Archibald Douglas

Amy Touchet Blout

Elizabeth Touchet Griffen

Christian Touchet Mervyn

Mary Touchet

Elizabeth Brydges
(1615–1679)

— m —

James Touchet
Lord Audley
3rd Earl of Castlehaven
b. 1612

Lucy Touchet
m: John Ankill

Dorothy Touchet

Frances Touchet

George Touchet

Mervin Touchet

Lucy Davies
(1615–1679)

m: Ferdinando Hastings
6th Earl of Huntingdon

NOTES ON DATES, SPELLING AND GRAMMAR, AND CURRENCIES

DATES

At the beginning of the sixteenth century, all of Europe used the Julian calendar, named after Julius Caesar. In October 1582, most countries in western Europe shifted to the Gregorian calendar, named after Pope Gregory XIII. To make the conversion, they skipped ahead ten days and then resumed consecutive dating in a twelve-month cycle. After that, English dating, which remained in the old Julian system, was ten days behind the rest of western Europe. For example, June 20 in France was June 10 in England.

To complicate matters further, continental Europe advanced its year on January 1, whereas England took March 25 to be the first day of the new calendar year. For example, an English woman would date a letter "10 March 1592," whereas a Spanish woman would date a letter written on that same day "20 March 1593." Countries that used the Julian calendar were said to use the Old Style (O.S.) of dating, whereas those on the Gregorian calendar were in the New Style (N.S.), and when people wrote letters between England and the European continent, they would frequently mark their dates "O.S." or "N.S." to help keep things straight. England remained on the Julian calendar until 1752.

In this book, the Old Style dates are retained, but New Year's is taken to be January 1, so years have been modernized, while days and months remain in the old style. Dates are rendered in the Americanized format of month-day-year, for example, December 31, 1594.

SPELLING AND GRAMMAR

Spelling and punctuation were not standardized in England until the eighteenth century, and even then, standards evolved gradually. In this book, printed book titles are represented as they appeared in the sixteenth and seventeenth centuries, but the spelling and grammar of all quotes from printed works and manuscripts have been modernized and standardized according to today's conventions. Abbreviations have been expanded and modernized. All spellings have been converted to standard American English conventions.

CURRENCIES

In the sixteenth and seventeenth centuries, England used a currency system based on pounds (£), shillings (s), and pence (d):

£1 = 20 s

1 s = 12 d

The UK and Ireland shifted to a decimalized currency system on February 15, 1971.

There is not a simple or clean formula for converting money in the past to modern values. Inflation is just one complication, but money did not buy the same things in sixteenth-century England that it buys today, not only because there were different commodities but because commodities had a different value. For example, in preindustrial feudal Europe, a horse was essential for both tilling fields and transportation, whereas today horses, though prized, serve a different function in society and are therefore valued differently.

Monetary value, however, can still be a useful marker. For this reason, monetary amounts are listed in this book as they were in the sixteenth and seventeenth centuries and are followed by a modern equivalent estimate generated by the online Currency Converter: 1270–2017, provided by the National Archives in the United Kingdom. This amount is also presented in current US dollars based on the online XE Currency Converter. These amounts should not be read as precise but are merely intended to provide a rough comparison for modern readers.

Mark what radiant state she spreads,
In circle round her shining throne
Shooting her beams like silver threads:
This, this is she alone,
Sitting like a Goddess bright
In the center of her light . . .

I will bring you where she sits,
Clad in splendor as befits
Her deity.
Such a rural Queen
All Arcadia hath not seen.

John Milton, *Arcades*
For Alice, Dowager Countess of Derby, c. 1632

INTRODUCTION

Today, the Spencer family name is known the world over, and Althorp, their ancestral estate, is the home of the ninth Earl and Countess Spencer. A small island in an ornamental lake on Althorp's grounds is the final resting place of the earl's sister, Diana, Princess of Wales. When the summer days turn warm and before the autumn chill sets in, visitors flock to the colossal estate to pay their respects to the "People's Princess," tour the Spencer home filled with works of art and artifacts, and daydream about what it might have been like to grow up in one of the world's most famous houses or even to have one of the world's most famous last names. Some visitors push their imaginations deeper into the past, to the Althorp of the eighteenth century, when it was the childhood home of Georgiana Cavendish, Duchess of Devonshire, who in recent decades has come alive again as a protagonist in books and films. Georgiana certainly made a splash in her era and Princess Diana remains a beloved figure to this day, but it was another young Spencer woman who first put the family on the map.

When Alice Spencer was born at Althorp on May 4, 1559, the estate was nothing more than a modest manor home in the middle of some of the best pasture lands in the northern hemisphere, and its owners were a family of sheep farmers. Alice was born the youngest daughter of a country knight, and by the age of twenty-one, she had become among the first of her family to join the ranks of the English aristocracy by marrying Ferdinando Stanley, heir to the earldom of Derby and great-great-grandson of King Henry VII. Her last name may have changed and her social circle broadened, but she never forgot where she had come from.

It can be tempting to see Alice's life as an origin story of a family that is now a dynasty, but to look solely through that lens would be to miss so much. Alice Spencer, who used the title Dowager Countess of Derby for most of her life, lived fully and assertively in her own time, maintaining an unwavering devotion to preserving and elevating the status of the people she loved.

The detailed experiences of a woman's life in the sixteenth and seventeenth centuries can be challenging to know, in large part because the absence of female voices has left lacunae in the historical record. Yet Alice and her three daughters are among the best-documented women of their time, with the obvious exception of Queen Elizabeth I. This is principally because Alice was extremely litigious and, through her legal pursuits, we can trace her actions, motivations, and desires. At the end of Queen Elizabeth's reign, Alice waged a thirteen-year-long inheritance lawsuit against her estranged brother-in-law while negotiating advantageous marriages for her daughters, petitioning the courts, and serving as a patron to some of the most famous poets of the era. In the 1630s, toward the end of her life, she once again entered the legal fray, this time in defense of her eldest daughter, Anne, when she came forward with the horrific account that she had been sexually assaulted by a servant and that her own husband had orchestrated the act. The subsequent trials were among the most scandalous events of the age, and the experiences of these women provide a critical insight into the history of sexual violence and the price of survival.

Alice's life presents an alternative to the modern perception that women in the patriarchal past were typically complicit in allowing their fathers, husbands, and the culture at large to push them around like pieces on a chessboard. Alice was not a feminist, but she was an operator and a woman who was cognizant of the power that came with her social status, power she was eager to wield. More important, she understood how to use that power to advocate for both herself and those around her. She did not break down any barriers or fight to change the system; what made her remarkable was how effective she was at successfully navigating that system. When she was most vulnerable, she took control of her own life, and she raised her daughters to do likewise. Collectively they left a bounty of documented evidence that we can follow back into the past to see how women such as Alice made their way in a dangerous and hierarchical world with unrelenting resolve—and stunning success.

PART I

CHAPTER ONE

SPENCERS ON THE RISE

"A Mere Knight's Daughter"

It was a frosty winter day in 1636 when Alice Spencer, Dowager Countess of Derby, entered the tiny country church of St. Mary the Virgin. A patchwork of stone and brick with a stubby crenellated tower, the church had served the faithful in the village of Harefield, some twenty-five miles west of London, since the twelfth century. Alice herself had worshipped there for nearly four decades. Age and the cold winter had taken a toll on her body, but her mind was as sharp as ever. It was not piety that drew her to the church that particular day. The seventy-six-year-old Dowager Countess of Derby had come to inspect the tomb she had commissioned for herself. She determinedly made her way to the upper chancel, at the far end of the church next to the pulpit, and gazed upon the massive painted-stone monument that had just been completed to her exacting specifications. Alice could not leave something this important in the hands of her surviving family; she intended to prepare for her death with the same controlling eye and attention to detail she employed in all aspects of her life. Her choice of location ensured that her final resting place would serve as the backdrop to every sermon delivered in the small church. When the parishioners' minds wandered, their eyes would be drawn to the vibrant heraldry, carved canopy, and pious figures carved into her burial site. She must have taken pleasure in the thought that the stone behemoth would ensure that generations to come would be continuously reminded of her life, her deeds, and, most important, her family.

Two sides of the tomb were nestled against the heavy walls of the church, but Alice could walk along the front and foot of her memorial to inspect every detail of the carving. The effigy of her body, swathed in a red dress and with her hands at her chest pressed in a prayerful position, was laid on a carved stone curtain painted black. Three small niches supported the tablet on which her effigy rested, and tucked into each recess was a small kneeling figure of a woman in a matching red dress. The figures represented her three beloved daughters, who could be told apart only by the small heraldic crest carved next to each one. Alice, like her peers, read heraldry as a second language. It took only a passing glance to know who was who, although she might well have lingered over the crest for her eldest daughter. She would want to ensure that there were no indications of her daughter's disastrous second marriage. Alice had spent the last five years of her life desperately trying to sever any connections between her family and her disgraced son-in-law. She would never allow his badge to adorn the monument that would serve as the most prominent and enduring marker of her life.

Standing alongside her tomb, Alice looked down at the effigy of her own body with its long waves of hair cascading down around the shoulders. Her stone face was smooth and pale, revealing no sign of the passage of time; the carver had made her ageless. As Alice's eyes moved up toward the top of the tomb, past the carved black-and-gold tablets that recounted her own two marriages and the noble positions held by each of her long-dead husbands, her gaze reached the top of the green-and-gold carved stone canopy that arched up over her recumbent figure. Four crowned griffins, the symbol of the Spencer family, peered out in different directions from pedestals at the base of the dome. The tomb was topped with Alice's own coat of arms, flanked by supporters of another Spencer griffin, on the right, and the stag, a symbol of the Stanley family, on the left, representing her dear first husband. A countess's coronet sat atop the coat of arms, reaching up to Heaven. Alice knew that someday soon her body would be interred in the base of that tomb. The monument reflected everything she wanted to be remembered for, presenting her carefully crafted legacy for the ages. But there had been far more to Alice's life than any monument could portray.

Nearly 150 years earlier, Alice's ancestors could only have hoped that a member of their family would someday hold such a high place in aristocratic society. The Spencers of the early 1500s were midland farmers, shrewd and lucky enough to grow their modest lands and enterprises over time. Alice's grandfather William Spencer of Radbourn purchased the estate of Althorp in Northamptonshire, seventy-five miles northwest of London, in 1508 with money he had made in the sheep trade. At the time, the residence at Althorp was a large Tudor manor house, a two-story redbrick building with thick, exposed wooden beams and long, narrow windows. Though far from a lavish Tudor palace or the colossal estate Althorp would eventually become, it was a more spacious and comfortable home than most farmers in England possessed at the time. The high ceilings, private rooms, multiple fireplaces, thick roof, and decorative furnishings kept the Spencers warm in winter and set them apart from their neighbors.

The rules of feudal England dictated that land was the currency of power and the primary source of wealth. The ancient aristocracy passed their lands from one generation to the next and wielded power over tenant farmers, but men such as William Spencer, men with no titles, used their modest incomes to buy land when they could and thus gradually carved out their own small pockets of power. The monarch had the prerogative to grant land, which came with aristocratic titles as well, to families who had served the Crown. The arrangement made some families powerful, although not necessarily wealthy, and in turn bolstered their loyalty to the reigning monarch, an essential strategy for maintaining political stability. From the Crown's perspective, however, it could often be more lucrative to sell land to families such as the Spencers rather than to grant the privilege of ownership to peers. So when a feudal king wanted to go to war, for example, selling land was a quick way to raise money. After 1536, when King Henry VIII broke with the Roman Catholic Church and placed all ecclesiastical lands in England under his jurisdiction, the Tudor king had a bounty of lands to distribute, either to ensure the loyalty of noble families or to sell to gentry families and bring cash into the royal treasury. But the aristocracy feared that if more families could simply purchase land rather than inheriting it and thus gain local power, the social and political supremacy of the peerage would be threatened.[1]

The Spencers would soon become one of the families the ancient nobility was worried about. William became Sir William in 1529, when he was knighted by Henry VIII. He died just three years later, in 1532, and his son, John, inherited Althorp and the other parcels and estates his father had acquired. A knighthood was not hereditary, so John, like his father and grandfather before him, hoped that one day the reigning monarch would decide to grant him the same title in recognition of his loyalty and as an acknowledgment of his family's local influence. Capitalizing on the rich grazing lands he had inherited, John continued to invest in the sheep and wool trade, and by the middle of the century, he was one of the nation's leading providers of wool, mutton, and sheep. In 1545, he married Katherine Kitson, the daughter of Sir Thomas Kitson of Hengrave Hall, Suffolk, a wealthy merchant. Eight years later, John was knighted at Queen Mary I's coronation, making him Sir John and his wife Lady Katherine and enabling him to reestablish himself in the role his father had held.

English society, like that of the rest of Europe, operated on a strict hierarchy of social rank. The Spencers' knighthoods placed them in a social rank above other yeoman farmers, families who owned their own land but had not been granted knighthoods. Though knights were ranked higher than yeomen, yeomen were socially above tenant farmers, who only rented their lands. John's knighthood elevated his immediate family into the gentry, a class just below the nobility. Gentry families owned land and were granted coats of arms, although unlike the nobility's, the arms were not hereditary. Gentry families aspired to ascend into the nobility, which would enable the accumulation of hereditary titles, offices in service to the monarch, and typically control over larger portions of lands, which meant more rental incomes from tenants. A knighthood provided the potential for social stability for a single generation; a noble title provided social stability for the future. The English nobility, or peerage, contained another set of rankings; the lowest was baron/baroness; then viscount/viscountess; then earl/countess; then marquess/marchioness; and finally, duke/duchess. The sanctified inner circle of the ruling monarch and his or her immediate family sat at the top. John's elevation to the gentry meant that a place in the peerage hovered just above the Spencers, but the family still had work to do if they wanted to continue their rise.

John served as the sheriff and justice of the peace for Northamptonshire, two high-ranking local appointments granted by more powerful local noble families with the monarch's approval. John and Katherine were well positioned to maintain their new place in society, but, like most families of the age, they surely had hopes of improving their station. English gentry and peers in the sixteenth century thought in terms of multigenerational progress, understanding that sustainable change in feudal England happened only gradually and required careful planning—and, most important, a male heir. Katherine and John were already proud parents of a daughter, Margaret, but in 1549, the couple welcomed their eldest son and heir into the world and named him John. Katherine continued to spend most of the 1550s pregnant, ultimately giving birth to two more sons and five daughters by the end of the decade.

In May 1559 Katherine Spencer took to her birthing chamber for the ninth time. Mothers may have gained wisdom with experience, but no matter how many times a woman entered the birthing chamber, it was a terrifying and uncertain place. A midwife monitored Katherine in anticipation of the baby's arrival, and Katherine's female kin would have been there to hold her arms and wipe away her tears, blood, and sweat. When the time came, the women flanked Katherine's writhing body, holding her upright. As Katherine pushed and screamed, the midwife guided the child down, watching to ensure that the umbilical cord stayed clear of the baby's neck. As the baby was carried down and Katherine fell back into the arms of the women who had been holding her up, they saw that the Spencers had another girl to join their family of three sons and now six daughters at Althorp. They named her Alice.

As the youngest daughter of a local knight with eight other children, one might assume that Alice was frequently overlooked in the bustling family. But to a child with an active mind like Alice, Althorp would likely have seemed an Arcadian heaven, a comfortable nest in the center of verdant pasture lands and rolling hills as far as the eye could see. Her father had started planting oak trees near the house, many of which are still there today. The home teemed with servants who cleaned, chopped and stocked firewood, cooked, and attended to the needs of the family. Alice probably spent little time with her father, as he was occupied with the responsibilities of his local offices, managing the family's growing rental incomes, and overseeing the management of his valuable livestock. It would have been with her mother and the servants charged with caring for the Spencer children that Alice spent most hours of the day. Of all her siblings, Alice seems to have been particularly close to her sisters Elizabeth, eight years her senior, and Anne, a bit closer to her own age. The bonds they forged as children at Althorp would endure throughout their lives.

Beyond his business pursuits, John Spencer was invested in preparing his sons, particularly his eldest, to run the estate one day, while Katherine was responsible for overseeing the religious upbringing of the children, as well as their general education. This included all her daughters and sons, before the boys were sent away to school and after that to study law at the Inns of Court. The Spencers followed the norm for wealthy gentry families in ensuring that their sons received a formal education to prepare them for the responsibilities of local political office or a position as a clerk or secretary to one of the country's more powerful noblemen. They put the same care into ensuring their daughters received the standard education for gentry girls. Alice and her sisters had tutors to teach them to read, write, play musical instruments, draw, and embroider, all the skills that made refined young women desirable brides possessing the skills needed to manage their own estates one day. Whereas the children born to most noble households would have learned Latin and French, there are no sources to suggest that Alice and her sisters could read languages beyond English, and the Spencers were still a minor family of no particular distinction beyond their growing wealth. But all the Spencer girls were taught to read English, and their early childhood educations gave Alice, Anne, and Elizabeth their first glimpses of life beyond Althorp. That foundation was critical to the development of the devoted patrons of the arts they would go on to be, supporting an impressive array of poets, writers, and theologians.

The Spencer children's religious education would have been molded by the age of tumultuous religious change they were living through. Since the 1530s, the country had endured massive upheavals brought about by the Reformation, when Henry VIII had broken with the Roman Catholic Church to establish a Protestant Church in England. During her nearly five-year reign in the middle of the century, Henry's daughter, Mary I, firmly pulled the country back into line with Rome through her Counter-Reformation, but her half sister Elizabeth's ascension to the throne in 1558, a year before Alice's birth, meant the restoration of a Protestant Church in England. The Spencers were loyal subjects and seemed to adhere to the reigning monarch's religious policies. As conformists, the family returned to the observation of the new Protestant faith, attending the local church regularly. Alice only ever knew her family and her country as Protestant, but she was surely raised to understand that loyalty to the reigning monarch in all things was essential to survival, to say nothing of success.

As her father's wealth continued to grow, young Alice's daily life would have been removed from the chaos that lay just beyond her picturesque minia-ture realm, but the Spencers knew they needed to prepare all of their children to thrive in a harsh and uncertain world. Alice would only gradually learn of the disdain her family faced from those both below and above them in the social hierarchy. Since the end of the turbulent Wars of the Roses in 1485, Henry VII and his son and successor, Henry VIII, had enacted a series of enclosure laws that allowed landowners such as the Spencers to plant thick hedgerows and put up fences that prevented local people and tenants from accessing pastures, meadows, and forests, essentially converting common lands into private prop-erty. Sir John and his father quickly realized that their lands would generate far more money from sheep farming than from rents they might collect from tenant farmers. Under the Spencers in the sixteenth century, 27,000 acres in Northamptonshire were completely enclosed, forcing 1,500 people to abandon their rented lands and common pastures and cutting off access to firewood and kindling.[2] Local farmers and laborers detested the Spencers, as people starved while the Spencers' sheep grazed all day. Enclosure riots routinely ravaged the countryside as farmers dug up or burned the Spencers' thick hedgerows, at-tacked their flocks, and trespassed to gather essential food and fuel. But young Alice, who was not due to inherit or run the family lands, would have grown up protected from and largely oblivious to those disturbances.

Not only did the Spencers face disdain from the struggling tenant farmers, but the family was loathed by their "betters." In the second half of the 1500s, the members of the English aristocracy believed that they were facing a crisis as the numbers of peers decreased while the gentry class grew vastly wealthier. What money is in a modern capitalist society, land was in feudal Europe, and power came from controlling land as the source of everything: food, textiles, fuel, and rental income. Tensions grew between members of the old aristoc-racy and England's nouveaux riches, and by the time Alice was a young girl, the Spencers had become a highly visible emblem of the rising gentry. They had the land and money but not the titles. Without joining the ranks of the aristocracy, their sphere of influence would never extend beyond their mid-land farms. Alice's grandfather had started the Spencers on their upward tra-jectory when he had purchased Althorp and expanded their landholdings; the enclosure laws and their bountiful lands had enabled the family's rise—at the enormous cost to the tenant families around them—into the ranks of the gentry. Now Alice's mother and father needed to do their part to ensure that the family's future would be even brighter. It was time for their children to wed.

—◆—————◆—————◆—

Fertile land and fertile marriage were the two most powerful tools available to families such as the Spencers. Sir John and Lady Katherine enacted a two-part strategy in arranging the marriages of their children: first, to ensure a stable line of inheritance for the Spencer lands and the family's positions of local authority; second, to use their capital wealth to seek opportunities to marry into higher social circles. People often think that in feudal England sons were all that mattered, but this is untrue. Though the patriarchal social structure and practice of primogeniture meant that every family wanted a son as an heir to protect the descent of property and carry on the family name, daughters were often the key players in marriages that elevated family networks. Coverture practices, wherein wives took their husband's last names, have meant that over the centuries we often detach daughters from their natal families because their last names changed. But families looking to rise relied on the networks their daughters forged to advance their interests and status, and those were critical alliances that we miss if we follow only sons and natal surnames, such as Spencer. Sir John and Lady Katherine cared deeply about finding the best possible match for their son and heir, but it was their daughters who had the potential to elevate the family to breathtaking heights. The couple therefore devoted an enormous amount of time and resources to the marriages of their daughters.

Sir John and Lady Katherine's eldest daughter, Margaret, was in her early teens when Alice was born, and the couple had five more daughters whom they would need to place in good marriages. The timing of arranging matches for a family such as the Spencers was delicate, and they did not want to have too many daughters on the marriage market at once. Arranging good matches was a costly business, so it was to the family's benefit to space out the unions. The English laws of coverture stipulated that when a woman married, all her property, landed or movable, belonged to her husband, so providing a girl with a substantial dowry was a way to entice a husband of high status. Wealthy parents set aside money, lands, gold and silver objects (called plate), or even fine textiles to make up their daughter's dowry. Marriage contracts were typically negotiated between the parents of the bride and groom, and despite the popular misconception today, mothers often played a critical role in the negotiations.

Part of the marriage contract established the dowry, the cash, the leases, and the movable property, including the household goods and clothing the wife would bring to the marriage. The rest of the contract established any financial incentives the husband might provide for the wife for the duration of their marriage and establish what would happen if a wife outlived her husband. A contract often specified that if the husband died before the wife, especially if he did not have a written will, she could receive up to a third of the estate's value, called the dower portion (not to be confused with the dowry she had brought to the marriage). If the couple had children, the remainder of the husband's estate would typically go to the male heir. If a couple had no sons, the husband could dictate in his will if property would pass to the husband's next closest living male relative, such as a younger brother, to the couple's eldest daughter, or be split among daughters. Not unlike today, however, real life was messier than standard practices suggest, and inheritance disputes were common in England at the time.

English law, unlike the laws in other European countries at the time, also allowed for women with substantial means to negotiate something called a jointure in lieu of accepting a dower portion. A jointure specified properties to be held in reserve for the wife if she were to become a widow, and she could draw income from those lands for the rest of her life. A jointure could be settled at the time of the initial marriage contract or be negotiated later as a separate agreement. It could even go so far as to give a blanket promise of an annual cash income from any source for a wife, to be paid not just through her marriage but for the duration of her life. Sometimes a jointure even stipulated that a wife would receive certain revenues during the course of her marriage and continue to receive them after her husband's death. The value of a jointure could far exceed the one-third value of an estate granted by a dower portion, and the land was protected from her husband's mismanagement once it was placed in the jointure. He could never take out, sell, or grant leases on the lands held within her jointure without consent, typically by a male family member she had appointed to serve as her agent while she was married, although she would still be required to consent to changes made to her jointure. If a wife had a jointure, her husband could add to it over the course of their marriage, but he could not use it for his own benefit.

Whereas a modern-day prenuptial agreement establishes how assets should be divided if a husband and wife divorce, a jointure was intended to ensure that specific assets would be protected for the wife if her husband were to predecease her. Jointures were a mechanism that provided women with some independent financial security at a time when they usually possessed very little. And when a wife inherited her jointure, she often retained control over the lands even if she were to remarry. (Divorce was so uncommon at the time that marriage contracts did not include contingency plans in the event that a marriage did not work out.) A jointure not only provided wealthier women with a degree of financial protection but was also a sign that the bride, or whomever had acted on her behalf, had exerted considerable power in the negotiations.[3] Again, however, life was often messier in reality than on paper, and ill-informed wives could consent to the mismanagement of their jointures and lose everything.

In 1563, the Spencers arranged for a jointure in the proposed marriage between their eldest daughter, Margaret, and George Forman, the son of another Northamptonshire gentleman. The contract stipulated that the marriage had to take place by Michaelmas (the feast of St. Michael, held in late September) in 1565, and the jointure required Margaret to be paid the considerable sum of £200 per year (£47,000/$65,000 today) during their marriage.[4] The Spencers had the clout to establish a jointure for Margaret, but she was marrying into another local family, not an influential noble family. For reasons unknown to us, the marriage never took place, as sometimes happened, but the failed arrangement still tells us that the Spencers held the upper hand in their local marriage market and gives a sense of their early expectations.

By the time the arrangement lapsed, John Spencer III had come of age and Sir John and Lady Katherine shifted their focus to finding a wife for their son.

As he was their heir, the stakes were much higher. In 1566, he married Mary Catlyn, the daughter of another local gentry family. Her father was a judge at the Court of Common Pleas and ultimately became a judge of the King's Bench. Mary brought the income of several lucrative manors to the marriage, and she did not secure a jointure, a strategic win for the Spencers and their heir.[5] The estate would remain intact for John III and Mary Catlyn's heir.

With young John now married and Althorp and the family estates seemingly secured for the immediate future, Alice's parents again turned their attention to arranging marriages for their daughters. In 1570, Margaret wed a different local gentleman, Giles Allington.[6] Within a few years, Alice's sister Katherine married Thomas Leigh, Esquire, of Stoneleigh Abbey. Thomas was the third son in his family, but his father settled his estate by ensuring that all of his sons would inherit in equal parts. The Leighs were not from Northamptonshire, so that marriage marked a transition for the Spencers. Though Thomas Leigh was the son of a knight, a horizontal move along the social playing field, his family came from outside the county, were well connected, and like the Spencers, were quite wealthy. Thomas's father had made his fortune in overseas trade, so the Leigh-Spencer match brought two new fortunes together. Things were looking promising for the Spencers.

By the mid-1570s, Sir John and Lady Katherine were no longer satisfied with a family tree made up of local sheep farmers and merchants. From 1570 to 1580, the Spencers' profits from selling wool were at least £2,632 a year (£630,000/$870,000 today), and they were ready to reinvest the funds in marriages, not sheep.[7] Despite the simmering social tensions between establishment families and upstarts such as the Spencers, noble families needed to find wives with large dowries, and the Spencer girls came from one of the wealthiest families in the realm. As Alice was the youngest, she would need to be patient and wait her turn, but as a young woman in her midteens, she would have paid close attention to what was about to happen; marriage was practically a spectator sport, especially when her sisters' marriages could hint at her own future possibilities. Sir John and Lady Katherine made their first leap in 1574, with the marriage of their daughter Elizabeth to Sir George Carey. Carey was Queen Elizabeth's cousin, as his grandmother had been Mary Boleyn, Anne Boleyn's sister. Alice's new brother-in-law was an influential and well-connected man. By the 1570s, as the peerage continued to shrink under the frugal Queen Elizabeth, that was the perfect arrangement; men such as George Carey came with noble titles, while women such as Elizabeth Spencer came from cash-rich families.

The following year, 1575, Sir John and Lady Katherine arranged another lofty match when their daughter Anne married William Stanley, Lord Monteagle. Monteagle's father was Thomas Stanley, a younger brother of Henry Stanley, the fourth Earl of Derby. Though he did not enjoy the same landed wealth and status as his uncle's family did, Monteagle was well established nonetheless. The only potential blemish to his reputation was his religious affiliation. Lancashire, a northern county on the west of England, 165 miles south of Edinburgh and 250 miles north of London, was a hotbed of recusant Catholics throughout the sixteenth century, and the Stanley family played fluctuating roles in both suppressing and supporting the county's Catholic population. There was considerable speculation that Monteagle himself remained a practicing Catholic. Welcoming a wealthy Protestant woman into the family could only help the Stanleys improve their reputation. The Spencers were willing to overlook Monteagle's religion and focus on his noble family and lofty connections at court, suggesting that they cared more about gaining entrée to the aristocracy than about religious affiliation.[8]

✦━━━✦━━━✦

In 1580, it was finally Alice's turn, and Sir John and Lady Katherine arranged for her the most distinguished marriage of all their children. The twenty-year-old Alice was to be joined to Ferdinando Stanley, Lord Strange, heir to the fourth Earl of Derby. The young couple probably met at Anne and Monteagle's wedding, but they may not have known each other very well when their families began the negotiations. The details of their marriage agreement do not survive, but the marriage was a triumph for the Spencers. The Earl of Derby's family tree made the Spencers' own look like a sapling. Ferdinando was the great-great-grandson of Henry VII. His grandmother was Mary, sister of Henry VIII, who had been married to the King of France. With her marriage to Ferdinando, Alice Spencer left a rising gentry family and took her place among one of the sixteenth century's most prominent aristocratic families. Her in-laws controlled the county of Lancashire, a right that Thomas Cromwell had granted the third Earl of Derby in the 1530s in exchange for his support in suppressing the Pilgrimage of Grace, a Catholic uprising, and other recusant activities.[9] The Stanleys were also the Lords of the Isle of Man. The Crown had given the Stanleys the isle in 1406, and in 1522, the Privy Council had ruled that the isle was "not of the Realm of England," which gave the Stanley family complete control over the government of the isle as their own mini-kingdom.[10] Though the isle's population was relatively small, the independent control of the isle gave the Stanley family enormous clout among the English aristocracy. The Stanley family was subservient to the kings and queens of England, but controlling the Isle of Man made them kings in their own right, even if their rule extended over only a 220-square-mile island in the middle of the Irish Sea.

Alice's sister Anne's marriage to Monteagle had been the bridge the Spencers needed to gain access to his cousin, but the match was also supported by the queen's "favorite," Robert Dudley, Earl of Leicester. He had invested in a small portion of the Spencers' sheep enterprises a few years before, and the financial arrangement seems to have opened the door for a venture into the marriage market for both Leicester and the Spencers.[11] People speculated that the Earl of Leicester had sought to find a rich Protestant wife for the Earl of Derby's son to help stabilize his own political relations in the North. Ferdinando's ancestry meant that he was a potential successor to Queen Elizabeth, so his marriage was far more important than that of the average earl's heir. Leicester seized the chance to participate in arranging the match, thus making friends with the wealthy Spencers, bringing another young Protestant bride into the suspiciously Catholic North, and winning political favor with the Stanleys.

Alice and Ferdinando were probably married in the North in a chapel near Knowsley Hall, the Stanley family's seat in Lancashire. Everyone in attendance would have been sumptuously dressed in lush silks and velvets embroidered with shining silver and gold threads.[12] Sir John would have escorted Alice down the aisle to signal his blessing of the union. Alice and Ferdinando would have stood side by side at the front of the church with all eyes upon them. Ferdinando looked like the quintessential heir to an earldom. His wavy brown hair grazed the tops of his shoulders. The sharpness of his hairline matched that of his tightly pointed goatee. Just above his light blue eyes, his forehead was marked with a pronounced mole. Alice stood to his left. Her dark hair matched her equally dark eyes, and her long thin nose came to a sudden curve at the end. Standing in front of the altar, they would have made a striking pair, but their families cared far more about what the union represented; they were about to witness a financial merger sanctified by God.

The minister asked Alice and Ferdinando if they would "forsake all others," to which they both responded, "I will." Sir John then gave his consent to the union, and Alice and Ferdinando proceeded with their vows. Ferdinando slipped a band on Alice's left ring finger, an act that would change both their lives. There would have been prayers and perhaps a service as outlined in the Book of Common Prayer, the state-sanctioned prayer book of the Protestant Church in England, or a short sermon offered by the minister. The conclusion of the ceremony meant the beginning of the revelry. Alice and Ferdinando embarked on their life together with an elaborate feast, musicians, theatrics, and dancing, as friends and family toasted to the happy couple. Though Alice and Ferdinando were at the center of the jubilation, the party was also for the Stanley and Spencer families, as both sides believed they had a chance at a prosperous future together.

The Earl of Leicester served as witness to "the match he made betwixt a mere knight's daughter and the noble Earl of Derby's son and heir."[13] The problem was, he had neglected to get approval for the marriage from the queen, who had the right to vet all marriages in noble families and was notoriously prickly about any conversation pertaining to the line of succession. Fortunately for Alice and her parents, the queen's displeasure was directed at Leicester and she ultimately approved the union between Ferdinando and Alice. She eventually forgave Leicester and accepted Alice into her nobility.

From the moment Alice took her vows, she was no longer just the youngest daughter of a "mere knight"; her new family ruled a kingdom of their own, and the expectations for her were high. The marriages of her brother and sisters had been stepping-stones along a path that led away from the sheep farm of Althorp and into the estates of Knowsley Hall and Lathom Hall, the Stanley ancestral homes. Alice would no longer be called Spencer but instead Lady Strange. Still, her new title would not erase her commitment to her family. If anything, her new name and title could open doors for those around her and indeed were expected to. Any children from her union would be born into the earldom of Derby, and royal blood would flow through their veins.

CHAPTER TWO

MARRIAGE AND MOTHERHOOD

"The Very Pattern of Right Nobility"

The twenty-year-old Alice found both love and power when she married Ferdinando Stanley, Lord Strange and heir to the Earl of Derby, in 1580. Of course, love between an aristocratic husband and wife often looked more like a mutual respect than the deep intimate connection people today expect marital love to be. Later in her marriage, Alice wrote to a friend to compliment her husband's "uprightness and honorable carriage," two qualities most wives in the sixteenth century would have been grateful to find in a husband.[1] Alice, like other young women of her station, had probably not been given a choice in her marriage, and in truth, Ferdinando had likely had little or no choice, either. Both understood their familial duties and seem to have assumed their roles as husband and wife with grace and compassion.

That is not to say that the transition to married life was an easy one, especially for Alice, who left her pastoral childhood behind to assume new responsibilities in a particularly powerful dynasty. Ferdinando's family controlled the northern English counties of Cheshire and Lancashire and the Isle of Man with enormous independence. Following the turmoil of the Wars of the Roses, the decades-long clash in the middle of the fifteenth century between the Lancaster and York families over which dynasty would rule England, the Tudors had actively sought to consolidate and centralize their power over the nobility. They were keen to prevent any noble families from acting as mini-monarchs and forced them to fall into line under the ruling king or queen. By the mid–sixteenth century, most noble families no longer enjoyed the kinds of medieval privileges they had been accustomed to when they had governed their local regions with relative autonomy. But the Stanleys' blood relationship with the Tudors, coupled with their wise choice to submit to the reigning Tudor monarch and avoid causing trouble in London politics, meant that they continued to hold their ancient privileges.

Though Elizabeth I ruled the realm from London, people had taken to calling the Stanleys' household the great "northern court."[2] Lathom Hall had been their ancestral home, but the family routinely moved among Lathom, Knowsley Hall, and New Park, creating a compound of estates comprised of vast parks, tenant farms, pasture lands, and local villages. In the early fifteenth century, Knowsley had been a hunting lodge, but the Stanleys had expanded the building to include a state dining room to host Henry VII there in the later part of the century. That modest lodge was turned into a second grand estate and today is home to the nineteenth Earl and Countess of Derby. Lathom Hall was lost to the family after the Civil War in the 1640s, as the Earls of Derby supported the losing Royalist side. But in Alice and Ferdinando's time, each estate was just a short ride from the others, which allowed the young couple and their household to move around the Stanleys' northern lands with ease. Alice had left all that was familiar in her childhood home of Althorp to settle in and begin to build her life as a lady of the North.

The Stanley households were run by teams of stewards and servants, with Alice's father-in-law at the helm. In fact, the Earl of Derby maintained one of the largest households in England. His home was practically a small village in itself and would likely have seemed overwhelming to Alice as she tried to settle in. In the second half of the sixteenth century, most noble families downsized their staff to minimize their payroll and cut down on the number of mouths to feed. By the end of the century, most grand estates had fewer than a hundred servants, but Alice's father-in-law was the exception;[3] not only did he cling to his medieval governing rights as a landed magnate but he also maintained his household according to medieval custom, keeping up to 140 staff in attendance. He had teams of treasurers, grooms, waiters, clerks, yeomen, and any other possible position one could imagine to handle every aspect of his estate in an organized and hierarchical manner. The earl's estate was so large that his estate officers were not just servants to the Stanleys but had amassed enough wealth, land, and status to manage smaller estates of their own. That was a far cry from the relatively modest hierarchy of the Spencers' home. Twice in the 1580s, Queen Elizabeth called on the Earl of Derby to serve as her ambassador to the court of the King of France, and each time he took most of his household with him, leaving Ferdinando and Alice to manage the remainder in his absence.[4]

Alice found herself firmly planted in one of the only medieval households left in the realm, and it clearly made an impact on her. Though she would not have been responsible for the detailed management of the bustling household, she paid close attention to how the estate was run, as someday Ferdinando would inherit the entire enterprise and she would need to be ready to play her part. Years later, when at the helm of her own household, Alice would structure it in a similar fashion, with a commitment to the rather outmoded operations, roles, and even theatrics of service that her father-in-law clung to. She, too, would keep a relatively large staff, although far smaller than her father-in-law's, and organize the household offices in accordance with this medieval structure.[5] As a young girl, Alice's education had been designed to prepare her to be a charming wife, but what she was beginning to learn at Knowsley was calculated to transform her into a countess.

✦━━━━━◆━━━━━✦

Alice may have had a lot to learn about the inner workings of a complex household, but she understood that the most important thing she could do to support the Stanley estate was to give Ferdinando heirs. The couple wasted no time in trying to conceive and were extremely fortunate that Alice became pregnant within a few months of their marriage. She would undoubtedly have noticed with pleasure that she had ceased her monthly bleeding, giving rise to great expectations, although that alone could not confirm a pregnancy in the sixteenth century. Her hopes may have been strengthened by morning sickness, as well as swelling and tenderness in her breasts, and her corset may have started to hurt her as her chambermaids were unable to pull it as tightly as usual due to her growing waistline. But it would not have been until the fourth or fifth month that Alice knew for certain, when she first felt the little flutter in her belly of the baby's first movement. That was the "quickening," and it was the moment when, Christians believed, babies received their souls and came to life. In Alice's world, only after the quickening did a woman know for certain that she was pregnant.[6] During the 1580s, Alice gave birth three times, and though the couple would certainly have prayed for sons, Alice safely delivered three beloved daughters. Anne was born on July 16, 1581, followed by Frances, born in May 1583. Their youngest daughter, Elizabeth, was born December 23, 1587.[7] Each pregnancy brought a similar routine to Alice's life, and each safe delivery was a sign of her healthy fertility.

Like most things in the sixteenth century, pregnancy was shrouded in custom and superstition, and women (and men) had been imparting "wisdom" to pregnant women for centuries. For Alice, as for many elite women of the time, pregnancy brought a certain rhythm to her life and household. The cooks at Knowsley, Lathom, and New Park would all have been instructed to ensure that Alice's meals included more meat and fewer spices. Old wives' tales warned that too much red wine or strawberries could cause blemishes on the baby's delicate skin. Alice would likely have followed any advice her own mother shared, too. Regardless of the dietary restrictions, nothing was more important to the development of Alice's babies than her "maternal imagination." She was expected to spend considerable time intentionally thinking about the shape of her baby, picturing in her mind's eye the formation of a healthy little body, praying for a boy (although a healthy daughter would be welcomed, too), and using her own spiritual devotion to nurture the baby's soul. Today, it may be easy to scoff at beliefs like this, but it is important to understand the humanity of Alice, her family, and her contemporaries. For Alice and Ferdinando, pregnancy could bring great joy, but it was also an extremely perilous time in a woman's life. Alice faced a 6 to 7 percent chance of dying in childbirth and about a 14 percent infant mortality rate.[8] Motherhood was the most important role women like Alice would ever hold, and as such their contemporaries went to great lengths physically, mentally, and spiritually to keep mother and baby as safe as possible.

For women of Alice's rank, the birthing chamber was a sacred female space, and men were not permitted to enter the room. Given her financial resources, Alice and her stewards would have spared no expense to transform the room into a place that met Alice's physical needs and could comfortably prepare her for her delivery. Shortly before the baby was expected to arrive, she confined herself to her birthing chamber for her "lying-in," the final phase of her pregnancy. For her first pregnancy, she did her lying-in at her childhood home of Althorp and gave birth to her daughter, Anne, there. It was not unusual for women to want to be close to their mothers, especially during their first pregnancy. During her lying-in, Alice was surrounded by her mother, sisters, close female friends, a local midwife, and other female servants. Fresh air and natural light were believed to be dangerous during a delivery, so dark heavy fabrics covered the windows, and candles were kept glowing around the room. The attending women prepared "caudle" (broths and mulled wines) in the chamber for Alice to drink. Clean linens were neatly folded in preparation for the delivery. The women kept watchful eyes over Alice and prayed for her and her baby while embroidering swaddling clothes for the baby. In the days before the intensity of labor, the birthing chambers of noblewomen were quiet, calm, gentle spaces of profound femininity.

That tranquility disappeared with the onset of labor. The women rapidly tended to Alice's needs, offering continued prayers and physically holding her as delivery was imminent. Alice's mother or closest female relative, such as one of her married sisters—Anne, Katherine, or Elizabeth—would likely have been the one to actually deliver the baby, with a midwife watching to help should the baby need to be turned in the womb. Alice did those same things for her own sisters and friends and would someday do them for her daughters. Even the volatile birthing process was cloaked in female ritual and companionship. She gave birth to her next daughter, Frances, at Wormleighton Manor, a second home of the Spencer family, just twenty miles southwest of Althorp. Elizabeth, however, was born in the north, at Knowsley Hall.[9] After each delivery, Alice's baby stayed with her in the birthing chamber for the first week of the child's life.

Though it was a time of bonding and recovery for Alice and her baby, Ferdinando celebrated. In the week after Alice gave birth to their youngest daughter, Elizabeth, Ferdinando went on several overnight trips to hunt venison for the family feasts. During the course of the week, Lathom was buzzing with guests coming for the Christmas holiday and celebration of Elizabeth's birth. Alice's sisters Anne and Katherine were both there, along with their husbands, friends, and a troupe of players, for a grand entertainment. A week later, baby Elizabeth traveled with her father and family to the local church for her baptism. Their eldest, Anne, had been baptized at the parish church near Althorp, but Frances's and Elizabeth's baptisms were both in the North. Alice, like all elite mothers of the age, did not attend any of her daughters' baptisms, as she remained in her lying-in chamber for several more weeks to heal.

The first week of February 1588, Alice emerged from her chamber, and again the extended family gathered, this time for Alice's churching ceremony. In the medieval period, when England was still a Catholic country, churching was the service for the mother to be spiritually cleansed after childbirth. With the Protestant Reformation, however, many male church leaders saw the ritual as superstitious, yet women refused to abandon the practice. Childbirth was so steeped in female tradition that many women demanded to follow the customs of their mothers, grandmothers, and other ancestors. As a result, in Protestant England, churching was recast as a thanksgiving for the mother's health and survival. After Elizabeth's birth, Alice was churched by the bishop of Chester. Ferdinando, the bishop's wife, and Alice's sisters Anne and Katherine, along with other friends, were in attendance. The party remained with Alice and her family for three days.

Throughout the 1580s, Alice's life revolved around her three pregnancies, the safe delivery of each of her daughters, and the joyful feasts and celebrations that marked the end of each pregnancy with her husband, her sisters, friends, and now her daughters. Each safe delivery left a glimmer of hope that someday the couple would welcome a son into their growing family.

Before her eldest daughter, Anne's, birth in the summer of 1581, all anyone could do was hope that Alice would prove herself able to deliver a child safely. Becoming a mother solidified her place within the Stanley family, for which she would be handsomely rewarded. Ferdinando and Alice's marriage agreement does not survive, but in the winter of 1582, Sir John Spencer and Ferdinando's father, Henry, fourth Earl of Derby, amended their original agreement. By proving her fertility, Alice had earned a jointure. On February 1, 1582, the two men signed a document specifying "the competent and sufficient jointure to be had and made sure unto the said Lady Alice." The intent of the agreement was "for the advancement and preferment of such issues both males and females as to the said Ferdinando Lord Strange shall get of the body of the said Lady Alice Strange." Henry offered financial incentives for Alice and Ferdinando to have children together, thus securing their family lineage. When the couple had been married, the Earl of Derby had promised them three years' worth of rental income on some land valued at "four score thirteen pounds 13 schillings," or £1,040 (£213,000/$294,000 today), and with that document, he had enabled them to continue to collect that income indefinitely as their own.[10] But the new contract did not end there.

The Earl of Derby promised to set aside a list of manors, pastures, and meadows in Shropshire, Cheshire, and Lancashire that would be protected for Alice's future use "from and after the decease of the said Earl then to the only use and behalf of the said Ferdinando Lord Strange lawfully begotten for and in the name of part of the jointure of the said Lady Alice his wife." When the current earl should die, Ferdinando would have "full and perfect power and authority" to collect revenues from the lands protected by Alice's jointure. If Ferdinando predeceased Alice, she would assume ownership over them for the rest of her life, whether she remarried or not. The Earl of Derby would be permitted to continue granting leases on the land during his life, but if Ferdinando, Alice, or one of her appointed agents should inquire about the financial state of the leases, the earl was granted six months to notify them of any losses to income. As was customary in such contracts, the document also outlined specific lines of inheritance and contingency plans if Alice and Ferdinando's children did not outlive their parents and made extra accommodations for any sons the couple might have. The agreement, however, did not neglect their daughters, as each girl would receive a share of £2,000 (£410,000/$567,000 today) at the time she married.[11]

That document changed the trajectory of Alice's life, ensuring financial stability for herself and her children if she were to outlive Ferdinando. It also deepened and strengthened the connection between the Stanley and Spencer families. For the aristocracy, marriage was just the first level of commitment between two families. The second level was achieved when a child was born, as he or she embodied the joining of their bloodlines. And now a share of the

Stanleys' most valuable asset, a sizable portion of their northern lands, had been set aside for Alice and her children. In the feudal world, that was the fullest expression of multigenerational shared interests. There was only one person who would have been angered by the contract: William, Ferdinando's younger brother. Alice's new jointure claimed a portion of his ancestral lands and moved them out of his reach should Alice and her children outlive William's father and brother. Familial devotion and the bonds of brotherhood might have ensured that William accepted his station within the family, but greed and a sense of entitlement were always a threat to peaceful family life among the aristocracy.

The Stanley family were no strangers to conflict. Ferdinando's mother, Margaret, had left her husband and sons in 1567, shortly after Ferdinando's younger brother, William, had been born and five years before his father, Henry, had inherited the earldom. In that period, it was not unusual for noble husbands and wives to spend time apart, traveling on estate business or visiting relatives, but it was less common for marriages to completely disintegrate. According to Margaret, the couple had long endured "diverse breaches after diverse reconciliations," but marital arguments were hardly a reason to dissolve a noble union in the minds of the Elizabethan peerage. Margaret had gone to court to attend the queen, as Margaret's mother and Queen Elizabeth had been first cousins; Margaret's grandmother was Mary Tudor, Henry VIII's sister. Margaret claimed that upon her departure, her husband, "by anger or grief, broke up house" and remained with their children in the North. Margaret would never forgive Henry for refusing to accept her familial responsibility to the queen and taking her sons away from court. Her animosity was fueled by the belief that Henry intended the move not just to separate her from her sons but "devised to get my jewels from me."[12] The couple remained legally married, but Margaret stayed in London, in service to the queen, while Henry, Ferdinando, and William resided in the North, visiting the capital on rare occasions when politics and business required it.

Henry might also have preferred to stay in the North because of concerns about the dangers of being too close to the queen, in both the physical and familial senses. Connections to Elizabeth I, as with all monarchs of the time, were a double-edged sword. A royal bloodline brought Margaret and her sons social and political status, but it also brought constant suspicions of potential plotting, and those suspicions were enough to get some people executed. There was never a straightforward way to handle that, so although Margaret may have felt she was better off proving her loyalty as a courtier to her royal cousin, Henry felt safer far away in the North.

The arrangement continued for many years, until Margaret overstepped her bounds by advocating that Queen Elizabeth choose a husband. In Elizabethan England, nothing was more of a political hot-button issue than discussions about the queen's marital status. She had had many suitors and proposed matches early in her reign, but as the years advanced, it seemed that she was likely to remain unwed and thus never produce an heir. The queen's final suitor, the Duke of Anjou, came to London in the late 1570s, and courtiers started taking sides about whether Elizabeth should marry the Frenchman or not. For the queen in her forties, however, discussion about her marital status and potential heirs meant that people were meddling in the line of succession, over which she wanted sole control. The queen forbade any conversations about the subject, but Margaret was openly vocal in favor of the match.[13] If Elizabeth married and produced children, Margaret and her sons would move down the line of succession, so she might have believed that her advocacy could never be seen as plotting. What tipped the scales against Margaret, however, were rumors circulating that she had "tried to discover by means of witchcraft . . . whether the queen would live long," something Margaret vehemently denied.[14] It was forbidden to "seek to know . . . how long her Majesty shall live . . . or who shall reign . . . after her Highness's decease . . . by casting of nativities [astrological charts], or by any prophesying, calculation, or other unlawful acts."[15] Henry's fears for his family came true, and Margaret's bloodlines and actions put them all at risk. Margaret was arrested in 1579, just as the Spencers and Stanleys were finalizing the match between Alice and Ferdinando. Never was there a better time for Ferdinando to marry a young Protestant bride and start a family in the North.

Ferdinando's need to form a connection with an unquestionably Protestant family was exacerbated by the fact that his mother observed the old religion and his father also maintained a lax attitude toward Catholicism in Lancashire and Cheshire. William Cecil, Lord Burghley, the queen's chief advisor, noted "seditious rumors scattered round the country. Common prayer not continued in my [the Earl of Derby's] house as it was. The churches in the country near my Lord's house, either not served with curates, or none suffered to preach in them."[16] Henry promised to maintain a tighter control over local religious practices, but the truth was that Alice had come to a dangerous and unstable place. Her father-in-law had been suspected of recusancy, and in the first year of Alice's marriage, her mother-in-law was in prison. Margaret was eventually released early in the 1580s and remained in London, although she was never able to cast off the queen's suspicions. The best thing Alice could do for herself, her husband, and their families was to give birth to, and raise, loyal Protestant children.

In her new role, Alice was also expected to serve as a conduit to power for her Spencer family, as it was assumed that her advantageous marriage would open more doors for them. In 1581, Lord Burghley agreed to take Alice's younger brother Richard into his service. Richard understood the opportunity and humbly thanked Lord Burghley by saying "What greater patron could I have to look after my interest?"[17] The next year, Burghley sent Richard to Germany to act as a diplomat for the queen. Though Alice's marriage alone had not created the opportunity for her brother, it had certainly contributed to strengthening the reputation of the Spencers and reinforced her and Ferdinando's own connection to the powerful Cecil family. In the sixteenth century, even more than today, a rising tide lifted all boats.

That kind of patronage worked in many directions, and each member of the extended family had a role to play. In 1582, Alice's brother-in-law Sir George Carey successfully wrote to Burghley on behalf of Alice's father, seeking Burghley's assistance in swaying the queen to name Sir John Spencer sheriff of Northamptonshire. Carey wrote, "I am therefore bound and forced most humbly and earnestly to beseech your Lordship to favor and pleasure both him and me."[18] If one member of the family secured favor, it reflected positively on everyone. Throughout the 1570s, Sir John and Lady Katherine Spencer had paid for their daughters' husbands, purchasing entry into an elite patronage network. In the 1580s, the investment was paying dividends.

On November 10, 1581, there was a rupture in the network, however, when Anne's husband and Ferdinando's cousin, Sir William Stanley, Lord

Monteagle, died. Five years later, Anne remarried, to Henry, Lord Compton. Though it was surely a relief to everyone that Anne remarried another well-connected peer to stabilize her place in society, wedded bliss did not last long. About a year after their wedding, the names of two of Lord Compton's servants appeared on a list of "Knaves, Papists, and Harbourers of Priests," meaning that they were either secretly supporting Catholic networks in England or sheltering priests in their household.[19] In another document from that same year, Lord Compton himself was identified as "like to prove a dangerous man" to the realm.[20] Those were treacherous lists to be on, and Alice would surely not only have feared for her sister's safety but also have resented any negative light cast on her own family for being so closely connected to Lord Compton.

Alice and her sister Anne had been allies since childhood, and the two women tried to put on good faces and continued to execute their roles and responsibilities as noble ladies, despite the rampant speculation about their connections to Catholic families. In 1586, as their families faced the scandal of knowingly employing recusants, Lady Compton and Lady Strange traveled to court in an attempt to preserve their reputations as best they could. The Elizabethan gossip mill was aggressive, however. A bureaucrat named Nicholas Burden reported in a private letter that the sisters had paid a hospitable visit to the French ambassador, offering the commentary "For Lady Strange, I can say nothing. The rest are all too bad members and need to be looked into." Burden then suggested that someone should warn the ambassador to "keep better company."[21] Anne's husband, Lord Compton, worked hard to prove his loyalty to the queen and served as one of the men who removed Mary, Queen of Scots from her castle in 1587 to stand trial against Queen Elizabeth.[22] He was able to avert any direct accusations despite the rumors and suspicions, and when he died two years later, Ferdinando served as one of his pallbearers.[23] Alice and Ferdinando firmly stood by the people they cared about, both the living and the dead. That became a defining quality for Alice throughout her life.

⬥—⬦—⬥

Despite their landed wealth and high social standing, Alice and Ferdinando understood how unstable and volatile their place in the world really was.

Motherhood and Protestant devotion were two critical attributes for Alice, while Ferdinando consistently presented himself as a loyal subject of the queen and dedicated local patriarch. As the heir of a noble house with a long history, Ferdinando had been raised to understand that acting as a patron of the arts could reflect the greatness of his position. Now, as a married couple, Ferdinando and Alice enthusiastically embraced the vibrant literary and theatrical outpouring that was thriving in England at the time. Alice became her husband's eager student in learning about the arts, building upon the early education she had received and her innate respect for literature and music. Today, we recognize that Alice and Ferdinando lived during the historical moment of the Renaissance, but that term was not used to describe the age until the mid–nineteenth century. Alice and Ferdinando routinely funded poets and playwrights, both because it was expected of people of their rank and because it brought them joy. They understood that the honey-tongued flattery of writers and performers seeking steady funding could paper over Alice's more humble roots and Ferdinando's fraught bloodlines and provide both an ego boost and a reputation boost. They did not support poets because they were thinking about posterity; they were concerned with what made them look good in the moment and what the labels of "patron" and "patroness" could do for their reputations and thus that of their entire family network.[24] On a far less cynical note, they, like their peers, genuinely delighted in the wit, power, and enchantment of well-written words.

Ferdinando's tenure as a patron of the arts began in the late 1570s, just before he married Alice, when he funded a troupe of acrobats called Lord Strange's Tumblers. The troupe routinely performed throughout England, and in the winter of 1579–1580, Lord Strange's Tumblers were invited to perform for the queen at Whitehall during the Christmas festivities. That was around the time of his mother's fallout with the queen, so it was an ideal way for Ferdinando to try to soften the queen's heart toward him by providing whimsy with costumed men whirling and twirling through the court during the merriment of the holidays. Though Margaret remained in prison, none of the queen's anger seemed to have been directed toward Ferdinando, his brother, or his father.

After her marriage, Alice joined Ferdinando as a fixture in the thriving literary and theatrical scenes. In 1591, Edmund Spenser dedicated to Alice "Tears of the Muses," a poem in his *Complaints: Containing Sundrie Small Poemes of the Worlds Vanitie*, published a year after his iconic epic poem *The Faerie Queene*.[25] In the introductory letter to the poem, Spenser spoke to common themes of honor and nobility when he wrote to Lady Strange, "The things that make thee so much honored of the world as thee be, are such, as (without my simple lines' testimony) are thoroughly known to all men; namely, your excellent beauty, your virtuous behavior, and your noble match with that most honorable Lord, the very pattern of right nobility." He then offered a different motivation for his desire to write for her. He explained that he also felt a "private band of affinity, which hath pleased your Ladyship to acknowledge."[26] Spenser used the work to suggest that despite the difference in the spelling of their surnames, Alice Spencer and Edmund Spenser were relatives. Ultimately, he made plain the most obvious reason to attach Lady Strange to his work: "That by honoring you they might know me, and by knowing me they might honor you." He also dedicated poems in the volume to Alice's sisters Anne and Elizabeth, making the same claim. Through their elite marriages, followed by more than a decade of life as noblewomen and mothers, the Spencer sisters had become influential ladies in their own right, and Edmund Spenser was trying to affix himself to their status and thus win their favor as well as the esteem of anyone who might think he was their relative.

Spenser was not the only writer to court the attention and tout the honorability of the young Lady Strange. In 1593, Barnabe Barnes wrote one of his six epistles to the Lady Strange in his most famous work, the book of poetry called *Parthenophil and Parthenophe*. In his dedication to Alice, Barnes hailed her "beauty" and in the end acknowledged:

> *All British ladies, deign my muse's suites*
> *Which unacquainted of your beauty craves*
> *Acquaintance, and proceedeth*
> *T'approach so boldly, and behaves*
> *Her self so rudely daunted at your sight*
> *As eyes in darkness, at a sudden light.*[27]

Barnes attempted to appeal to Lady Strange's vanity by expressing that her beauty was so vibrant, it could practically blind any woman at first sight. What he really wanted to do was secure her as a future patron.

As with Ferdinando's patronage, it is impossible to confirm whether Alice funded any future works by the specific writers who courted her, yet she continued to be associated with writers and performers and would be for the rest of her life. The wider Stanley family had a long history of supporting writers over the course of the fifteenth and sixteenth centuries, as did most English aristocrats, but their dedication to it ebbed and flowed over the century, while Ferdinando and Alice remained wholly committed to it, as writers continued to herald them throughout their lives.

Lord Strange's Tumblers evolved into a more serious acting troupe, taking the new name Lord Strange's Men, as the young lord and his new bride embraced the growing trend of supporting writers and performers of the day. The 1580s saw the establishment of numerous acting companies, each funded by a nobleman and one by the monarch herself: the Lord Admiral's Men, Lord Pembroke's Men, the Earl of Essex's Men, the Earl of Leicester's Men, and the Queen's Men. Lord Strange's Men emerged within this scene, and Ferdinando ensured that his players worked with all the popular playwrights of the time: Robert Greene, Christopher Marlowe, and Thomas Nashe, among others, very likely including William Shakespeare.[28] Lord Strange's Men performed more than two hundred times, primarily in the 1580s and early 1590s, and many of the performances are mentioned in Philip Henslowe's diary. Henslowe invested in and managed the Rose Theatre, a famous stage built just a few years before the even more iconic Globe Theatre, so the regular mention of Lord Strange's Men in his meticulously kept diary indicates how well connected Ferdinando and his troupe were in the theatrical world. The troupe traveled around England, although the majority of their performances took place in London.[29] The surviving records make it impossible to prove a direct link between Ferdinando and Shakespeare, but the contexts of the performances also make it impossible not to recognize that it was a small world of players, playwrights, and patrons and intersections had to have occurred. For example, there survives today only one copy of the first printed quarto edition of *Titus Andronicus*, in the collections at the

Folger Shakespeare Library in Washington, DC. The title page explains that the text is "as it was played by the Right Honorable the Earl of Derby, Earl of Pembroke, and Earl of Sussex, Their Servants."[30] This suggests that players from each of the troupes came together for a performance of the play at some point before the 1594 printing.

Though it is impossible to trace the detailed connection between Ferdinando and Shakespeare through records of the men themselves, following the activities of playing companies does allow for more clarity. Actors and writers in all the major troupes moved from company to company throughout the 1580s. Then, by the early 1590s, some members from Lord Strange's Men and the Admiral's Men combined to form the dominant troupe of the last decade of Elizabeth's reign, the Lord Chamberlain's Men—although Ferdinando continued to sponsor his own players as Lord Strange's Men. The Lord Chamberlain's Men was Shakespeare's company, and "the Bard" becomes much easier to trace from there (although still an elusive figure).[31] By the end of the 1580s, Ferdinando's troupe of actors, no longer acrobats, had garnered an impressive reputation and had performed at court six times in the winter season between 1591 and 1592. There is considerable uncertainty about precisely how involved patrons were in the operations, performances, and, most tantalizingly, creative pursuits of the companies they funded.

With three young daughters, it is likely that Alice spent most of her time consumed by childbirth and estate management, not players. But Lord and Lady Strange did not just fund theatrics; they hosted them as well, indicating that at the very least they did not just want their names on a troupe for status alone but genuinely enjoyed the arts. Between May 1588 and August 1590, companies such as the Earl of Essex's Men, the Queen's Men, the Earl of Leicester's Men, and Lord Strange's Men performed twelve times at Knowsley, Lathom, and New Park. And when they came, there were grand festivities as the family hosted large parties of friends, families, and visitors. An unidentified troupe of players, probably Lord Strange's Men, performed the week Alice gave birth to Elizabeth in the winter of 1587–1588. Alice was still confined to her birthing chamber, but Ferdinando and his glittering estate celebrated the birth of Elizabeth with feasts and performances. In September 1588, the Queen's Men performed at New Park to mark the return home of

Henry, fourth Earl of Derby, from a diplomatic mission to Flanders. That time Alice and her daughters were in attendance. And during the weekend of September 12–13, 1589, the Queen's Men and the Earl of Essex's Men visited Knowsley Hall. The troupes "played all night" on Saturday. Sunday, following a sermon, the Queen's Men performed in the afternoon and the Earl of Essex's Men provided the night's entertainments. Unfortunately, no other accounts of the performances survive and we do not know what was performed. Lord and Lady Strange and their young daughters resided at Lathom in February 1590 and were treated to theatrical entertainments on the last day of the month. In June 1590, after they relocated the household from Lathom to Knowsley, the Queen's Men were once again on hand to entertain the Stanleys.[32]

The details of all those gatherings are infuriatingly sparse, but the routine appearances of those major playing companies at Lathom, Knowsley, and New Park (more than two hundred miles from London) tell us that the finest theater of the Elizabethan Age was woven into the fabric of the Stanleys' household. On May 6, 1593, the Privy Council granted a new license to Lord Strange's Men, giving Alice and Ferdinando renewed permission for their celebrated players to tour the country.[33]

CHAPTER THREE

TREASON AND MURDER

"Rebellion and Insurrection Might Be Stirred Here"

In late September 1593, the old Earl of Derby's health began to rapidly decline, and it became clear that his death was imminent. Alice and Ferdinando needed to start preparing for their new responsibilities that lay ahead. On September 21, 1593, just days before his father died, Ferdinando wrote to Robert Cecil asking for his assistance to encourage Cecil's father, Lord Burghley, and the queen to "bestow the office of the Chamberlain of Chester upon me, in respect I fear my father's life will not be long." A son would often go on to hold the offices his father had held, but the appointments were still up to royal discretion. Ferdinando then humbly asserted that he was "hoping her Majesty will think me worthy of the place having followed her the whole course of my life without any reward at all." Ferdinando had prepared his entire life to someday assume his father's positions, and he would do all he could to ensure a smooth transition. Alice also had a role to play, and she added a tender note to the bottom of the letter: "Sweet Cousin, you must receive my commendations to your lady and yourself, and for my sake, I pray you further this desire."[1] She used the term "cousin" to imply a closeness and familiarity, not an actual family relationship. Alice and Ferdinando were a united couple, deploying a two-pronged strategy: Ferdinando would address the politics head-on, and Alice would gently strum the strings of friendship that bound their families together. They were a couple ready to rise.

Henry Stanley died on September 25, 1593, and Alice's life was changed forever. Alice had spent thirteen years as a lady in his bustling household, and now she and Ferdinando would wear the coronets of the ancient and noble

Stanley family. At thirty-four years old, the youngest daughter of a sheep farmer assumed her new role as the Countess of Derby and Queen of the Isle of Man. Now that their three young daughters, Anne (12), Frances (10), and Elizabeth (5) were the daughters of an earl, Alice could anticipate the radiant futures that lay ahead of them.

Ferdinando was determined to prove to his peers and his people that he was his own man, not just an extension of his troubled mother and father. Alice, too, was an extremely different woman from her mother-in-law, Margaret, now Dowager Countess of Derby. While Alice and Ferdinando seem to have always enjoyed a loving union and served as a presence in the lives of their daughters, Henry and Margaret Stanleys' strained separation early in their marriage had created a rift in the family. Ferdinando did not spend much time in his mother's household, which was for the best, considering her reputation. It was important to Ferdinando and Alice that, more than anything else, they show themselves to be loyal subjects of Her Majesty.

Their good intentions, however, could do only so much against the dark shadows cast by the Stanley family's Catholicism. In July 1593, mere months before Ferdinando ascended to the earldom, a local man, William Goldsmith, confessed to Robert Cecil that he had been asked by Catholic plotters about Ferdinando Stanley's loyalties and if "Lord Strange were much at court and in what grace with the queen?" Catholics on the European continent had long wondered if backing the Stanleys' claim to the throne could restore Catholicism in England. Goldsmith responded that to his knowledge, Lord Strange had no interest in Catholicism, let alone treason. Goldsmith then told Cecil that the Catholic plotters believed Ferdinando to be of "no religion," although he would "find friends" if he were to take up their cause.[2] Rumors like these could destroy Ferdinando and Alice's good standing with the queen and put their lives in danger. The couple knew they would have a lot to prove when Ferdinando assumed the earldom to reassure the queen and her court that the new Earl of Derby was a loyal Protestant.

As a means of combating the rumors, the new earl and countess decided it best to avoid any comment on religious matters at all and let their actions speak for themselves. They employed Protestant chaplains and publicly attended church. In truth, that strategy was naive. It was impossible to be a family with a direct blood relationship to Queen Elizabeth, hold a clear claim on the Tudor throne, and think that people would assume their best intent. When it came to the Stanley family, it was better to assume that everyone was watching—and talking. Robert Parsons, an exiled English Catholic leader among the Jesuits in Europe, published a book in Antwerp, noting "The Earl of Derby's religion is held to be doubtful. Some think him to be of all three religions (English Protestant, Calvinist, and Catholic), and others of none . . . but others do persuade themselves that it will do him hurt, for that no side, indeed, will esteem or trust him."[3] Those doubts about his true religion, coupled with his father's reputation for leniency toward Catholic recusants and his mother's earlier arrest, made Ferdinando, Alice, and their daughters vulnerable. They would soon be forced to take a stand.

On October 10, 1593, Alice and Ferdinando were busy preparing for Henry's elaborate funeral. Their plans came to a sudden halt when a man named Richard Hesketh knocked on their door at New Park, claiming he had a message from one of Ferdinando's cousins. Ferdinando and Alice did not know Richard, but they were well acquainted with his family. The Heskeths resided in Lancashire and had been visitors to the Stanley estates over the years. Now that they controlled the earldom of Derby, Ferdinando and Alice anticipated that local families and relatives would seek out their patronage, so Richard Hesketh's appearance on their doorstep seemed quite harmless, however poorly timed.

Unbeknown to Ferdinando and Alice, Hesketh had spent the better part of the 1580s on the European continent, having traveled all the way to Prague. He had taken the vows of the Jesuit order and returned to England with instructions to "Signify unto [the earl] in general you have a message of importance to import to his lordship, from special friends of his."[4] Hesketh neglected to specify that those "friends" were actually Cardinal William Allen in Rome and two English Catholic exiles in Brussels, Sir William Stanley (a distant relation) and Thomas Worthington. The group had been plotting the meeting with Ferdinando for more than a year before his father's death. Ferdinando's ascent to the earldom had occurred just weeks before Hesketh's arrival, and the group did not want to wait too long to determine the new earl's religious loyalties. Though none of the men had ever met Ferdinando, many Catholics on the continent believed Lancashire to be "the best Catholic country that ever you came in."[5] Could this new earl, who carried royal blood in his veins, be the powerful Catholic who would finally help them overthrow a Protestant queen?

Richard Hesketh had traveled to England for three reasons. First, the plotters hoped that "rebellion and insurrection might be stirred here in this realm, and consequently her Majesty and the state of the realm brought to final destruction." Second, he was to try to find noblemen and -women who "might be withdrawn from their natural obedience to her Majesty, their sovereign Lady, and to raise rebellion against her Highness." Last, his primary target was "to persuade the said Lord Strange to take the diadem and crown upon him, and consequently to depose her Majesty." The plotters believed that it was essential for Ferdinando to seize the crown before the queen died in order to "prevent competitors."[6] The plotters did not know Ferdinando personally; they only knew of his bloodlines, the wild rumors about his father's Catholic toleration, and his mother's downfall. They were willing to take a gamble that Ferdinando's personal religious leanings were more in line with his father's than they actually were. Only a single prayer attributed to Ferdinando, written in 1588, has survived, and it speaks to the strife that weighed on his heart and soul:

> Let peace and justice embrace each other. O Lord, let England be to thee
> a second Israel, consider the immortal threatenings of our enemies, and
> suffer them not to exercise their tyranny upon us.[7]

Ferdinando prayed that enemies from abroad would not attempt to disrupt the "peace and justice" he longed for in England.

Hesketh approached his initial introduction to Ferdinando with caution and humility. The men exchanged the customary pleasantries and watched each other closely. If Hesketh felt that Ferdinando was unfriendly toward him, he had been instructed to politely end their meeting. Ferdinando later said that he had made a point of asking the stranger if he was "acquainted" with anything nefarious, "which he protested he was not."[8] Hesketh merely asked that Ferdinando pick a time and place to meet again the following week, which Ferdinando did, as he had not been given any reason to distrust Hesketh during their brief introduction. The men arranged to meet the following Thursday at nearby Brewerton Green. Ferdinando and Alice had no idea that he had just blindly accepted an invitation to participate in a treasonous plot against the queen.

A week later, Ferdinando arrived in the village to meet with Hesketh as planned. Hesketh had brought his brother Bartholomew to the meeting as well, but Ferdinando's "cousin," who had allegedly asked for the meeting, was nowhere to be seen. Once the three men were introduced, the Hesketh brothers made Ferdinando an offer: Jesuits abroad on the European continent would help Ferdinando secure the throne of England for himself and his family if he "be a Catholic and that he would bind himself to restore, advance and perpetually maintain the Catholic religion in our country."[9] Ferdinando Stanley would knock his cousin Queen Elizabeth off the throne and become King of England; Alice Spencer would be queen, and their three daughters could be in line for the throne. The plotters had already envisioned the details of Ferdinando's coronation and imagined that if the earl

> *join with Sir William Stanley, Worthington, and other traitors for the performance of the treasons aforesaid, such enemies and strangers as they would bring into this realm, would crown [Ferdinando] King of England at their first meeting with him; and for that purpose they would bring with them a hallowed crown for the said Lord Strange, and Lord Strange at his coronation [he would] take an oath to restore and maintain the Catholic religion, otherwise he should be no lawful King.*[10]

The conversation alone was treason, and there was no way Ferdinando could pretend it had never happened. He had now twice met with a Catholic plotter, although he later attested that if he had initially suspected any threat to the realm, he "would not have failed of informing her Majesty thereof."[11] Yet there he was, and if word of the encounters got out, he, Alice, and their family would be in grave danger. No one would believe that Ferdinando was innocent of plotting in the name of his own Tudor line despite his lifetime of loyal service to the queen; his parents' reputations ensured that. Ferdinando and Alice would be seen as traitors and their daughters' lives thrown into chaos.

Shrewdly, Ferdinando asked the Hesketh brothers to allow him time to consider their offer. He quickly made arrangements for the three men to ride to London together, as he knew the only way to cast off any association with the plot was to turn the conspirators in himself. Before his swift departure for London, he must have confided in Alice to alert her to his plan and the danger they were in. She would also need to start carefully and quietly shoring up powerful allies to attest that the Stanleys were victims of, and not accomplices to, a potential plot against the queen. From the North, Ferdinando discreetly sent letters to members of Queen Elizabeth's government denouncing the meeting and pleading with officials to arrest the two brothers on their arrival in London. Ferdinando was livid and explained in his letter to Robert Cecil that Richard Hesketh had tried to use him as a pawn as he went about "in malice as he doth to draw the government from me to himself."[12]

Though Ferdinando was enraged and surely terrified, he would need to stay calm and collected as the three men traveled together for several days to make the 220-mile journey south. He needed to keep a watchful eye on the Hesketh brothers so that he could bear witness and divulge every detail possible to the queen and Lord Burghley when the trio reached London. Queen Elizabeth and her Privy Council would see him as either a loyal agent or treasonous plotter, and he would have to endure a few days of rigorous travel to find out which it would be. Meanwhile, Alice would need to suppress the nauseating anxiety of uncertainty until she heard from Ferdinando. There are no records telling us how she spent those emotionally grueling days, but she likely busied herself with the affairs of the estate and her young daughters, while both desperately waiting for and dreading a knock on the door. Much to Alice and Ferdinando's relief, the Hesketh brothers were apprehended by the queen's men almost immediately upon their arrival in London and removed from Ferdinando's custody.

While Ferdinando remained in London to face the dramatic and traumatic situation head-on, Alice continued to serve her husband from the North as an active agent for her family. She wrote to Robert Cecil, again taking a softer tone than did her husband, who addressed the court assertively, denouncing the perpetrators. She started by reminding Cecil of their long friendship and preemptively thanked him for his support: "It is no little comfort, my good cousin, to me that my Lord finds you so good a friend." She went on to explain, "I doubt not but my Lord [Ferdinando] shall be crossed in court and crossed in his country, but I imagine his uprightness and honorable carriage will, by the means of so good friends as your father and yourself, upon whose love and kindness he chiefly and only doth rely."[13] Alice had been a countess for only a few weeks, but she recognized that she, too, held a position of authority and would need to wield it to effectively garner support. She was not just trying to protect Ferdinando; her entire family was in danger if they could not convince Queen Elizabeth's court of their innocence in the plot.

Alice's and Ferdinando's petitions worked, and the Hesketh brothers were imprisoned in the Tower of London, where they confessed the full story of the plot after being tortured. On November 29, 1593, they were executed as traitors. Ferdinando's and Alice's prayers were answered when the queen expressed her gratitude to them for their loyalty and they were permitted to remain freely in the North. She even insisted that the indictment against the Hesketh brothers reflect "that my Lord Derby, being by him moved, did presently apprehend the party, and made it known to her Majesty."[14]

Thankful that they had evaded danger, the couple turned their attentions to their life in the North, hoping that they had proven their loyalty to the queen and the Protestant faith, although in truth, it would take time to earn back her trust fully. By the winter of that year, she had yet to name Ferdinando the Chamberlain of Chester, the position previously held by his father. Ferdinando feared that he would have to live in "disgrace" but knew he and Alice would need to be patient.[15] Soon word would spread across England and the continent that the Earl and Countess of Derby would not be friendly to Catholic recusants.

✦—·—◆—·—✦

With that horrific affair behind them, it was time to lay Henry Stanley, fourth Earl of Derby, to rest. He was buried in the family chapel at Ormskirk on Tuesday, December 4, 1593, just five days after the executions of the Hesketh brothers. As the heir, Ferdinando rode alone in the funeral procession, cloaked in black velvet. Alice and her daughters trailed behind and also wore black velvet, and Henry Stanley had called for "blacks" (mourning cloaks) to be given to one hundred local people to wear at his funeral, creating a dramatic and somber band of mourners. The Lord Bishop of Chester presided over the grand service.[16]

As Alice sat quietly in the church and watched her husband make the offering, she must have been overwhelmed by the events of the last month. She had waited her entire adult life to sit next to Ferdinando as the Countess of Derby, and the fear of having that taken from her, of what could have been taken from her three beautiful young daughters, was unimaginable. The physical toll of the anxiety would dissipate in time, but her memory of the fear never would. The funeral was not just about saying goodbye to her father-in-law; it was also a time to try to put the horrors of the last month behind her. She was now a countess, wife, and mother, with the queen's full grace. Sitting in the Stanley family chapel, with her family safe inside, must have offered her the hope of God's grace now, too.

Her prayers were quickly answered. That winter, she became pregnant again. If the child were a boy, he would be born Lord Strange, heir to the earldom of Derby, just as his father had been; if a girl, she, like her sisters, would someday marry into a noble family. Alice was in a position to see only possibilities.

In December 1593, Lord Strange's Men took to the stage for the first time as Lord Derby's Men. The troupe performed three times that month, traveling to the Midlands for performances in Leicester and Coventry and at Caludon Castle. The Earl and Countess of Derby wasted no time in resuming their normal activities, underscoring their public personas as patrons of the arts and leaders in local politics.

As spring 1594 arrived in the North, Alice's pregnancy started to show and the household began preparing for the impending birth of what everyone hoped would be a male heir. Ferdinando resumed his rigorous rides and hunts around Lathom, Knowsley, and New Park. He spent his days thundering through lush northern fields, now all lands that belonged to him. After the grim autumn and dark winter, it felt as though life was finally flourishing. But that Arcadian dream was about to come to a swift end.

It started with an actual nightmare. Alice awoke with a jolt in the darkest hours of the night of April 4, 1594. Ferdinando had been frantically crying out for his beloved wife. She tried to comfort him and wake him from his frenzied dream. He had been dreaming that his pregnant wife was dead. Alice reassured him that she and the baby were both healthy and thriving and it was all a bad dream. Eventually the couple settled back into slumber.

The next morning, the fear from the night before was gone and Ferdinando again went riding. He later claimed that when he returned to Knowsley that evening at about "six o'clock at night, there appeared a man who twice crossed him [walked by him twice] and when he came to the place where he saw him, he suddenly fell sick."[17] He took to his bed and again had a horrible nightmare, dreaming he had been stabbed in the heart. Rumors would later circulate that the nightmares had been brought about by the mysterious encounter with the strange man, and Ferdinando's dreams were haunting premonitions. On Saturday April 6, Alice moved her husband to their primary estate of Lathom and the household steward called for a Dr. Case from Chester.

Chester was a good thirty miles from Lathom, and Alice and her servants knew it would be some time before the doctor arrived. They were right; it took a full week for the physician finally to get to Lathom. In the interim, Alice's anxieties about her husband's health grew. He could not keep any food down, and he constantly cried out in agony. They decided they needed to do something to try to ease his pain, so they turned to a local "cunning woman," known only to us as Jane, for help.

In the sixteenth century, there was a blurry line between medicine and magic, and cunning women and men were the practitioners who walked that line. Alice, Ferdinando, and most everyone around them believed that magic was real, but they made distinctions between different kinds of magic. Black magic, such as curses and hexes, was done to cause harm, but white magic could cure ailments and sickness, keep pregnant women safe, and even help someone find a lost item. Cunning folks used herbal remedies, incantations, and charmed amulets to wield their powers. Faith in those practices was deeply ingrained in Alice and Ferdinando's culture, and it was possible to be a good Protestant and still rely on the practice of white magic.

Initially Alice believed that Ferdinando's sickness had been brought about by his rigorous exercise, "which his honor took four days in the Easter week."[18] Conventional wisdom for Alice and her family would have been that if Ferdinando had fallen ill from natural causes, such as overexertion, or had been poisoned by the mysterious man he had encountered at Knowsley Hall, Dr. Case, a physician, would have been able to help. Medical knowledge at the time was based on a belief that humors (liquids) in the body needed to be in balance to maintain health. Ferdinando's constant vomiting meant that he had too much bile in his system, and bloodletting or enemas would be used to rebalance his humors to restore health. If, however, the mysterious man at Knowsley had bewitched Ferdinando, only a witch could remove the curse. Alice would not take a chance on her beloved husband's recovery and thus called both a cunning woman and a physician.

During the week between the time Alice sent for Dr. Case and his arrival, Jane, the local cunning woman, tried to heal Ferdinando. Alice also relied on local medical practitioners who were less esteemed than Dr. Case and household servants to care for him. Alice ensured that he was given chicken broth to try to provide some sustenance, while Jane worked with herbal potions and even fashioned a wax figure with a heart drawn around the belly. If someone had been cursed, one possible cure was for the practitioner of magic to draw the hex out of the bewitched and transfer it to something or someone else. With the wax figure, Jane was trying to do just that. Nothing worked, and Ferdinando's condition worsened. Alice and others attending Ferdinando would have seen that as a sign that Ferdinando's ailment was caused by something other than witchcraft, but as Ferdinando grew sicker, some of his last moments of lucidity were while Jane was treating him. As a result, throughout his illness, when he could speak, he shouted in agony that he had been bewitched.

Throughout the week, Ferdinando refused to be bled because he firmly believed his sickness had been brought about by witchcraft. But Alice, desperate for his revitalization, permitted other treatments to try to rebalance Ferdinando's humors and purge him of toxins. As Alice feared that he might have been poisoned, perhaps by Catholic recusants in retaliation for his role in thwarting the Hesketh plot, she and her attendants tried to treat him with a bezoar stone and "unicorn horn," although neither treatment worked.* They administered glisters (enemas), intended to draw the humors downward, and for a brief time, it seemed that Ferdinando was somewhat relieved. Comfort did not last long, however, and his health continued to deteriorate. For days, Ferdinando's attendants attempted to balance his humors by continuing to administer glisters and forcing him to consume manna (a dried tree gum used as a laxative) and scabious (herbaceous) waters. As his aching body started to swell, they gave him medicines to induce sweating as a form of purging and coated his body in oils and plasters (concoctions of medicines that hardened on the skin), but nothing helped. In truth, those treatments may have made things worse.

On April 11, 1594, Alice frantically put quill to paper and drafted a letter to Robert Cecil: "bear with me . . . for my senses are overcome with sorrow. It hath pleased God so to visit my Lord with sickness, that there is little hope of recovery."[19] Her husband lay dying, and she had never been more terrified for herself, her three young daughters, and her unborn child. Just as she had done before, she wrote to her powerful friend at court in the hope that she would be able to count on him if the worst happened.

Between bouts of illness, on Friday, April 12, a week after falling ill, Ferdinando dictated his last will and testament from his deathbed. Custom dictated that his younger brother, William, would inherit the title of the earldom and Lathom and Knowsley Halls, the family's ancestral homes, but Ferdinando desired everything else to pass completely intact to Alice. William would become the sixth Earl of Derby, and retain control of the family's ancestral estates, but all of the landed wealth and income would pass to Alice and their children, essentially giving his brother the shell of an earldom. If the child Alice carried was a son, Alice would keep everything her jointure entitled her to and the infant would inherit the remaining entirety of Ferdinando's landed power. If the child was a daughter, the couple's eldest daughter, Anne, would

---

* Bezoar stones are small balls of partially digested food, hair, and other substances removed from a ruminant animal's stomach. "Unicorn horn" was almost certainly ground horse hoof or deer horn. Both bezoar stones and "unicorn horn" were common ingredients called for in various folk recipes for remedies to treat poisoning. My thanks to Dr. Joel Klein, Molina Curator for the History of Medicine and Allied Sciences, at the Huntington Library, for helping me identify "unicorn horn."

inherit everything else except for Alice's portion and what had been secured for her use by the terms of her jointure.

In some ways, Ferdinando's deathbed will defied custom as, in principle, noble families wanted their estates to remain intact. Ferdinando wanted Alice to keep everything in her jointure as her own property, hewing it off from Stanley holdings, but that was precisely what a jointure was designed to do. Severing the remaining lands from the earldom's three primary estates was unusual, although not unheard of in feudal England.[20] His decision demonstrates a deep devotion to his wife and daughters and hints at a disdain toward his brother. The earl spent his final days planning for the futures of the beloved women in his life until he began sinking into violent fits.

Dr. Case finally arrived at Lathom on Sunday, April 14, and did all he could to treat Ferdinando. He inserted a catheter as a final attempt to purge Ferdinando, but "no water appeared."[21] In the end, Alice helplessly looked on as her husband "fell into a trance" and "he cried out against witches and witchcraft, reposing his only hope of salvation upon the merits of his blessed savior."[22] On Tuesday, April 16, after eleven days of agony, Ferdinando called for Alice. He softly said his final goodbye to her. He also asked her to give a jewel with his coat of arms on it to Dr. Case, who had worked so hard to save him. Then Ferdinando, Earl of Derby for only seven months, slipped away, as his "nature declined and his honor most devotedly yielded his soul to God."[23] Stoically, Alice "most honorably performed" her husband's final wish and thanked the doctor for all he had done.[24]

On April 28, Alice's brother-in-law Sir George Carey wrote to members of the queen's Privy Council that people in Lancashire made "greater presumptions that the late Earl of Derby was bewitched [rather] than poisoned."[25] Either way, the popular assumption was that Ferdinando's death was caused by foul play, perhaps as retaliation for his having handed the Hesketh brothers over to the queen. Though the circumstances surrounding his death could suggest poisoning, it is also possible that a routine illness combined with aggressive attempts to purge him and rebalance his humors contributed to his death.

Alice, however, could not afford to waste any time with wild gossip about poison and witches. Regardless of the cause, Ferdinando was dead and she was alone, guided only by the instructions in her husband's will, the deep wish that the baby inside of her was a son, and her own steadfast character. As her husband's spirit left his body, she became the fifth Dowager Countess of Derby, as her mother-in-law remained the fourth Dowager Countess of Derby. Alice would need to make a plan for herself and her daughters, but first she needed to say goodbye to her husband.

Once again, funeral arrangements had to be made. Ferdinando was buried on May 6, 1594, just two days after Alice's thirty-fifth birthday, near his father in the chapel at Ormskirk. The scene was all too familiar, and Alice must have found it hard to believe that she was there again less than a year later, this time a widow. She was beside herself, unable to control her temper and despair. After the funeral, she again wrote to her friend Robert Cecil, this time to apologize for being so inhospitable to him when he had attended the services, explaining that she hoped he "will take in good worth the short entertainment [he] found, and bear with what was amiss, since grief of mind, and my troubles were the cause."[26] Alice must have caused quite a scene at her husband's funeral because she wrote a remarkably similar letter on June 27, to the Earl of Shrewsbury, another powerful nobleman, with the exact same apology, word for word, that she had given to Robert Cecil. She also added that she was "holding myself much blame worthy that I sent not to you before, but I will amend that error hereafter, and crave of you that as you have begun, so you will continue an honorable friend to me and my children."[27] She could not afford to let her grief jeopardize her relationships with her most powerful allies.

Alice's broken heart was not her only problem. Not surprisingly, William, her brother-in-law and the new Earl of Derby, was outraged by his brother's will. He believed that inheriting the title should mean inheriting all of the lands as well. Alice's title of dowager countess may have suggested that she held a firm place within the Stanley family and the aristocracy, but she understood how vulnerable she and her daughters truly were. In the 1590s, the right patronage could do a lot for a pregnant widow, but it could not entirely protect her from the patriarchal laws of the realm.

Then, in the midst of that shock, the worst happened; Alice miscarried. The brokenhearted widow had no time to mourn, however. Without a male heir to inherit the lands, it was certain that her brother-in-law would contest Ferdinando's will, as patriarchal English law made it far easier to defeat a female heiress than even an infant male heir. William might even seek to contest the legality of Alice's jointure. And if he succeeded, Alice and her daughters would lose everything.

As she braced for what would surely be a brutal fight, Alice carried out one final act to pay tribute to her idyllic life with Ferdinando: on May 27, 1594, Lord Derby's Men made their last performance in Winchester, this time under the name Lady Derby's Men.

CHAPTER FOUR

AN UNRELENTING LAWSUIT

"My Sole and Only Executrix"

A lice's brother-in-law George Carey led an initial investigation into the
causes of Ferdinando's death and reported that the doctors insisted that
"the disease could be no other but flat poisoning," yet people in the northern
counties remained certain that witchcraft was the cause.[1] Carey, however,
could not identify anyone to charge with murder. As William prepared to
contest Ferdinando's will, Alice knew that her contemporaries would start
picking sides and factions within the peerage would form. She needed to prepare for the battle of her life, a battle whose outcome would also determine
the trajectory of her daughters' lives.

Petitioning powerful courtiers would not be enough. Alice would need
to cultivate the right persona: a blend of a docile widow enmeshed in the
highest circles of the nobility, mother of three daughters of royal descent, an
honorable dowager countess who commanded respect for her rightful place
in this hierarchical world, and a much-admired patron to some of the greatest poets and artists of her day. Her familial and social connections would
also not be enough; she would need to assert herself as poised and worthy
of the riches and lands marriage and motherhood should have assured her.
Though it would be a treacherous tightrope act, it would not be impossible.
Women had long managed to survive and even thrive in that patriarchal
world, Elizabeth Hardwick, later Elizabeth Talbot, Countess of Shrewsbury,
known as Bess of Hardwick, being among the most famous. Perhaps no one
exemplified the fact better than Queen Elizabeth, a strong, assertive woman
capable of assuming the command style of a king when the occasion called

for it, yet never allowing her subjects to forget it was a powerful woman who sat on the throne.[2] There would be moments when Alice, too, would need to assume the power of a man to be the mother she needed to be. She could not afford to be too deferential, docile, or passive, all traits traditionally revered in women. If she could move beyond the traumatic memories of Ferdinando's final days and the agony of her miscarriage to embody the image of the ideal noblewoman who was not afraid of the power her station afforded her, she might emerge from her despair with her life intact.

The celebrated poet of the age Edmund Spenser was the first to help promote precisely this version of Alice in his 1595 epic poem, *Colin Clouts Come Home Againe.* He dedicated the saga to Sir Walter Raleigh, but Alice, the recently deceased Ferdinando, and two of Alice's sisters all made appearances in the allegorical poem. Spenser personified the flower Amyntas as Ferdinando, while Alice was Amaryllis:

> *There also is (ah no, he is not now)*
> *But since I said he is, he is quite gone,*
> *Amyntas quite is gone, and lies full low,*
> *Having his Amaryllis left to moan.*
> *Help, O ye shepherds help ye all in this,*
> *Help Amaryllis this her loss to mourn:*
> *Her loss is yours, your loss Amyntas is,*
> *Amyntas flower of shepherd's pride forlorn:*
> *He whilest he lived was the noblest swan,*
> *That ever piped in an oaten quill:*
> *Both did he other, which could pipe, maintain,*
> *And eke could pipe himself with passing skill.*[3]

Spenser mentioned Ferdinando's skill with a quill, referencing his literary and theatrical patronage and a few minor attempts he himself had probably made at writing.[4] But his primary focus was on Alice's grief at losing her beloved husband, and he commanded the "shepherd," a reference to the nobility in general, to help *Amaryllis.*

Spenser also made allusions to Alice and her sisters Elizabeth and Anne as three flowers among the lush garden of the aristocracy:

> *No, less praiseworthy are the sister three,*
> *The honor of the noble family:*
> *Of which I meanest boast myself to be,*
> *And most that unto them I am so nigh.*
> *Phyllis, Charyllis, and sweet Amaryllis:*

Elizabeth was Phyllis, Anne was meant to be Charyllis, and again, Alice was Amaryllis.[5] The poet went on to articulate the unique qualities of each "flower":

> *Phyllis the faire, is eldest of the three:*
> *The next to her, is bountiful Charyllis:*
> *But the youngest is the highest in degree.*
> *Phyllis the flower of rare perfection,*
> *Faire spreading forth her leaves with fresh delight,*
> *That with their beauties amorous reflection,*
> *Bereave of sense each rash beholders sight.*
> *But sweet Charyllis is the paragon*
> *Of peerless price, and ornament of praise,*
> *Admired of all, yet envied of none,*
> *Through the mild temperance of her goodly rays*

Spenser painted Elizabeth and Anne as beautiful and sweet-natured, but the youngest sister was the "highest in degree" because Ferdinando Stanley had the highest rank in the peerage of all the Spencer sisters' husbands.

> *But Amaryllis, whether fortunate,*
> *Or else unfortunate may I aread.*
> *That freed is from Cupid's yoke by fate,*
> *Since which she doth new bands adventure dread.*

Shepherd whatever thou hast heard to be
In this or that praised diversely apart,
In her thou mayest them all assembled see,
And sealed up in the treasure of her heart.[6]

The Alice we see in Spenser's verses is exactly how she needed to be seen at that moment. As Amaryllis, Alice was gentle, honorable, situated in the most esteemed echelon of the aristocracy, yet vulnerable as she was about to face a dreadful situation. Spenser eloquently entreated other courtiers to remain steadfast in defense of the noble widow.

Alice would need all the help she could get as she began an ambitious legal battle against her brother-in-law, William Stanley, sixth Earl of Derby. She had her own extended family on her side. Her brother-in-law George Carey wrote to his wife, Alice's sister Elizabeth, mocking William and calling him a "nidicock" (fool).[7] Strategic marriages and the negotiation of jointures for her daughters could serve as the strongest weapons in Alice's arsenal, but she also needed to secure the favor of powerful men. Fortunately, she showed a remarkable aptitude for navigating complicated legal terrain; Ferdinando had prepared her well. She was ready to execute her power as a countess and mother to protect her daughters, herself, and their collective interests.

The legal systems at the time were indisputably patriarchal, but by the end of Queen Elizabeth's reign, English land law was in a state of flux as two legal systems had emerged: common law courts and equitable courts. Common law and equitable courts not only coexisted and overlapped, they also frequently contradicted each other. Common law was the overarching law in England, based on cases and precedent. It included traditions of primogeniture and coverture. Equitable courts, overseen by the Chancery, however, dealt with individual cases that required special consideration based on the belief that the general application of common law made it far too broad to reasonably apply to every situation. Equitable courts took unique circumstances into account and had the authority to override common-law decisions. By the 1590s, there was a growing trend in inheritance suits for courts to favor directly descended female heirs-general (the deceased's daughters) over collateral male heirs (the deceased's younger brothers).[8] Though William counted on the common-law court to rule in favor of his male claim to the house of Stanley, Alice's best hope was that an equitable court would follow more modern trends and over-rule him.

The first document everyone turned to for insight was Ferdinando's will, drafted from his deathbed on April 12, 1594, just four days before he died. In it, he named his "well-beloved wife Alice Countess of Derby my sole and only executrix."[9] Aristocratic husbands frequently made their wife their sole exec-utrix on the assumption that she would always act in the best interest of her children and would know how to manage their estates properly.[10] Ferdinan-do's will explicitly expressed his desire for his landholdings to remain intact. If the child Alice carried was a son, he would inherit all properties at his birth. Alice would get her dower claims and retain control of the estates placed in her jointure and manage all the other estates during their son's minority. If Alice miscarried, which she did, or had a girl, Ferdinando wanted her to have complete control over his estates, beyond those in her jointure, for her life. After Alice's death, Ferdinando envisioned that his estates should then pass in entirety to

> [my] eldest daughter the Lady Anne Stanley and the heirs of her body lawfully to be begotten. And for default of such issue the remainder thereof unto Frances my second daughter and to the heirs of her body lawfully to be begotten, And for default of such issue, the remainder unto Elizabeth my third daughter and the heirs of her body lawfully to be begotten.[11]

Oddly, nowhere in his will did Ferdinando mention his brother, William, the Stanley collateral male heir, by name. That was rather unusual, and no sources survive that reveal the personal feelings of either brother toward the other. But it is easy enough to assume that William did not appreciate inher-iting an earldom in name only, although he gained control of the family seats of Knowsley, Lathom, and New Park. He would not sit by and allow a sheep farmer's daughter and her three girls to take control of his noble ancestors' lands.

The basis of William's contestation of Ferdinando's will was the argument that his grandfather Edward, the third Earl of Derby, had entailed the family lands in Lancashire in March 1570 for sixty years.[12] An entailment was a mechanism that legally bound land together and outlined the desired line of succession, making it impossible for a reckless heir to start selling off portions of the family estates. Once lands were entailed, they could not be legally separated. In feudal Europe, entailments were a crucial tool aristocratic families used to ensure multigenerational control over lands. William argued that Ferdinando's will conflicted with the entailment and that Ferdinando had had no right to give control of the Stanley lands to a Spencer woman. He also argued that some of the lands in Alice's jointure had been entailed and could therefore not be separated from the rest of the estate, contending that his father and brother had not legally been able to promise certain lands to Alice. But Alice had her jointure (signed by William and Ferdinando's father) and Ferdinando's will to prove that the two preceding Earls of Derby had promised her, and then her daughters, those lands.

Because applications of land laws were so uncertain due to the two often conflicting court systems, there was no clear and obvious answer to the dispute. Alice and William would have to build their own teams of powerful friends, allies, and judges in an attempt to persuade the courts to read the evidence in his or her favor. In October 1594, two stewards, one appointed by William and one by Alice, delivered "one trunk with evidence sealed by them on behalf of the said earl and countess" to Thomas Egerton, Master of the Rolls, a high-ranking position in the equitable courts.[13] Egerton was from Cheshire and in the 1580s had served as a chief legal advisor to Henry, fourth Earl of Derby, William's father and Alice's father-in-law. Both William and Alice knew Egerton from his time in service to the Stanleys, and both parties believed that he would remain impartial and do his duty to the legacy of the Stanley family, although Alice and William both believed they represented that legacy.

William was desperate to gain the upper hand and knew he needed to line up strong allies of his own. On January 26, 1595, he married Elizabeth de

Vere, a daughter of Edward de Vere, seventeenth Earl of Oxford, and Anne Cecil. Elizabeth called Robert Cecil "uncle" and William Cecil, Lord Burghley, "grandfather." Although Cecil and Burghley had been good friends to Ferdinando and Alice, William hoped that by marrying Elizabeth, he would shift their allegiance; they would not want to see Elizabeth, the new Countess of Derby, as the lady of an impoverished estate. Unfortunately for William, Elizabeth was never very fond of him, nor did she care for the North. While he firmly planted himself at Lathom, Elizabeth remained at court in London, carrying on several not-so-discreet love affairs. Alice faced the situation head-on and candidly pleaded to Robert Cecil, "I hope, my Lord, your father's wanted favor will not be drawn from me by any means or persuasions, albeit I hear of a motion of a marriage between the earl, my brother, and my Lady de Vere, your niece, but how true the news is, I know not, only I wish her a better husband."[14]

Despite William's marriage to Elizabeth, Cecil and Burghley were quite happy to stay out of the Stanley inheritance suit, for the most part, although they did seem to favor Alice at times. Burghley served as Lord Treasurer on Queen Elizabeth's Privy Council, was her most trusted advisor, and also oversaw the Court of Wards. Once, after delaying a hearing in the suit between William and Alice, he explained to his son, Robert, "I have done nothing in this cause but what my conscience did prescribe me. And if the Earl shall think otherwise of me, as I doubt he may be thereto led, yet he shall understand that I gave my child to him, but not my conscience, nor my honor, which no blood shall ever gain of me."[15] Marrying into a powerful family seemed to have served Alice far better than it had William.

In March 1595, those alliances had hardly been tested when William and Alice appeared to reach an accord. William agreed to give Alice her dower: one-third of Ferdinando's freehold lands for her use during her natural life. He also agreed to pay her £5,000, Anne £8,000, and Frances and Elizabeth each £6,000, a cash payout totaling £25,000 (£4.2 million/$5.8 million today). He also agreed to provide £100 annually (£14,000/$20,000 today) for maintenance to each of his nieces until they turned twenty-one or married.[16] Alice and her daughters would live extremely well upon that money and would also likely become four of the most desired brides in the realm.

It did not take long, however, for that initial settlement to unravel. Alice had already begun to grant leases on properties she considered to be part of her jointure before she and William had hashed out the details, and William argued that her new leases were in violation of existing leaseholds. If Alice controlled the leases, she would profit from the rents, and the youngest daughter of a knight would be transformed into a forceful dowager countess. Too much was at stake for her to give in to her brother-in-law's complaints, and she remained unwavering in her certainty that her powerful allies would help her defend her claims to those lands through her jointure. Though Alice had agreed to accept her dower, she also expected to maintain control over the leases she had recently granted on some of her jointure lands, and she had no intention of allowing William to collect a single penny from what she believed to be hers. Their agreement was not as comprehensive as either party initially believed and thus was short lived.

William continued to file claims in common-law courts, while Alice petitioned through Thomas Egerton in equitable courts. Beyond the emotional toll of a protracted inheritance suit, the whole thing was getting expensive. Disputes over the Isle of Man served as the death blow to the accord. In 1406, King Henry IV had granted the "lordship of Man to Sir John Stanley," and the family had controlled the isle ever since. In 1522, a Chancery council had determined that the Isle of Man "was not part of the Realm of England, nor was governed by the law of this Land."[17] William claimed his Stanley rights as the King of the Isle of Man; Alice claimed that it was part of her dower, granted to her by Ferdinando's will, and she was its queen. On August 31, 1594, three inhabitants of the isle sent a petition requesting the rebuilding of the castles of Rushen and Peel on the island. They addressed it to both "right honorable the Earl of Derby and the Lady Alice Countess Dowager of Derby" because no one could ascertain who ruled the island.[18] The Privy Council then complicated matters when they saw Ferdinando's death as an opportunity to take back the Isle of Man for the Crown. By August 1595, Queen Elizabeth had seized control of it, and with no legal settlement, neither Alice nor William could fight the queen. The March agreement between William and Alice fell apart completely.[19]

Queen Elizabeth now not only controlled the Isle of Man but also held the wardships of Alice's three daughters, because minors of elite families became wards of the Crown if their father died. Their mother would need to petition the Court of Wards and Liveries to have her custodial rights restored. That was often just a formality, but the Stanley daughters, with their royal bloodlines and wealthy Spencer relatives, were an enticing investment for the Crown. Though the girls likely continued to live with their mother, whoever controlled the wardship of the Stanley daughters could arrange their marriages and reap the profits of their marriage contracts. Anne was fourteen, Frances was twelve, and Elizabeth was almost eight.

As the 1595 agreement started to unravel, Alice petitioned the Court of Wards to regain custody of her daughters. It was crucial to Alice that she remain their legal guardian—and not just out of a mother's love. By arranging the marriage of each of her three daughters, Alice would have three opportunities to secure other alliances that could further their collective cause. The queen, however, might use each marriage to secure loyalty and stability with a noble family of the realm or even as a diplomatic tool if she opted to wed a Stanley daughter to a foreign courtier, denying Alice the chance to build her own family alliances. Alice loved her daughters, yet she also understood that they were pawns in a formidable game, and she was determined to be the one to control them.

Despite William's marriage to one of their own, Alice was hopeful that the Cecils would remain her allies, as William Cecil, Lord Burghley, oversaw the Court of Wards. The stakes had just become even higher for Alice, as her mother-in-law, Margaret Stanley, also called Dowager Countess of Derby, died on September 29, 1596. Margaret bequeathed some of her own dower lands in Lincoln to her granddaughters, but because the queen held their wardships, the lands became the property of the Crown. Alice would need to get custody of her children to be able to control their marriages and now their landed income. She continued to petition her allies, and the strategy continued to work. On March 14, 1597, thanks in large part to Lord Burghley's favor and support, Alice received a "Surrender from the Queen on the advice of the Mr. and Council of the Court of Wards and Liveries . . . of the wardships of Ladies Frances and Elizabeth Stanley."[20] (Anne had already come of age.) The grant not only gave Alice full custody over her daughters, it also included a portion of the lands Margaret had left them. It was a major victory for Alice, but she would not stop trying to recover the remaining portion of her daughters' inheritance from their grandmother. She would never walk away if she believed she was entitled to more, even if it meant finding a subtle way to challenge the queen.

A few months later, Alice pleaded to Robert Cecil that an "auditor took of the lands descended to my daughters by the death of their grandmother." She asked, "Wherein if it please you to undertake some pains, and to use your best means to effect it, I shall acknowledge myself much beholden and will in all honorable kindness deserve so kind a favor." She hoped he might help restore to her daughters what was rightfully theirs. Not wanting to sound greedy or imply that she wanted to attempt to take something from the queen, she proposed that "the lands to be leased from her Majesty to me, during the minorities of my two daughters, no benefit will accrue to me more than the rents thereupon reserved," meaning she would not sell the lands and would profit from their rental income only until her daughters came of age or married, at which point her daughters and their respective husbands would receive the income.[21] Alice once again presented herself as a dutiful and desperate mother who was doing the honorable thing to secure the inheritance her daughters were entitled to. The strategy worked, and Cecil took up her cause. On January 14, 1598, Alice received a grant for the remainder of the lands.[22]

Those wins were a major boon to Alice, not just personally but also in her fight against her brother-in-law. With control over her daughters' wardships, she could now freely negotiate their marriage settlements and thus secure a greater network of male allies. Her daughters' husbands would each be motivated to take up her cause against William to further their own estates. And until each daughter was married, Alice was entitled to collect and control the rents on their inheritance from their grandmother. Those privileges were an important reason why Alice initially opted to remain a widow, as coverture laws dictated that her second husband would have the right to assume control over everything she had, including her daughters. Not marrying was part of her early strategy, and Alice had fared well on her own, with the help of the Cecils. Regaining her daughters' wardships gave her a moment to catch her breath, but as the lawsuit against William dragged on, she began to consider a new strategy. Perhaps it was time to find a new husband for herself who would be willing to fight on her behalf, giving her deeper access to the male-dominated legal sphere. She could not rely on the kindness of powerful friends forever, and the right man might be financially incentivized to share the potential rewards with her and be good to her daughters. Alice began to explore her options.

In 1600, Alice found just the man she had been looking for. He was the lawyer and judge whom she and William had each entrusted with their earliest evidences: Thomas Egerton. What better way to ensure a successful outcome than to marry the man at the helm of the equitable courts? The fact that he had started his legal career in the Stanley household just made the match that much sweeter and surely infuriated William.

Born in 1540 as the illegitimate son of a housemaid, Alice Sparks, and Sir Richard Egerton, Thomas Egerton was taken in and raised by a Cheshire lawyer. He was an intelligent boy, and his benefactor nurtured his talents, ultimately sending him to Oxford and then to study law at Lincoln's Inn in 1560, the year after Alice was born. There Thomas was a well-read, self-made man with a bookish love and passion for erudite debate, all traits his contemporaries saw as honorable. In 1576, he married Elizabeth Ravenscroft, the daughter of the man who had raised him. The marriage was a happy one and the couple had three children: Thomas, John, and Mary. Thomas's career continued to flourish, and in the 1580s, Queen Elizabeth appointed him to a series of legal posts while he also served as an advisor to Henry, fourth Earl of Derby, which was how Alice first met him.

Thomas continued to rise through the ranks of the Elizabethan state, and just a few days before Ferdinando died, Queen Elizabeth appointed him her Master of the Rolls, a high-ranking court clerk responsible for maintaining all the court's records and supervising all the lower-ranking clerks. Two years later, in 1596, Queen Elizabeth appointed him to the esteemed post of Lord Keeper of the Great Seal, but he also assumed the responsibility to act as lord chancellor, without the second title or salary. Beyond providing legal advice and service to the Crown, the Lord Keeper was responsible for keeping the seal matrix of the monarch's Great Seal, to be affixed to any document or charter the queen approved. As acting lord chancellor, Thomas was also the head of the entire equitable court system, making him one of the most influential judges in the realm. The queen's treasury was depleted, and to save money, she had developed a habit of appointing men to lesser positions and expecting them to take on higher responsibilities. Though the queen respected and trusted him, Thomas's humble origins also motivated her to withhold the higher title from him.

Thomas's first wife died in 1588, and in 1597, he remarried to Elizabeth More, the daughter of a knight. Their happiness, however, was short lived. On August 23, 1599, his eldest son and heir died from wounds sustained while fighting in a brutal English campaign to suppress the Irish. From his deathbed, the son wrote to his father, although Thomas did not receive the letter until his son was already gone: "Upon my brother the hope and fortune of your house stands, which I pray you be careful to advance, for your memory that lives after you."[23] Just five months later, Thomas's second wife, Elizabeth, died, leaving him heartbroken. At sixty years old, Thomas was single again and his unmarried twenty-one-year-old second son had become his heir. Suddenly the advice from his deceased eldest son took on new meaning, and Thomas knew that he needed to focus on expanding his estate.

In October 1600, Alice married Thomas Egerton, only nine months after his second wife's death. This was not a love match but a shrewd selection by Alice of a husband who would personally benefit in securing her victory over William. Alice, however, had not navigated six years of a tumultuous widowhood just so her new husband could exert his patriarchal legal rights over her and her unwed daughters. When Alice married Ferdinando, she had been from the "lesser" family; now she was the Dowager Countess of Derby, standing to inherit a windfall of lucrative estates and lands. She was fully aware of everything she brought to the negotiating table, and so was Thomas. He agreed to grant her a jointure, which he would continue to add to after they secured her inheritance.[24] Alice also continued to use the title Dowager Countess of Derby for the remainder of her life, even years later, when Thomas began receiving new titles of his own.

The Stanley-Egerton union became a double threat to William when, just a few months after their wedding, Thomas and Alice arranged a marriage between his son and heir, John, and her middle daughter, Frances. That was a bold move, and although historically stepsiblings did marry each other on occasion, by the late sixteenth century, it was far from the norm. Convention, however, mattered far less to Alice than did legal triumph. She held parental and custodial rights over her daughters, and she intended to use them. Because she had a jointure, she would pass lands to her daughters, while Thomas would pass lands to his son. Within one generation, Thomas's grandchildren stood to control massive landed wealth, and he would be the founding patriarch of a great English dynasty. The Lord Keeper would surely assist the Dowager Countess of Derby in finding a way to bend a flexible land law in his new family's favor, especially now that the outcome directly benefited his own heirs.

As Alice and Thomas were sorting out the new merger of their aspirational agendas, the queen was busy making her own plans for Alice's family. Anytime someone from the aristocratic class married, the monarch had the privilege to approve or deny the match, and it seems that Queen Elizabeth had expressed an opinion about the fate of Anne Stanley, Alice's eldest daughter. The queen's interest in Anne's matrimonial fate may have been why Alice and Thomas decided to secure a marriage between Frances and John, rather than Anne and John, for fear that they would agitate the queen if she had plans for Anne. After all, Anne, as the eldest Stanley daughter, occupied a spot in the line of royal succession to the Tudor throne. The older the queen got, the more anxious she became about her possible successor, and she could invoke her royal prerogative to weigh in on Anne's marriage prospects. Alice was helpless as the queen's statesmen pursued diplomatic marriages for her daughter. At one point, Queen Elizabeth considered marrying Anne to the Duke of Muscovy, touting Anne as "one of the daughters and heirs of our cousin the Earl of Derby, being of our blood royal and of greater possessions than any subject within our realm."[25] The arrangement fell through, however, when the queen learned the young duke was five years younger than Anne. Had the Russians accepted the match, Anne would have been shipped off to Moscow, far from Queen Elizabeth's court and away from any claim to her throne, and Alice would have had to say a painful goodbye to her eldest daughter. She did not want to sit idly by and lose her daughter, but she knew better than to go head-to-head with the queen. When the Muscovy match fell through, Queen Elizabeth seemingly lost interest in placing Anne in a marriage, leaving it up to the young woman and her family.

Alice's marriage to the Lord Keeper and the union of their children were major weapons in her suit against William. The earl's legal expenses were mounting. Robert Cecil estimated that William needed "to raise at least £30,000 [£4.1 million/$5.7 million today] to settle his legal debts."[26] The most obvious way to generate money was to start selling lands, and Thomas and Alice were ready to buy. Thomas purchased the lands of Ellesmere in Shropshire from William, land that had originally been part of Alice's jointure arranged by Henry, fourth Earl of Derby, and her father after Anne's birth but had been contested at the onset of their inheritance suit. Though Alice and Thomas may have had a chance to win back the land if their protracted suit ever reached a final settlement, purchasing the land directly from William would alleviate any potential future question or dispute over ownership. Because they could afford to do so, it was the fastest and clearest way to start shoring up their properties. Alice sat back with a Cheshire-cat grin as her brother-in-law was forced to sell the estate to her new husband.

William was not ready to give up, however, and he began a suit to try to win back the Isle of Man from the Crown in the hope that the queen might change her mind and restore his family's ancient claim to rule the isle. He could not appeal directly to Queen Elizabeth; he needed to follow the proper legal channels. He was forced to turn to the Court of Chancery because it was the court that had initially secured the Stanleys' claim to the island in 1406. The court eventually ruled that the Stanley family, as an entity, not William himself, did have a rightful claim. William was given the option to purchase the island from the Crown for £2,000 (£275,000/$380,000 today). The Chancery, however, also determined that the Stanley daughters held an equal claim to the island, and it does not appear that the Stanley women paid anything for their share, suggesting that the court viewed them as the rightful heirs of the

Stanley family.[27] The court then divided control of the Isle of Man: half went to William, and the other half was split into thirds among Anne, Frances, and Elizabeth. Even though William promptly filed suit against the decision, the judges ultimately ruled again in favor of the Stanley daughters. Alice's choice of a second husband was proving to be a good one.

As the Chancery council debated the issue of the Isle of Man, they came to a very important conclusion. In scrutinizing Ferdinando's will in order to reach a verdict, they determined that

> *And first by the same deed and will and all the part thereof it appears that the said Earl [Ferdinando] meant to make provision for all his 3 daughters and not for the eldest alone, for so first he expressed the consideration of his conveyances to be the love which he beared to his 3 daughters and named them particularly likewise that the same should continue unto them all as it is limited.*[28]

The decision meant that the Stanley daughters became coheiresses with the rights of heirs-general, meaning that Anne was not the sole heir as the eldest but all three daughters were equal heirs. Alice would retain control of some of the lands for her life, but her daughters would equally split everything else granted in Ferdinando's will. For years, Alice had fought in defense of Ferdinando's will, with the understanding that his properties would pass to her and then to Anne. But the Court of Chancery's new reading of things meant she would be the mother of not just one heiress but three coheiresses. However unexpected the ruling was, Alice had no intention of fighting the Chancery's interpretation of the will, as the decision ensured that each of her daughters would be equally provided for. Of course, because Thomas's son had married Alice's middle daughter, the decision meant that his heir was also well provided for.

In the end, William bought out his nieces' shares in the Isle of Man for an unknown sum probably close to £30,000 (£4 million/$5.5 million today).[29] Alice had secured a victory in the fight over the isle that anyone else would have considered a triumph, but she would not leave it at that. William had regained his Stanley right to rule the island, but the Crown still controlled the churches there. Since Henry VIII's break with the Roman Catholic Church in the 1530s, the Crown had owned all ecclesiastical lands. So Alice petitioned the Crown to grant her letters patent to the abbey lands on the Isle of Man for forty years, which she was granted on March 17, 1606.[30] The grant gave her the right to collect the income from the abbey lands of the Isle of Man, an act that did not just increase her family's wealth and status but poured salt into the wounds of her estranged brother-in-law. As the wife of the Lord Keeper and Dowager Countess of Derby in her own right, Alice had become a fierce feudal aristocrat, never letting an opportunity to control more land pass her by. She continuously demonstrated her ability to think creatively as well as a staunch unwillingness to leave anything on the table; despite William's obsession with regaining control of the Isle of Man, it had not occurred to him to petition for the rights to the abbey lands. Alice outplayed him on every level.

The establishment of the Stanley daughters as coheiresses changed their standing in the marriage market, and Alice wasted no time in capitalizing on their glittering new prospects. It was the perfect moment to lure husbands for Anne and Elizabeth. The details of how Anne's marriage came about are frustratingly lost, but by the end of March 1603, she was married to Grey Brydges, Lord Chandos of Sudeley.[31] Under the original terms of Ferdinando's will, Elizabeth, his youngest daughter, stood to inherit anything only if her mother and two older sisters died and left no legal heirs, but the Chancery decision had now made her a prized bride, too.

Alice settled on the honorable but debt-strapped Hastings family, the Earls of Huntingdon, as the ideal place for her youngest daughter. Elizabeth and Henry Hastings, the family heir, married on January 15, 1601, and she brought with her a dowry of £4,000 (£550,000/$760,000 today). Though the inheritance suit had been initially settled, there were still details to finalize, and Alice would need all of her sons-in-law to remain motivated to advocate for their brides. And as none of the Stanley daughters had children yet, the long-term future of the settlement could not be determined. Shortly after the marriage between Henry Hastings and Elizabeth, Alice cheerfully wrote to the groom's grandfather, the fourth Earl of Huntingdon, to celebrate the potentially bright future for both of their families, exclaiming that she sent her "honorable respect, both to the good of the young couple, and the increase of their estates."[32] As Alice and Thomas continued to deliver success, Elizabeth ended up with a jointure.[33] Alice knew as well as anyone that a jointure would not always guarantee ease if Elizabeth were to become a widow, but it remained a woman's best chance of financial security in an uncertain future. It also demonstrated the position of strength that Elizabeth's side brought to the marriage negotiations. The Hastingses were a powerful family of the Midlands, so their willingness to agree to set some lands aside for Elizabeth that would be more valuable than a standard dower portion shows the incentives they were willing to offer to secure a match between Elizabeth and Henry.

Once the Court of Chancery had settled the dispute over the Isle of Man and Alice had maximized the marriage options for herself and her daughters, she and William came to a final agreement about the inheritance in 1602, and the deal was solidified in a Private Act of Parliament in 1607. The settlement stated that William would pay the heirs-general £20,400 (£3 million/$4.1 million today), to be divided equally among them: £8,000 cash, £11,200 for lands in Middlesex that he would purchase from them (but they would retain control of Colham and Eynsham), and he paid £1,200 (£165,500/$220,000 today) for lands that he had illegally sold to parties outside the family before the resolution.[34]

After nearly ten years, the fighting finally ceased, and as the properties came rolling in, Alice and her daughters could at last put the upheaval of Ferdinando's death behind them. Alice had transformed her fears into hopes, and then those hopes became plans. She had not accomplished it alone. With the help of Thomas Egerton and her other powerful allies, Alice had masterfully navigated a harrowing inheritance suit. She had cultivated a network and reputation that facilitated those alliances and bided her time to use marriage as a strategic tool for herself and her daughters at precisely the most opportune moments. The young Alice, who had been the littlest Spencer daughter, running to keep up with her older brothers and sisters in the verdant fields of Althorp, was gone, replaced by a tough, uncompromising woman who knew what she was entitled to and who was respected enough by powerful men and the queen to enable her to hold on to it. Alice had prevailed; her daughters were safe. Now it was time to focus on using their newly won wealth, status, and stability to expand her family's influence at court.

PART II

CHAPTER FIVE

A RENAISSANCE FAMILY

"Yea, Such Daughters and Such a Mother"

On the afternoon of Friday, July 31, 1602, after weeks of frenzied preparation, Alice and Thomas stood just outside the front entrance of their grand manor as a hush fell over the entire village of Harefield. Everyone was poised and waiting for a special visitor to arrive. Harefield, situated in Middlesex, twenty miles northwest of London, was a verdant landscape compared to the gritty capital city. The Colne River, a tributary of the Thames, served as the western border of the small village, and its waters nourished the rich pastures and woodlands surrounding it. Shortly after their marriage, Thomas and Alice had purchased Harefield Place from the Newdigate family. Though less lavish than Knowsley or Lathom Hall, the couple intended Harefield to serve as one of their own country estates. Surrounded by a moat, Harefield Place was a picturesque medieval estate with large, heavy wooden doors and an impenetrable facade. Any minute, the rural manor would be transformed into a royal palace, everyone straining to hear the first beats and rhythmic thunder of the traveling entourage, signifying the queen's arrival.

Queen Elizabeth had chosen Harefield Place as a stop along her semiregular summer progress. English monarchs frequently fled London during the summer months, when the crowded city grew hot and malodorous. If there were an outbreak of the bubonic plague, as happened periodically until the mid–eighteenth century, kings and queens would also go on progress to try to escape the disease. A royal progress was intended to be a festive time, filled with feasts, entertainments, dancing, and hunts, although the queen and her court could govern from anywhere should the need arise. It was also a chance to tour some of the palatial manors of the nobility and live off their hospitality. Though it was a great honor to host the monarch, doing so was an enormous expense. The progress also brought the queen closer to her common subjects, who might never visit London, letting them see her magnificence in person and demonstrating that their ruler was never far from them. The size of the party fluctuated as courtiers came and went from the royal entourage, but the group typically hovered around fifty guests, not including the vast numbers of personal attendants and grooms needed to maintain the entourage as well as the horses, carts, coaches, and wagons that transported them and their luggage. From the road, the royal progress looked like a traveling carnival.

The stop in Harefield was early in the queen's summer progress that year. The group had left Greenwich on July 28, stopping first at Lambeth and a minor manor near Kew.[1] The royal court's time at Harefield would be the first significant stay-over, and they would be Thomas and Alice's guests for several days. Extravagant gifts for her majesty had to be secured, theatrical entertainments written, musicians hired, and feasts planned. Alice and Thomas ordered chickens, pigeons, veal, geese, rabbits, ducks, pigs, partridges, trout, and lobster, among other fixings, spending more than £220 (£30,000/$42,000 today) on the three-day feast alone.[2] Yet any monies spent would have been considered an investment in the future of the fledgling Egerton dynasty.

While Alice and Thomas surely wanted to outshine any of Queen Elizabeth's other hosts that summer, the couple also hoped that the queen would support the marriage of their children—his son, John, and her daughter Frances— to each other. The family was fully committed to the match, but as descendants of Henry VII and daughters of an earl, Frances and her sisters were expected to secure the queen's blessing before their marriages. Everyone at court knew that Thomas and Alice had already begun to make the arrangements for their children's wedding, so to ask the queen at that point, though technically required of their rank, looked more like an afterthought than an act of humility. Thomas and Alice were worried that they had irritated their queen by neglecting to ask for her blessing earlier in their conversations. The aging queen surely had more pressing matters on her mind, such as her own succession plans, but customs still needed to be observed. A grand entertainment could be just the occasion to remind the queen of their devotion to her, as there was nothing like music, theatrical performances, dancing, and feasts to calm any annoyance Queen Elizabeth might feel toward the Egertons. Lavish gifts, of course, could also help remind her majesty of Alice's and Thomas's affection.

Alice and Thomas commissioned John Davies to write and orchestrate the Harefield entertainments, as he had an established reputation for writing household entertainments and they did not want to take any chances on a lesser-known writer. They needed everything to be perfect for their queen and the other guests. Alice had spent her young adulthood learning the art of aristocratic entertainment from the Earls of Derby at Knowsley and Lathom Halls, but it had been eight years since Ferdinando's death. Now, at forty-three years old, Alice, with her new husband at her side, would at last assume the role of the great hostess. Alice and her writer for hire transformed the entire village into their stage, and the queen's entertainment began on the road into Harefield. When the royal entourage reached the dairy on the way to Harefield Place, they were greeted by two cheerful characters: a bailiff named Richard and a dairymaid named Joan, probably played by young members of neighboring noble or gentry families or high-ranking members of their households. The duo joked about the strangers passing by:

> **Joan:** All this night I could not sleep, dreaming of green rushes, and yester-night that chatting of the pies . . . but what make you in this company, I pray?

> **Bailiff:** I make the way for these strangers, which the way-maker himself could not do; for it is a way was never passed before. Besides, the Mrs. of this faire company, though she know the way to all men's hearts, yet she know the way but to a few men's houses, except she love them very well, I can tell you.

They regaled the party with accounts of all the craftsmen who had been furiously preparing the estate. Joan then teased the queen:

> **Joan:** My Mrs. charge me earnestly to retain all idle harvest folks that passed this way, and my meaning was, that if I could

hold them all this night and tomorrow, on Monday to carry them into the fields and make them earn their entertainment well and thrifty.

The bailiff and the dairymaid presented the queen with a jeweled rake and fork, dazzling props to jokingly imply that the queen should work in the fields to "earn her entertainment." The playful exchange reminded the cosmopolitan courtiers that they had left London and were now entering her majesty's pastoral realm.

The queen accepted the gifts and proceeded down the dirt country road toward Harefield Place. When she reached the front of the estate, she was met by two other characters: Place, wearing a colored robe that matched the bricks of the estate, and Time, with yellow hair, in a green robe, holding an hourglass that had stopped running. Clever wordplay ensued as the two spoke indirectly to the queen:

Place: Let me see, your wings are clipped, and for ought I see, your hourglass runs not.

Time: My wings are clipped, indeed, and it is her hands hath clipped them. . . . I am her Time, and Time were very ungrateful, if it should not ever stand still, to serve and preserve, cherish and delight her. That is the glory of her time and makes the Time happy wherein she liveth.

Place: And doth she make Place happy as well, Time? What if she makes thee a continual holiday, she makes me a perpetual sanctuary. Doth not the presence of a Prince make a cottage a castle and the presence of the Gods make every place a Heaven? . . . Were I as large as the hearts that are mine owners', I should be the fairest palace in the world. . . .

Time: In good time do you remember the hearts of your owners? For, as I was passing to this place, I found the heart, which . . .

was stolen by one of the nymphs from one of the servants of this Goddess.

Place then gave the queen a diamond in the shape of a heart and welcomed her inside. If Alice and Thomas had done their jobs well, their guests would be enchanted by the opening pageantry, setting a whimsical and relaxed mood for the rest of the royal visit. Alice and Thomas wanted the royal entourage to think of Harefield as a delightful respite from the pressures of London.

✦━━━━━━━✦━━━━━━━✦

The court remained at Harefield for three rainy days, during which time Alice and Thomas whispered commands to the household staff to ensure that the jubilation indoors was vibrant enough to keep the dreary weather and any royal dissatisfaction at bay. By all accounts, the visit was going well and Queen Elizabeth was "in her merriest vein"—that is, until Alice finally got up the nerve to ask the queen directly if she might be willing to accept her two oldest daughters, Anne and Frances, as ladies of her privy chamber, "and to bestow them in marriage where she thought fit, or at least to give her leave to bestow them." The queen saw through Alice's show of humility, knowing full well that Alice and Thomas had already been making plans for Frances's marriage. Queen Elizabeth quickly grew "exceedingly passionate and commanded silence on that behalf," refusing to respond one way or another. Alice and Thomas were left suspended in uncertainty, and court gossips reported that the couple was "nonplussed and know not how to proceed."[3] Their best choice of action was to abort the conversation as gracefully as possible and smile through the rest of the entertainments in the hope that the sprightly shows would color the queen's memory of the awkward exchange. Of course, more gifts might also help.

The steady midsummer rains prohibited any outdoor activities, but Alice and Thomas ensured that their guests would be amply delighted with a variety of amusements. Beyond the standard minstrels, dancing, and sultry conversations that normally accompanied feasts, a dozen singers from the Boys of the Chapel performed for their guests, as did acrobatic tumblers.[4] The entertainments continued with an extravagant display of hospitality and wealth as Alice and Thomas had arranged for a lottery for the queen and all thirty-four of the noble ladies attending that weekend. A lottery blended often mediocre poetic verse and song with a gratuitous distribution of gifts. They were typically choreographed, but the precise rules remain unclear.[5] At Harefield, Alice and Thomas secured the gifts, Davies probably wrote the verses, and because no expense was spared, a performer was hired to narrate the event.[6] A gentleman dressed as a mariner appeared before the group and sang a tale of a Spanish ship that had recently been raided by the English. The story went on to playfully explain that the gifts the ladies were about to receive were the bountiful treasures taken from the Spanish, although it is unclear if the gifts had been preselected for each woman or were randomly distributed.

The queen was cast as Cynthia, a character based on Artemis, the Greek goddess of the hunt, and the ladies were her nymphs. The queen went first as the mariner sang out, "Fortune must now no mire in triumph ride;/The wheels are yours that did her chariot guide." The queen then received a Wheel of Fortune, a lavish prop sumptuously set with diamonds. The Wheel of Fortune was an ancient symbol made popular during the Renaissance, and the story was that a powerful woman would spin the wheel and determine the fates of those around her, making it the ideal token for the queen. As the hostess and mistress of the house, Alice went next: "You thrive, or would, or may, your lot's purse./Fill it with gold, and you are ne'er the worse," upon which she received a purse. Other lots included a looking glass, a mask, and a pair of gloves. On and on it went, as the ladies received their gifts and the verses were sung. Though there may have been whispers about Alice's clumsy exchange with the queen, the music and seemingly ceaseless distribution of "Spanish booty" probably hushed many of the gossips. The queen's good mood that evening surely signaled that no harm had been done, allowing Alice and Thomas to breathe a little easier.

On Monday, August 3, the final day of the visit, the party prepared to embark on the next leg of the queen's progress to Hitcham Manor in Buckinghamshire, the estate of Sir William Clarke.[7] Alice and Thomas gave the queen a parting gift, a vibrant "robe of rainbows," that had cost £340 (£45,000/$62,000 today) to commission. The entire robe was made of silver cloth, and the dramatic sleeves were adorned with rubies and pearls.[8] Such an extravagant token said just as much about the host and hostess as it did about their royal guest; the shimmering gems were a reflection of the Egertons' dynastic ambitions. When they commissioned the piece, they could not have known that it would rain during the queen's entire visit; when they eventually gave her the gift of the rainbow robe, it must have felt like the perfect poetic ending to the occasion. The robe was so stunning that some believe it was the inspiration for Queen Elizabeth's "Rainbow Portrait."[9] In an effort to hold on to the whimsical realm Alice and Thomas had worked so hard to maintain throughout the entirety of the visit, the robe was accompanied by a poem, likely rewritten by Davies on-site to reflect the realities of spending time in Harefield those rainy summer days:

> *Commeth Iris, and unbidden guest,*
> *In her moist robe of colors gay;*
> *And she cometh, she every stays,*
> *For the space of forty day.*
>
> . . .
>
> *From her rainy robes he took,*
> *Which here he doth present to you.*
> *It is fitt it should with you remain,*
> *For you know better how to reign.*

Iris was the rain, an uninvited guest whose presence made it feel as though the ceaseless showers lasted forty days, a reference to the great flood in the Old Testament. When the rain finally cleared, however, a rainbow appeared as a fitting tribute to the queen, and thus she wore a robe made from it.

Place reappeared to bid the troupe farewell:

Place: Sweet Majesty, be pleased to look upon a poor widow, mourning before your Grace. I am this *Place*, which at your coming was full of joy; but now at your departure am full of sorrow. I was then, for my comfort, accompanied with the present cheerful *Time*; but now he is to depart with you; and,

> blessed as he is, must ever fly before you: But alas! I have no
> wings, as *Time* hath. My heaviness is such, that I must stand
> still, amazed to see so great happiness so soon berest me. Oh,
> that I could remove with you, as other circumstances can!

And with that, Alice, Thomas, and the village of Harefield watched the queen depart. The enchantment of the Harefield entertainment dissipated as the court rumbled out of sight. Those three days had cost the Egertons more than £2,000 (£275,000/$380,000 today), but they seemed to have been worth every penny.[10] Courtiers wrote to their friends and associates in the months that followed, recounting the queen's enjoyment. One report of the stay at Harefield happily recalled, "We are frolic here in court, much dancing in the privy chamber of country dances before the queen majesty, who is exceedingly pleased therewith."[11] Shortly thereafter, John Egerton and Frances Stanley were married. Despite her uncomfortable exchange with the queen, Alice got her way; the fledgling Egerton dynasty had been given a royal blessing.

❖━━━━━◆━━━━━❖

The jubilation was short lived, as the entire country experienced a surge of smallpox that summer, lasting into the winter. By December 1602, some members of the household staff of Harefield Place had been infected, though Alice and her family remained healthy.[12] Smallpox was a constant threat in that period, and people lived in fear of the disease. No one knew the cause, nor were there standard successful treatments, but the symptoms were undeniable; whereas high fevers and body aches could denote numerous other ailments, there was no mistaking the aggressive red rash that rapidly spread down the body. Smallpox was not always a death sentence—Queen Elizabeth had survived the illness in 1562—but the high mortality rate, along with the competing advice of physicians and healers, meant that any infection brought fear into the household. Alice, Thomas, and a portion of their household packed up and fled the village to take up residence in the Rolls Chapel, the grand library where the Court of Chancery records were kept in London. During an outbreak of the bubonic plague, people would avoid the crowded metropolis, but smallpox was so common that the Egertons were just eager to get away from Harefield and were fortunate that Thomas's political appointments and their family's vast fortunes and connections offered myriad options of retreat. (Their infected servants were not so lucky.) As Master of the Rolls, Thomas had possession of the chapel and the residential apartments there, and the location was the ideal temporary residence for the couple. Their move to "the Rolls" also reminded people, especially Alice's estranged brother-in-law, that the Court of Chancery was just one of the seats of her new family's power. Whether she needed help to defend Ferdinando's will or to escape smallpox, Thomas and his court would protect them.

The association between the Egertons and the Chancery became increasingly important in the coming year. The queen's summer progress proved to be her last, and by early spring 1603, she grew dangerously ill. With no heirs of her own, Elizabeth's imminent death meant a seismic shift for the English throne, but the sixty-nine-year-old queen refused to name a successor in the early days of her illness. The Tudor family tree did not have many branches, and the succession of the English throne was the greatest affair of the state. Elizabeth could have chosen a descendant of her Aunt Mary as her heir. The Stanley family were direct descendants of Mary's line, although Alice's brother-in-law William, the current Earl of Derby, would have taken precedence over Alice's daughters.

At the end of her life, the queen finally named her heir. She would entrust her throne to her Scottish cousin, James VI of Scotland. James VI was the son of Mary, Queen of Scots, and a direct descendant of Margaret Tudor, as well as the great-great-grandson of Henry VII, Queen Elizabeth's grandfather. She had followed the instructions in her father, Henry VIII's, will. After all the betrayal and intrigue that had played out between Queen Elizabeth and her cousin Mary, Queen of Scots, in the end it would be Mary's Protestant son who sat upon the English throne. When Queen Elizabeth died on March 24, 1603, James VI of Scotland also became James I of England.

For forty-five years, England had been ruled by a towering, unmarried woman. King James had a wife, Anna of Denmark, and children of his own, two sons and a daughter. Although he was a direct descendant of the Tudor line, his surname was Stuart (or Steward in the Scottish spelling), denoting yet another shift in the succession of the English throne and the establishment of a new monarchial dynasty. Even though the throne passed smoothly and peacefully from Queen Elizabeth to King James, it was a seismic shift. The Tudor age was at a close, and the English peerage looked hopefully but cautiously toward the future.

The Stuart succession also put the monarchy out of reach for Alice's daughters and signified the start of a new era in England. As Keeper of the Great Seal and a member of the Privy Council, Thomas would have been consumed by affairs of state, but Alice would also have had a role to play in navigating the new regime. For the English nobility, politics was a family business; Alice not only understood that, but it defined her sense of her place in the world. A new monarch could bring Alice and her daughters new opportunities.

Even though the same man sat on the thrones of both England and Scotland, legally they remained separate kingdoms. Each country maintained a separate Parliament and different political and legal practices. The English and Scottish peerage also remained distinct, meaning that King James would either allow English nobles to maintain their current appointments or appoint new English nobles to fill the posts. Before he made up his mind, he would first need to meet the noble families of England and observe life in his new southern realm.

When the royal family set off to make their way south from Edinburgh to settle in London, it was the ideal moment for noble houses up and down the country to dazzle the Stuarts. As the journey was mapped out, aristocratic families began to plan grand entertainments to host the new monarch and his family. Alice and Thomas well knew after their turn hosting Queen Elizabeth the previous summer that accommodating a monarch could be an expensive endeavor. Though Harefield would not be a stop along the Stuarts' southern progress, they were still asked to lend their support. Robert Cecil turned to Thomas Egerton for help readying his own estate, explaining "I am not able to furnish my house at Theobald of all such necessary conveniences for his Majesty's reception without the help of my friends. I am bold to pray your Lordship to suffer me to borrow some of your silver dishes" and other fine serving pieces.[13] Queen Elizabeth had only recently been laid to rest in Westminster Abbey as wagons of silver dishes, fine tapestries, and embroidered silks were transported between England's stately homes in preparation for the new royal family's arrival.

Alice and her family must have been elated when it was decided that Althorp would be a stop along the royal progress south. Her brother John, heir to her father's growing estate, had died in January 1600, and since that time, Alice had grown close to her nephew, Robert Spencer, who was now lord of the manor. Robert continued to expand the family sheep business, while also serving as a member of Parliament and Sheriff of Northamptonshire, eventually being knighted as a member of the Order of the Garter, the highest order of knight, although he still did not yet have a hereditary noble title. Over the years, Alice had written to him to offer advice, as well as asking for his help in securing political appointments for men in her service, and Robert had reciprocated with news from court. Robert had also been a guest in attendance during the lavish Harefield entertainment, so he knew his aunt and new uncle were experienced hosts to a royal entourage. Robert had been a widower since his wife, Margaret, had died in 1597, and his children were still quite young at the time of the Stuart succession, so he would need help in managing the royal visit. Who better to turn to than his commanding aunt Alice and her powerful husband?[14]

King James traveled separately from his wife and children in order to arrive in London earlier, so the Althorp entertainment was only for Anna of Denmark, the new queen consort, and the nine-year-old royal heir, Prince Henry. Queen Anna had a reputation as a lover of art and literature and worked to instill the same passions in the young prince. It would be a perfect opportunity to introduce the foreign queen to a cadre of English writers. So Alice, Robert, and Thomas commissioned Ben Jonson to write the masque. Jonson soon became a favorite of the new queen, going on to regularly pen court entertainments at the request of Queen Anna and Prince Henry. Alice and her family were not only patrons of the arts but also skilled cultural matchmakers, which only widened their impressive sphere of influence.

The festivities at Althorp took place in June 1603, less than a year after the Harefield entertainment. Jonson's work was not a literary masterpiece, but its tone was lighthearted and playful. The Spencers did their best to ensure that their new queen and prince saw England as an enchanted, and thus enchanting, kingdom. The character of Satire greeted the queen and prince:

> *Look, see: (beshrew this Tree)*
> *What may all this wonder be?*
> *Pipe it, who that list for me:*
> *I'll fly out abroad, and see.*

> *That is Cyparissus' face!*
> *And the Dame hath Syrinx' grace!*
> *O that Pan were now in Place*
> *Sure they are of heavenly race.*[15]

Other characters included a fairy and an elf. There would be plenty of time for serious exchanges, but that was the moment for the extended Spencer family to introduce themselves to the new royal family, and there was no better way to do so than with beauty and whimsy. Alice had left Althorp nearly twenty-five years earlier, at the age of twenty-one. At that time, the Spencers had been on the brink of social and political advancement, and Alice's marriage to Ferdinando was an essential step in their ascent. Now forty-four years old, Alice was no longer just the youngest Spencer daughter; she was the Dowager Countess of Derby, the mother of three young noblewomen, wealthy in her own right, and the wife of one of the most powerful men in England. Her sisters were also countesses, and her nephew, now head of the Spencer family, continued to increase his standing as one of the wealthiest men in England. At the beginning of that century and monarchy, Althorp was no longer a mere sheep farm but a worthy setting for a lavish welcome for the new queen and prince to their kingdom.

＋—•—＋

The royal progress south was just the first of a series of festivities and ceremonies held that summer, and Alice and her family were there for all of it. On July 2, 1603, just a few weeks after the Althorp entertainment, Alice and her daughters again met with the queen, this time at a feast at Windsor Castle to commemorate the installation of the Knights of the Garter. Alice, Anne, Frances, and Elizabeth, "being all of them most sumptuous in apparel and exceedingly rich and glorious in jewels like the wearer," took their place in line to "perform their homage unto her highness, with great reverence, kneeling one by one, kissed her majesty's hand, being hard to discern whether the mildness of the sovereign or humility of the subjects was greatest."[16] As she curtsied to Queen Anna, Alice's memory may have flickered back to her awkward exchange with Queen Elizabeth at Harefield, just a year before.

The arrival of the Stuarts brought a fresh start, and Alice and her family certainly made a good first impression. As the queen consort (meaning that she was queen by marriage) rather than the regnal queen (the ruler by birthright), Anna of Denmark was far less formidable than Queen Elizabeth had been. Though King James touted a vision of a more absolutist rule than his royal predecessor had, he also maintained a far more jovial, borderline lascivious, court culture than Elizabeth had. Prior to his ascension to the English throne, King James had published two books, *The True Lawe of Free Monarchies* and *Basilikon Doron*, laying out for everyone his precise approach to kingship, which included an interpretation of the divine right of kings that read more like absolutist rule than English politics had customarily allowed for.[17] Men such as Alice's husband would ensure that his absolutist urges were checked by the long-standing legal and political customs of England.[18] On the other hand, for much of the previous decade, the English aristocracy had secretly obsessed over who would inherit the "Virgin Queen's" throne, and after forty-five years with a single woman as the head of state and the Church of England, the Stuarts brought a return to a more traditionally gendered order of monarchy and court culture. In a sense, the shift coincided with a new phase in the lives of Alice and her family. Though the Dowager Countess of Derby would never sit submissively in the shadow of her husband, Thomas, together the Egertons would do their duty to maintain order and advance their new blended family, just as they hoped the Stuarts would do for England.

At his coronation, James I won the favor of his English peers by granting a slew of new titles and knighthoods. Promoting the families who had served Queen Elizabeth was a good way to ensure that those English statesmen remained loyal to their new Scottish king. Alice's nephew Robert Spencer was made Baron Spencer of Wormleighton on July 21, 1603, finally establishing a hereditary title for the Spencer family; her husband, Thomas, was also elevated into the peerage with the rank of baron, with Ellesmere granted as his baronial name. English noble titles typically have a territorial designation, and Ellesmere is a village in Shropshire. More significantly, Ellesmere was one of the first leases that Thomas had reacquired for Alice in her inheritance suit against William Stanley, as the Stanley family had previously held the land rights and the village had been designated part of Alice's jointure from the Earl of Derby. Now Alice not only profited from the rents in Ellesmere, she was married to Lord Ellesmere. Technically, that made Alice Lady Ellesmere, but a baroness was a lower rank than a countess, and Alice continued to use Dowager Countess of Derby as her dominant title, although she surely enjoyed adding the new title to her collection.

Along with a new title, King James also officially named Thomas Lord Chancellor, the head of the Chancery, the highest equitable court in the realm. As Queen Elizabeth's Master of the Rolls and Lord Keeper of the Great Seal, Thomas had been acting as lord chancellor but without the title or the salary. He relinquished his two lower posts of Master of the Rolls and Keeper of the Great Seal and turned his attention to reorganizing the courts and expanding judicial prerogative under his jurisdiction. Once he stepped down as Master of the Rolls, he lost his residential privileges at the Rolls, so he leased York House, an even larger London town house on the desirable and cosmopolitan street running along the Thames called The Strand to use as his London residence. He and Alice divided their time between Harefield Place and York House, often spending time apart, as most aristocratic husbands and wives did. Thomas's work with the courts kept him in London, and Alice frequently traveled to visit her three daughters, each of whom, within a few years, was running her own large household and beginning to have children.

Those homes became the epicenters for each family's patronage circle. Anne and her husband, Grey Brydges, Lord Chandos, made Sudeley Castle in the Cotswolds of Gloucestershire their primary residence. Chandos was the patron of a network of local poets and loved to throw large and expensive parties, earning him the nickname "King of the Cotswolds." Elizabeth settled in Leicestershire, dividing her time between the two ancestral homes, Castle Donington and Ashby de la Zouch, of her husband, Henry Hastings, where she continued the family tradition of supporting local poets and writers. Since Frances's husband, John, was also her stepbrother, Alice and Thomas were perhaps most directly involved in their lives. They spent considerable time in London, as John also held various posts in King James's court, and in 1604, the couple acquired the sprawling estate of Ashridge in Hertfordshire.

Both generations of the Egerton family not only were patrons of writers but also began buying and collecting books and manuscripts, building one of the most important English libraries of the era. Though there is no evidence that Alice herself was actively involved in book collecting, certainly a flurry of masterworks came through her door. Thomas collected newly printed books and pamphlets, such as those produced by one of his secretaries, John Donne. Like a true gentleman of the period that would ultimately be labeled the English Renaissance, Thomas also bought manuscripts of ancient and medieval texts as part of the rising desire to "rediscover" the past, with a new appreciation of history, language, and learning. The crown jewel of his collection was a lavishly illuminated manuscript of Geoffrey Chaucer's *Canterbury Tales*. Chaucer himself had overseen the production of the manuscript in the early 1400s. Today, we call this book "The Ellesmere Chaucer," and it is probably the most important manuscript in the English language, being the most complete and beautiful contemporary version of the tales, as well as the first work of literature written in Middle English at a time when most works in western Europe were written in either French or Latin.[19] With illuminations in vibrant pigments and gold and miniature paintings of each of the pilgrims next to the opening of each tale, the large manuscript was, and is, a staggering work of visual and textual art. For Thomas and Alice, it was a trophy and a material reminder of their status and influence, but their books also represented something even more significant.

Alice and Thomas embodied the ideals of their thriving cultural moment, just as Ferdinando had, as well as a reverence for the written word. For people such as Alice, patronage and collecting were ways of being seen, and she enjoyed being illuminated by the shine from the thriving literary world around her. Beyond that, however, she had learned from Ferdinando that literature and theater could serve as conduits to one's own humanity. For Alice and her peers, being well versed in music, literature, and history was an essential part of nobility, and Alice ensured that her daughters inherited more than just their father's lands and income.

Like his father, John Egerton built a library at Ashridge, and Frances actively collected her own books, kept in a private book closet. Her collection grew to 241 printed books and manuscripts, a remarkably large private library for the age, ranging from Bibles and homilies to *Diverse Plays by Shakespeare* and a volume entitled *The Life of Queen Elizabeth*. There were also Turkish histories, maps, books in English and French, and recently printed works on the Court of King James. There were books about spirituality, religion, and politics. John Donne created a small book of poems for Frances, which was bound in white with her initials emblazoned on the cover.[20]

Frances used her books for more than private reading and collecting; she also used them to express her fondness for other members of her family.[21] She often loaned her books to her sisters, and they in turn helped her library grow. In 1632, her sister Elizabeth, who also maintained a small collection of religious sermons and poems, gave her a copy of *The New Covenant, or the Saints Portion*, a compilation of sermons. Frances also gifted books from her library to her servants and children. They became sentimental keepsakes, as one small octavo volume of *A Progresse of Pietie*, printed in 1600, shows the signature of her young daughter, Alice, on the title page. On the page before is the fledgling scribble of her son's signature, followed by the Latin words *Me tenet ex dono matris suae* (Given to me by my mother).[22] The front cover of the little book bears a gold stamp in the shape of an eagle standing over a baby in a basket. That was the Stanley family heraldic badge, but Frances adapted the symbol for herself by adding flowers and leaves around the baby.

In turn, each of Alice's daughters made patronage a centerpiece of her own family's endeavors. At least twelve works printed between 1591 and 1637 include a humble dedicatory epistle to Alice or one or more of her daughters. Over Thomas's lifetime, seventy-five works were dedicated to him. Writers and clergymen constantly touted Alice or her daughters as, for example, a "most virtuous lady, the worthy patroness of learning" or some variation thereof.[23] Beyond tributes to each woman's virtue and learnedness, they were also celebrated for their piety, nobility, beauty, and other vague attributes designed to flatter them and encourage their financial support. It was a symbiotic relationship wherein writers tried to profit by name-dropping and Alice and her daughters gained social capital for being celebrated as patrons of the arts and religious works.

In actuality, most of the dedications were fairly superficial. There were two dedications, however, that meant more. The first came from Sir John Davies, who had penned the Harefield entertainment for Queen Elizabeth's 1602 visit. In 1609, he paid his respects to Alice and her daughters in the dedication of his *The Holy Roode* or *Christs Crosse*:

> *To the Right Honorable, well accomplished Lady, Alice, Countess*
> *of Derby, my good Lady and Mistress: And, to her three right Noble*
> *Daughters by Birth, Nature, and Education, the Lady Elizabeth,*
> *Countess of Huntingdon, the Lady Frances Egerton, and the Lady Anne,*
> *Wife to the truly Noble Lord, Gray, Lord Chandos, that now is.*[24]

Though a number of dedications made to Alice alone touch upon the themes of "birth, nature, and education," Davies made a point of stressing that all four women shared those qualities. By emphasizing their birth, he acknowledged that for Anne, Frances, and Elizabeth, these traits had come from their mother. After all they had been through, it surely meant something special to be lauded in print as a close-knit and honorable mother and daughters.

In 1616, Thomas Gainsford, a soldier, translator, and historian, took this idea even further in the dedication of his *The Historie of Trebizon, in Foure Bookes*. Gainsford wrote a brief epistle at the opening of each of his four books to one of the women: the first to Alice, the second to Elizabeth, the third to Frances, and the last to Anne. It is the one he composed for Elizabeth, Countess of Huntingdon, at the beginning of the second book that marks the significance of his choice to dedicate the collective work to them:

> *I thought it most befitting to look out for some handsome props of*
> *supportation, and so have placed the Daughters in one circle with the*

> *Mother: Yea, such Daughters, and such a Mother, that me thinks you*
> *move together like faire Planets in conspicuous Orbs and from whose*
> *influence can proceed nothing but sweet presages . . .*[25]

Whether he realized it or not, Gainsford celebrated the women by expressing the most important bond Alice held throughout her life: her connection with, and her influence over, her daughters.

＊━━◆━━◆━━◆━━＊

Almost a decade before Gainsford published his dedication, some of Alice's family had gathered to celebrate the conclusion of the struggle that had brought them so close together. In 1607, Parliament finalized a Private Act that officially brokered the end of Alice's inheritance suit against her brother-in-law William. Though the two parties had reached a preliminary settlement in 1602, the legal entailments and complications over the jurisdiction of the Isle of Man meant that Parliament had had to rule on the final details. The Act came down precisely as Thomas and Alice had anticipated, which meant that Alice, her coheiress daughters, and their respective husbands could finally put the Stanley inheritance suit behind them. Alice and her daughters had been waiting for that moment for thirteen years, and they were not about to let it pass without commemorating the achievement and all that Alice had done to secure their bright futures. Henry and Elizabeth, now titled the Earl and Countess of Huntingdon, invited a small party to Ashby de la Zouch to celebrate.

It had been thirteen years since Ferdinando's death, and it must have felt particularly appropriate to mark the end of the grueling inheritance suit with a glittery spectacle that put the forty-eight-year-old Alice at the center of it. While Ferdinando had been alive, her power had been completely derived from him; her life had been circumscribed by what it meant to be the Countess of Derby. Now, even though Alice had remarried, she moved through the world by her own force and made decisions for other people. A family gathering and entertainment in her honor would not just celebrate the end of the lawsuit but was a moment for Alice to revel in the woman she had become.

Alice arrived at Ashby for the festivities in late July. According to accounts, she traveled the hundred miles north from Harefield without Thomas, but it is likely that he joined her there.[26] Anne may not have been in attendance and may have been pregnant at the time, but Frances was there to celebrate with her mother and younger sister. Alice's older sisters Elizabeth and Anne were also in attendance, as were a few other close friends.[27] The revelries began with a hunting trip in Leicester Forest. The party brought with them "two gallons and three pints of claret wine, and a gallon of sack, and one gallon of [borage] wine," so it is safe to assume that a good time was had.[28] The next evening, the party gathered in the Great Chamber at Ashby for a performance written by John Marston. When Alice had hosted Queen Elizabeth at Harefield and Queen Anna at Althorp, the grandeur had been all for her royal guests. This time, Alice was the guest of honor at a masque that celebrated her successful work in securing the status and fortunes of her daughters. The players danced before her, and the lyrics of their performance were a testament to the matriarch Alice had become:

> O we are full of joy no breast more light,
> But those who owe you theirs by Nature's right
> From whom vouchsafe this present. 'Tis a work
> wherein strange miracles & wonders lurk
> For know it Lady whose ambition towers
> Only to this to be termed worthy of yours
> whose forehead I could crown with clearest rays
> but it her praise is, she abhors much praise.

Alice's daughters were a reflection of her accomplishments as a mother and countess, so Marston's entertainment also used the language of heraldic imagery to celebrate the union of the Stanley and Hastings lines in the Earl and Countess of Huntingdon:

> But every night upon a Forrest side
> on which an eagle peach they aide
> and honor her with their most raised light [29]

and again:

on the top of which in a fair oak sat a golden
eagle.[30]

The oak was a symbol of the Hastings family, as Henry Hastings was the Keeper of the Royal Forest in Leicester. Notably, in 1607, he had also assumed the post of Lord Lieutenant of Leicestershire, another benchmark career advancement for the family. The eagle was a symbol of the Stanley family, and like her sister Frances, Elizabeth used the crest throughout her life, although she added oak leaves and a small acorn to the basket. Alice and her family heard their heraldic symbols come to life in Marston's entertainment as a testament to their honor and lineages.[31]

The Ashby entertainment also included a lottery, a means of lavishly bestowing gifts upon the ladies, harkening back to the grand entertainment Thomas and Alice had hosted for Queen Elizabeth at Harefield Place. Each of the fourteen women sang her own stanza before receiving a valuable token, as the men looked on. As the guest of honor, Alice opened the lottery by singing:

As this is endless, endless by your joy:
Value the wish and not the wishers toy,
And for one blessing past God send you seven,
And in the end the endless joys of heaven.
Till then let this be all your cross
To have discomfort or your loss.[32]

Presumably she was then gifted a jeweled cross or something of the sort. Her daughters, sisters, and close friends then followed with their own stanzas and gifts. The fourteen women danced in the candlelight, sang, and showered one another with jewels and fine tokens. It was an opulent scene.

We do not know what Alice thought as she reveled in the Great Hall of her youngest daughter's estate, watching the enchanting performance in her honor and dancing in the lottery with her daughters, sisters, and friends. But it is easy to imagine that she must have felt an immense sense of accomplishment and pride. Her three daughters had grown up to become ladies at the helms of their own grand estates, each having secured a fine husband with monies hard won by the shrewd decisions Alice and Thomas had made. Perhaps Alice ached a little for Ferdinando. How could she not wish he were there to see the women their daughters had become and to watch his bride at the center of her own performance? This youngest daughter of a country knight had transformed into a formidable woman, who wielded marriage and literature as her weapons and emerged triumphantly from the gladiatorial arena of a fiercely contested inheritance suit. She did not know it at the time—no one could have imagined, sitting in the candlelit Great Hall of Ashby de la Zouch—that the family would have to endure unimaginable horror before they could be reunited like this again. But that was still years away. On that summer night in 1607, Alice and her family danced triumphantly.

CHAPTER SIX

A WOMAN IN CONTROL

"Her Humorous, Proud, and Disdainful Carriage"

The jubilation of the summer celebrations and the legal triumph of Alice and her daughters could only temporarily distract from a scandal brewing elsewhere in the family. Alice's older sister Anne, who had attended the celebration at Ashby and been her close friend all her life, now sought her family's help as her marriage imploded. Anne's first marriage, to Sir William Stanley, Lord Monteagle, had been the bridge the Spencer family had used to wed Alice to Ferdinando, but Lord Monteagle had died in 1581 after six years of marriage, leaving Anne a childless widow. Within just a few years, she married Henry, Lord Compton, but that marriage had also been cut short when Compton had suddenly died in 1589, leaving Anne again a widow, this time with a five-year-old son. For her third husband, Anne married Robert Sackville, Lord Buckhurst, heir to the earldom of Dorset. Another Spencer daughter had made an astronomical rise, and, like her younger sister, Anne shrewdly played the game of building aristocratic alliances. Just as Alice and Thomas married their children to each other, so Anne and Sackville eventually consolidated their own wealth by marrying her son, Henry, to his daughter, Cecily. But by the spring of 1606, it was hard to imagine how Anne and Sackville had ever been capable of such long-term, pragmatic thinking, as their relationship was becoming more of an uncomfortable spectacle every day.

Dynastic unions were virtually never about affection or even compatibility. Once the unions had been secured and the monies and lands had been settled, social proprieties were the only strings tethering Anne and Sackville to each other, and eventually, those bonds began to weaken. Sackville grew increasingly frustrated with his wife's extravagant tastes and expenditures, lamenting that "This certain yearly allowance she had merely for her apparel, and thereby she need not perish for want of clothes. . . . I, myself, paid all the pages to all the women servants attending her, and defrayed all her charges and extraordinary expenses of physics, or any journeys by water or land, or any required she gave at any house she lay."[1] At the same time, Anne was fed up with Sackville's complaints about her spending. Much like Alice, Anne entered her later marriage from a position of financial strength, so although the laws of English coverture may have stipulated male authority and female subservience, the complex nature of jointures and personal and familial status meant that second and third marriages for women such as Anne and Alice did not follow a simple patriarchal script.

Unhappy aristocratic husbands and wives frequently set up distinct households but remained legally bound in marriage. By the spring of 1606, Anne was eager to live apart from her husband, while Sackville was determined to curb what he saw as his wife's extravagant lifestyle and force her to submit to his will. According to Sackville, he repeatedly offered financial incentives for reconciliation, which were met with "her continual violent tempestion sues in domestial conversations (greater than flesh and blood could endure)."[2] The couple could no longer carry on a simple conversation without exploding into a fight, so Anne turned to her high-ranking youngest sister, Alice, and younger brother Sir Richard Spencer to negotiate on her behalf. Sackville regarded Alice as an "honorable lady" and Richard as a "discreet gentleman," so everyone had hopes that the Spencer siblings could bring a suitable resolution to the matrimonial breakdown.[3]

Alice and Richard first sat down with Sackville to press for some easement of his expectations of his vivacious wife, as it was becoming clear to everyone that Anne had no intention of abiding by her husband's desire for the couple to resume cohabiting. He finally agreed that if she would return and live under his roof, he would remain quiet about her lavish spending. The Spencer duo then met with Anne to present the measured accord. Through the ordeal, Anne had lost all respect for her husband and continued to refuse to return to his home when she had other estates where she could live as she wished. Just as Alice and Thomas maintained multiple residences between London and their country seat in Harefield, other noble families also kept several households and migrated around the country to attend to personal and official matters. Rather than politely declining, however, Anne responded to his offer by writing up a series of what Sackville called "certain foolish rhymes" and "ridiculous compositions with kind of scornful answers": "The fool hath more wit then such a part to commit, Falentido Dilly," meaning that even a fool had more wit than her husband. Her second verse was "To this cunning piece of law, he that shooteth at a buzzard, may catch a dove, Falentido Dilly." The "dilly" at the end of each line was a common nonsensical refrain used at the time to give a verse a playful rhythm. "Falentido" was a silly way to say "'fallen dido,'" which in the colloquial English of the time would mean something like a "dead old duck.'"* Anne was mocking her desperate husband's attempt to catch her by likening him to a "dead old duck" who thought he could use the law to catch a buzzard of a wife, but she was actually a dove and would not be caught. Richard was angry at his sister for not taking the situation seriously, and Alice was also frustrated by her sister's childish response, as well as her own inability to negotiate a reasonable settlement. Though Alice certainly believed that her sister had earned the right to make demands in her marriage, the sisters disagreed about how to publicly conduct oneself, and Alice was not amused by Anne's penchant for overtly brazen behavior.

Exasperated, Alice and Richard abandoned any hope of reconciling Anne and Sackville, but Anne was far from done with her drama. She relocated to join the merriment of the royal court and to keep a distance from her husband, who appeared more emasculated with each passing month. By the winter of 1607, she was annoying everyone with her "importunities" and "storm," including the king and queen, who became desperate to get rid of her.[4] Anne and Sackville had become court jokes. The king teased Robert Cecil, Earl of Salisbury and Alice's friend, that Salisbury should marry Anne just to get her away from court. To sweeten the jest, King James jokingly promised that he would even use his "power to cause a solemn divorce to pass between the lusty lady and her husband and your lordship to be married to

---

*   My thanks to Patricia Fumerton, professor of English at the University of California, Santa Barbara, for helping me work out the joke.

her this Christmas, whereof his Majesty will defray the cost and dance at your wedding with all his children."[5] The situation was becoming embarrassing to everyone except Anne.

It was time to up the ante. In a joint letter, Ellesmere and the Archbishop of Canterbury again appealed to Sackville to put an end to the marital spat. Marriage fell under the scope of ecclesiastical law, and the Archbishop of Canterbury was the head of the ecclesiastical courts, whereas Ellesmere, as lord chancellor, was the head of all equitable courts. He was also Sackville's brother-in-law, so the family surely hoped that he could talk some sense into Sackville as men, brothers, and peers. Ellesmere and the archbishop made no attempt to hide their displeasure at having to intervene, explaining "that your said countess hath been since again with his Majesty, who referring her to us, she voweth that she will have us and never give us rest until we shall set down an order betwixt you." They implored Sackville to offer her "the sum of £1600 [£220,000/$304,000 today] per year until she shall please God so to unite your hearts, as that you may again with comfort cohabitate together."[6] Knowing how much Anne loved expensive things, Ellesmere and the archbishop thought that perhaps Sackville could bribe his wife into submission. After all, most aristocratic marriages were motived by wealth, not love, so a cash incentive seemed like a logical try.

Sackville refused to be pressured by "the unjust pretenses and unreasonable demands of my furious and turbulent wife," and he railed that "her ears are stopped and filled up with paltry cotton." He also offered a heated response to their request that he pay her off: "I do not think her worthy of the third part thereof who hath already spread so many false aspersions upon my deceased [father] and myself, as the foul sties thereof according to the nature of vulgar rumors and aptness of malignant impressions will stick fast in the minds of many."[7] Sackville's father had recently died in 1608, and Anne had been making disparaging comments about him at court. Sackville was furious over whatever she had said and believed that giving her more money would only reward her bad behavior, which he took as a betrayal of his family's good name. King James, the Archbishop of Canterbury, Lord Chancellor Ellesmere, Sir Richard Spencer, and Alice, Dowager Countess of Derby, had all failed to reunite the angry, melodramatic couple.

Though Anne and Sackville never reconciled, their feud ended just a few months later with Sackville's death on February 27, 1609. In his will, he addressed his fraught relationship with his wife: "whom without great grief and sorrow inconsolable, I cannot remember in regard of her exceeding unkindness and intolerable evil usage toward myself and my late dear right honorable good lord and father deceased, praying Almighty God of his mercy to forgive her as I do unfeignedly from the bottom of my heart." Rather than expressing anger and bitterness, he expressed sadness that she had been so cruel to him and to the memory of his father. Though he granted her forgiveness, it was surely more for his own sake so that he might die in peace. He permitted her to continue to use the household goods and jewels she had had from him for the duration of her life; she could then pass them on to her son, who was married to Sackville's daughter. He specifically mentioned five spectacular rings he had given her, three set with diamonds that she often wore on pins in her hair and two set with sapphires that were so fair they looked like diamonds. He permitted her to keep them for her life but insisted that they pass to his daughters after her death.[8] After years of a tumultuous row that had sucked in people at the highest level of state, on his deathbed, Sackville hoped that the union of their children would restore peace to his family and order to his estate. It may have worked, as Anne's behavior stopped fueling court gossip after his death, although she made no reference to the five rings or passing them to his daughters in her own will written before her death in 1618.

+------◆------+

Alice and Ellesmere were voices of reason and decorum in the marital spat between Anne and Sackville, but bringing a turbulent spirit to their later marriages was something the Spencer sisters had in common. Unlike Anne, Alice at least seemed to keep her brash attitude toward Ellesmere away from court. Like Anne and Sackville, Alice and Ellesmere had married only when it made strategic sense. It was her second marriage and his third and was a dynastic union, with no pretense of love between Alice and her new husband. And the decision to wed her daughter to his son had been designed to incentivize Ellesmere's continued work on behalf of Alice and her daughters. They shared a commitment to rising, but that was the extent of their common goals, and they did not even hold a uniform vision of how best to achieve it. Alice rose by strategic marriages for herself and her daughters, and although marriage was certainly a part of Ellesmere's plans, he secured his own place at court with royal appointments in the government and with focused study, hard work, and keen intelligence. Appointments to these types of legal and political offices were not an option for Alice. She inhabited her role as a countess with confidence and enjoyed the finest luxuries. In fact, when they first wed, Alice arrived at Harefield Place with forty servants to tend to the needs of her three daughters and herself, costing £650 per year (£90,000/$125,000 today).[9] The austere lawyer must have been gobsmacked by the sight of teams of staff parading trunks and furnishings through their home as he and Alice began to blend their families together.

Ellesmere may have thought that forty attendants for one woman and three girls was excessive, as would most of his peers, and he already maintained a well-staffed home with attendants for each member of the family, stewards and clerks to oversee the estate finances, an usher for the great hall, a cook, a baker, a butter boy, and grooms to take care of their horses, among various other posts.[10] Estates of that size required constant maintenance, which was a costly enterprise. In the first three months of 1606 alone, the family spent close to £37 (£5,000/$7,000 today) on basic repairs to York House, which included fixing floorboards, repairing wardrobes, covering seats in red leather or orange velvet, and even making an extra key to the water house (a building that contained a well) because Alice insisted on having her own. Seven of the nine expenses documented were at the request of Alice or her daughter Frances.[11] Whereas Ellesmere begrudgingly did what he had to do, Alice seemed to revel in it. As husband and wife, they never saw eye to eye about money.

That was probably in large part due to their different upbringings. The Spencers had become one of the wealthiest families in the realm. At Parliament, on May 8, 1621, Sir Robert Spencer, Alice's nephew, famously had a spat with the Earl of Arundel. Arundel and other long-established members of the aristocracy mocked Spencer as new money and the descendant of nothing but sheep farmers. Robert retorted that while his family had been raising sheep, "two honorable persons of [Arundel's] ancestors were condemned here in Parliament without being heard."[12] Robert's sarcastic comment was referring to Arundel's ancestors the Duke of Norfolk and the Earl of Surrey, both of whom had been executed for treason. The Spencers may have been new money, but at least they *had* money—and lots of it. Alice not only was a beneficiary of her family's wealth and status but also had amassed an enormous inheritance for herself, as well as an ancient title, and had created three coheiresses, each wealthy in her own right. Her large entourage mirrored, although on a far smaller scale, that which she had seen at Knowsley and Lathom when she had first been married to Ferdinando, in training for one day running her own estates. Though Ellesmere had been doing relatively well by securing important positions at court, true wealth came to him only when he married Alice. He had no extended family network, not even a new-money family, to prop him up. As an illegitimate child born a Catholic, he had a lot to make up for, and although he had earned immense legal and political influence, he was still a self-made man. Alice and Ellesmere were never on an equal footing, and that power imbalance plagued their marriage.

Not only were their upbringings and family histories contrasting, but they had differing experiences with religion prior to their marriage. Alice had learned much from the tribulations she and Ferdinando had faced due to his family's tolerance, if not outright embrace, of Catholicism. In Alice's mind, conformity with the state religion was the only way to survive. As an aristocratic woman, she could appoint her own private chaplains, which she did. On October 8, 1614, she appointed one Anthony Watson as her private chaplain to serve her at Harefield Place.[13] Later in her life, she also employed a chaplain named John Prichard.[14] Despite the printed sermons and theological texts scholars and clergymen dedicated to her, both of many of her personal chaplains were completely unknown, suggesting that Alice's personal religious practices were perhaps less staunch than those of her peers. She was not subversive or a recusant, but she seems to have been less pious than some other women of her day, including her two youngest daughters, Frances and Elizabeth, both of whom collected many religious books and routinely copied sermons as part of their regular worship practices. Conformity to the state religion was just one of the many ways Alice worked to maintain a good standing in the eyes of her peers and her monarch, regardless of who sat on the throne.

Things were not so simple for Ellesmere. As a young man who was known to have been raised a Catholic, he constantly needed to prove his religious loyalty to his queen and subsequently his king. As first Queen Elizabeth and then King James gradually entrusted him with more responsibilities within their legal and political courts, Ellesmere did not just conform to the state's Protestant religion; he shaped it. While in service to Queen Elizabeth, he oversaw the persecution of Catholics and Jesuits, perhaps most notably playing a role in the trial of Mary, Queen of Scots. He garnered a strong reputation for being a harsh adversary to those who held the old religion, and Elizabeth Russell, Dowager Baroness Russell, claimed that some people considered Ellesmere to be "an arrant hypocrite and deep dissembler."[15] As he moved further away from his Catholic roots, Ellesmere embraced conformity to the state religion, but unlike Alice's, his devotional leaning slanted more toward a moderate Calvinism, which included a disdain for the grand rituals of Catholicism. Under King James, the Church of England embraced some aspects of Calvinist theology but rejected the idea of predestination. That set men such as Ellesmere apart from the more fanatical Puritans, who adhered to a far stricter reading of Calvin's theology. Surprisingly in an age of radical religious reformation, religion was perhaps the only thing Alice and Ellesmere never seemed to fight about.

Alice and Ellesmere were bound by the sanctity of marriage and the myriad contracts that went along with aristocratic marriages, and they shared a bloodline in the children born to Frances and John. But for the majority of their relationship, Alice spent her time hosting grand groups of friends and family at Harefield or traveling to be with her daughters and their families. Ellesmere spent most of his time holed up in his chambers working at Harefield or at one of his London residences in service to the king and the Court of Chancery. He lamented Alice's frivolity, and although she may have been a dowager, she viewed him as just plain dour. The patriarchal culture of the times may have suggested that Ellesmere was the head of his family, but in a world where wealth and status could alter the balance of power in any relationship, the scales were tipped in Alice's favor.

They would stay away from each other as much as possible to preserve their good reputation, but that did not mean the marriage was remotely happy. In 1610, ten years into their marriage, Ellesmere hit a breaking point. He was two decades her senior, and at seventy years old, like many people of the age, he suffered constant battles with gout and kidney stones. Living with chronic pain, the fuse of his temper grew shorter. As his mental faculties slowly slipped, he became increasingly impatient with the frivolity of his wife in particular and the royal court in general. On several occasions, he tried to resign from his office, but the king refused to accept his resignation. The aging lord chancellor began taking steps to settle his estate and prepare for his death, fearing that Alice might try to make things difficult for his son and daughter from his previous marriage.

Always the detail-oriented lawyer, he started by drafting a memo he called "Some Notes and Remembrances for preserving and continuing of quietness between my wife and my son, after my death." He amiably began: "There is no worldly thing, that I more desire, than after my death, there may be no just cause or occasion of offense or unkindness between my son, whom I have made the executor of my last will and testament, and the countess of Derby, my loving wife." He then revealed two large promises he had made Alice upon the marriage. The first was that "she should dispose at her pleasure, all that I might be interested in by her marriage," meaning that Alice was to have complete control for the course of her life of any assets and lands that Ellesmere acquired as a result of her inheritance suit. Second, Ellesmere had promised to assign to Alice's jointure "a far greater quantity and portion of lands than my weak estate could bear" and said that he "would always endeavor to add such increase to that which I appointed for her as God should enable me," meaning that as he acquired lands from William Stanley as part of the inheritance settlement, he would add those lands to Alice's jointure; that was his way of acknowledging that their wealth really came from her first marriage.[16] Alice had not taken any chances in her second marriage, and she had established ground rules from the beginning to protect her landed interests. (These ground rules also disrupted the gendered dynamics of most marriages of the time.) Ellesmere's memo was intended to explain to his son and daughters why their stepmother was going to inherit control over so much land, leaving far less for them.

Being a man of his word, Ellesmere then outlined specific properties that belonged to her jointure and reminded her of their precise agreements. He then wrote a plea to Alice: "I do earnestly and heartily entreat and desire her to content herself therewith, and to be loving and kind to my son, and his wife, and their poor infants and little babies, to whom she is grandmother." He got a bit nastier at the end:

> But if my wife shall be instead by harkening to sycophants and shamed by sinister and lewd counsel; to fall into an unquiet willful and contentious cause, then I would have my son to pass and consider the declaration and directions here enclosed, and to use the same as the necessity of his occasion shall infer him, but otherwise to conceal and suppress it with silence, and manner to break or open the seal of it.[17]

Ellesmere wrote a second memo for his son, to be opened only if Alice contested any portion of his will and claimed more than the exorbitant amount of land he had promised her. The couple may have had some kind of understanding of decorum in their marriage, but Ellesmere did not trust Alice to maintain the facade in his death, and he wanted to arm his son with the vitriol he would need to defend himself and his sister from their stepmother. He entitled the document "An unpleasant declaration of things passed, between the Countess of Derby and me since our marriage and some directions for my son, to be observed between the said Countess and him, after my decease if he be enforced thereunto, as I fear he is like to be." In the memo, he expressed remorse for the excessive lifestyles Alice and her daughters maintained and wrote, "Immediately after our marriage, my family and household charge was much increased by reason of the train which the countess brought with her: namely for three daughters, and her and their attendants servants and followers (a wasteful company)." He considered the years he had spent married to Alice as "a punishment inflicted upon me by almighty God." He went on to lament that "it grieves me to remember . . . what reparations and sorrows I have suffered through her humorous, proud, and disdainful carriage, and by her turbulent spirit, and her curses railing and bitter tongue." He drew a parallel between Alice and her sister Anne, evoking the memory of the tumult that Anne had inflicted on her deceased husband: "The end of my life brings to me an end of these grieves, which I have passed with silence and endured with as much patience as I possibly could because I would not be a fabula vulgi [common tale] and I did take it to be a punishment inflicted upon me by almighty God. For had I not done, it would have appeared that as her sister Dorset and she be remained in blood. So their difference not in nature and condition upon consideration of those things thus passed." In the privacy of that desperate note to his son, Ellesmere confessed that he had secretly suffered the same bombastic berating from Alice that Sackville had so publicly experienced from her sister Anne.

Ellesmere's view of his wife left him distressed as he conveyed grim concern for his son's future: "I cannot but know that the end of my life will be the beginning of troubles to my son." He predicted Alice's course of action: "that this lady will handle as violent and strainable a course as can be devised against him and all that are descended from me, which if she do, then my son shall be thereby constrained to use all lawful means he can, to withstand her malice."[18] Ellesmere used the remainder of the document to speculate upon what precise actions of contestation Alice would take, which specific properties she would go after, and what her justifications of entitlement would be. That was his last-ditch effort to take the wind from Alice's sails and provide his son with a surplus of personal fodder to use against her if the situation arose. Ellesmere knew his wife, and he believed that Alice would want to control as much wealth and landed status as she could for as long as she was alive and would then someday die peacefully, knowing that her children and grandchildren would be set up to inherit it. Ellesmere, on the other hand, wanted his son to gain control over lands as quickly as possible. Poor Ellesmere was ready to die and did his best to put his affairs in order, but he would live for another seven years.

Whereas his memos painted a vivid picture of Alice as a volatile, greedy, and pernicious woman, no similar sources exist that describe Alice's own view of their marriage. Her actions, however, speak volumes. She demonstrated herself throughout adulthood to be a woman who actively fostered a persona of grandeur and had a shrewd desire to amass and control landed wealth and power. Whereas Ellesmere expressed exhaustion and feelings of having been browbeaten by his wife, it is easy to imagine that Alice would have defended her behavior by claiming that she was merely embodying the status she had earned and, according to Ellesmere, she criticized her husband for not doing the same. Throughout their marriage, Ellesmere's gender gave him one form of power over Alice, but he never expected her to be completely subservient to him because she outranked him. Elite marriages did not require affection, nor did they ever adhere to a simple gendered power dynamic, as husbands, wives, and their larger family networks always brought more than gender into the mix. Alice was never afraid of reminding Ellesmere of that, and as a result, their marriage was financially and dynastically successful, which was what she cared the most about, yet emotionally miserable, which was a disappointment to him.

Ellesmere wrote the final version of his last will and testament on August 16, 1615. The king continued to refuse to allow him to resign his position as lord chancellor. On November 7, 1616, the king tried to appease his ailing judge by elevating him to the rank of Viscount Brackley, but that did little to lift his spirits. Ellesmere did not care about a promotion; he longed for an end to his physical and mental decline. It was becoming clear to everyone at court that the end was near for the mighty judge, and just before King James finally accepted his resignation on March 5, 1617, he promised to grant Ellesmere an earldom. Ellesmere died ten days later, on March 15, 1617, as the papers were being drawn up. The details of his final hours and Alice's whereabouts are lost from the historical record.

Perhaps to no one's surprise, Alice contested his will. Ellesmere had been right about what made his wife tick. At fifty-seven years old, Alice was once again a widow, but her circumstances were far different than they had been the first time. Though the coverture laws of England made it seem as though wifehood or widowhood was a static state a woman found herself in, Alice's life proves otherwise. Her first experience as a widow was a perilous time of uncertainty and contention when she stood to lose everything, from her livelihood to her daughters. When Ellesmere died, there were no accounts of her appearing overwrought with grief at his funeral as there had been at Ferdinando's. She did not frantically line up male kinsmen to help her secure her place in the world because she did not need to. Alice was not the same wife to Ellesmere as she had been to Ferdinando, nor was she the same widow after his death; she was now a steady matriarch who had no need for any more husbands.

Out of respect for his long-serving lord chancellor, King James granted the promised earldom to Ellesmere's son, John, making him and his wife, Frances, the Earl and Countess of Bridgewater. Alice was surely pleased to have yet another of her daughters now a countess, but the new earl immediately faced conflict upon losing his beloved father. Ellesmere had made John his sole executor, as he had said he would. He had made provisions for his surviving daughter from his first marriage as well as their children. He had ensured that Alice would have everything she had brought into the marriage, as well as all the gifts he had given her, bequeathing

> *[to his] loving wife Alice countess of Derby, all the jewels plate goods and chattels, whereof she was possessed at the time of our marriage, and all such jewels as I have given unto her, since our marriage. And all other goods and chattels whatsoever, wherefore wherein I am, of have been, or might or ought to be possessed or interested by reason of the intermarriage between us.[19]*

Ellesmere's will also stipulated that if Alice should contest any aspect of her inheritance and jointure, all his "gifts and legacy unto her shall be utterly void and of none effect, and that then and thereupon she shall be utterly excluded to have or take any benefit or advantage at all."[20] He reminded his wife and son that they were to proceed in life cordially and quietly. Alice had never cared about his wishes in life, so it followed that she would ignore them after his death, and she filed a probate petition against the confirmation of his will. Her precise desires are unclear; she may have sought to limit the inheritance of Ellesmere's own daughter or perhaps she wanted to retain more control over lands in lieu of John's inheriting them. That seems particularly harsh, as in disputing Ellesmere's will, Alice was blocking her own daughter Frances from the inheritance as well. Alice's actions show that she was fixated on amassing as much wealth in her lifetime as possible, even at the expense of her daughter's family. If Alice was thinking dynastically, however, she might have argued that all the estates would ultimately pass to John, Frances, and their decedents anyway; what did it matter if she merely delayed the transference for a few decades? Decisions like that reveal Alice to be both colossally selfish and ingeniously proficient at understanding the long-term goals of the English nobility. Right or wrong, she was the embodiment of aristocratic ideals.

On February 7, 1618, the court passed a special probate of the will of Sir Thomas Egerton in favor of John, who had undoubtedly shared his father's tragic memo with the court. The court ruled that Ellesmere had been "sound in mind and in whole perfect memory" when he had written his will.[21] Bridgewater just wanted peace with Alice, probably at his wife's urging, so the challenge Alice made to the will did not void her jointure. She once again transitioned into widowhood, this time with enormous wealth and a lofty, stable position in society.

After Ellesmere's death, the marriage of Frances and John proved to be of even greater value to Alice. Bridgewater continued to be an advocate for Alice even after her petition against him failed, probably due to their shared affection for Frances. Alice was fifty-seven when Ellesmere died, and she would not bear any more children. Her two marriages had left her vast wealth combined with the titles of Lady Ellesmere and Viscountess Brackley, although she would only ever continue to use her highest rank, Dowager Countess of Derby. She had no need to marry for a third time. That same year, her sisters Anne and Elizabeth both died, leaving Alice as the matriarch of the Spencer and Egerton families. Now nothing mattered but protecting her daughters, her grandchildren, and their holdings. She entered the final phase of her life carrying all of her wealth, status, and experiences like arrows in a quiver, ready to battle anything or anyone who stood in her way.

✦━━━✦━━━✦

Alice did not have to wait long before her first fight. Her jointure came encumbered with some baggage in the form of Sir Edward Kynaston, a local Shropshire knight, which meant that she would need to spend just as much (if not more) time tending to her affairs as a landlord as she would the affairs of the royal court. The Kynastons, a minor landowning family, lived at Oteley in Shropshire.[22] Ellesmere had purchased some lands in the county from William Stanley in 1600, and it was from these lands that he had taken the name Lord Ellesmere. In his 1610 memorandum to his son and wife, he mentioned them: "I have also to my great charge and trouble recovered deeds of parts of the late earl of Derby's lands in Shropshire, which were detained by Sir Edward Kynaston. . . . All of which my mind is [Alice] shall enjoy and have benefit of."[23] Kynaston refused to acknowledge the boundaries between his lands and those belonging to Alice and Ellesmere. A continuous clash began in September 1616, when Kynaston and one of his men trespassed onto the land of one of Ellesmere's tenants. In doing so, they were in "clear breach of the said order."[24] They did so again in March 1617, just days after Ellesmere's death, which made it Alice's problem. She claimed that Kynaston and his men "carry away the wood growing and being upon the said parcel of land called Park Humfrey and with daily and frequent entries disturbed [Alice] and her tenants in the occupation thereof so as the same cannot be quietly enjoyed by her or them."[25]

Kynaston offered a different interpretation of the events. He acknowledged that he and his men had visited the tenants' homes in both September and March but claimed that in 1596 or 1597 he had been granted control of those lands, so that the tenants residing on the property were his. He also claimed that he had had permission to enter the property. As for the quarrel over Humfrey Park, Kynaston explained that he "came upon the part of the said tenement and then and there accepted a surrender of his estate and interests from the said [tenant] and then presently after departed without any disturbance of the said countess or any of her tenements," arguing that once he had learned that Alice held the leases there, he and his men had not taken any wood and he had left her tenants alone. He then told the court that he had been "much wronged thus to be molested and troubled without just cause" and he requested that the court dismiss the suit.[26]

A year later, Kynaston and Alice clashed again. The countess said that her tenants had complained to her that deer from Kynaston's hunting park had been wandering onto her land and had eaten £200 (£27,000/$38,000 today) worth of their crops, a devastating amount. Alice was not only agitated that Kynaston was again ignoring the boundaries of her property but concerned about the loss of food and income that threatened her tenants. Alice's local officer, Thomas Charleton, issued a statement upon her orders forbidding Kynaston from hunting on her lands. Alice also told her tenants to kill any Kynaston deer they found on her property. In 1618, Morgan Leigh, one of the countess's tenants, used greyhounds to kill one of Kynaston's deer that he found near his home. Kynaston threatened to fine Leigh £30 (£4,000/$5,500 today), not for killing the deer but for keeping greyhounds, which violated a law passed by King James I, as hunting with dogs was a privilege reserved for the upper classes. Leigh counterclaimed that Alice had given him permission to keep greyhounds, as if Alice's decrees held more weight than those issued by King James. He then threatened to tell the authorities that John Charlton, one of Kynaston's clerks, had killed a partridge on the countess's lands. Kynaston said that he would forgive and forget if Leigh would just "confess that he had killed Sir Edward's deer and done him wrong." Leigh apologized, and Kynaston dropped the whole thing.[27]

The peace was again short lived. In that same year, another of Alice's tenants, Robert Lowe, killed a deer that Kynaston and his hunting party had chased onto the countess's land. Lowe hid the deer in his house, and Kynaston and thirty men descended on Lowe's home, demanding that he hand it over. Lowe denied killing the deer, and the angry party left. Later, Kynaston sent two men to Lowe's house to look for the deer again, and they ransacked Lowe's barn. Eventually Lowe took the deer's carcass to Kynaston but claimed he had had nothing to do with slaying the animal.[28] Alice was livid that the local knight had had the audacity to accost one of her tenants. No longer content with trying to deal with Kynaston at his level, she took the fight to the highest levels of government. Men and women such as Alice served the Crown, but they also had responsibilities to their tenants, and Alice took all her roles seriously. The constant feuds with Kynaston were a nagging reminder that the life of a countess was not all holding masques and arranging marriages; squabbling occupied a large portion of her time and energy.

On November 12, 1618, Alice drafted a petition to Sir Francis Bacon, Ellesmere's successor as lord chancellor, protesting Kynaston's appointment to the Commission of the Peace. Always honey-tongued, Alice did not express malice but rather conveyed concern for the welfare of her tenants in Salop. She explained to Bacon that her desire to keep Kynaston out of powerful offices did not come from a "present disadvantage to her, but for the future good and freedom of others."[29] If he would not stop harassing her tenants, she would do anything in her power to prevent his advancement.[30]

Records show that that was not the last time Alice and Kynaston crossed paths. On December 6, 1627, John, Frances, and Alice drew up a contract among Kynaston; his wife, Mary; and several other local knights, which divided the cost of maintaining ditches that each party had constructed in Shropshire and also came to a precise agreement as to the property boundaries the ditches would demark.[31] Despite their numerous spats, Alice and Kynaston at least found ways to conduct business with each other, even if that business was to enforce the borders of their respective lands. Alice never tired of wielding the law against those who caused trouble for her or the people she was responsible for. But Kynaston was a mere nuisance compared to the ordeals Alice had faced and would continue to face in the years to come.

Alice was litigious and quick to feel slighted, but more important, she took her responsibilities as a great landowner seriously. She fought vehemently on behalf of her tenants to protect their rights and serve as a decent patron and landlord, recognizing how critical crops and firewood were to their survival. She did not believe that her tenants had a legal claim to her lands—after all, the Spencer family's wealth was due in part to the enclosure of common lands—but she did believe that she had a responsibility to those who rented her lands; she also had a disdain for Kynaston's disregard of the boundaries of her lands. Just as she petitioned powerful men to help advance her own causes, she did the same for others. In February 1604, while at the court of King James, she learned that villagers in Dent, Yorkshire, had asked the king to build them a school. Alice was moved to write to her friend Sir Julius Caesar, who had recently been knighted and made the ecclesiastical commissioner of Canterbury, to advocate for their cause. Alice wanted to help "the furtherance of so good a purpose to entreat your loving care" so that he might take up their request "with all convenient favor and for your good help therein." She concluded by saying that she "will not only be thankful, but ready when the occasion shall require, to requite the same."[32] She had every intention of returning the favor if he ever needed her to do so. She may have been fiery and difficult, but she was wholly devoted to her responsibility to support those she saw as dependent upon her.

Being part of the English aristocracy came with great privileges, such as landed wealth, a life without brutal menial labor, plenty of lavish entertainments, fine clothes, and estates, but it also came with responsibilities to one's tenants, one's monarch, and one's family. Whether a title was inherited or granted, a member of the nobility was expected to commit to a public and political life. Sometimes the only thing Alice could do was try to entice her kin to act a particular way, in the way she truly believed was in their best interest—even if they believed something different.

Henry Hastings, Earl of Huntingdon, famously loathed London and far preferred the pastoral retreat of his Leicestershire estates of Ashby de la Zouch and Donington Castle. Although he was an elected member of Parliament, he rarely went south to the capital. Instead, his wife, Elizabeth, often went to represent the family. Although those visits meant that Alice could see her daughter frequently, as Elizabeth traveled through Harefield on her way to London, Alice also believed that it reflected badly on the family if he continually shirked his responsibilities in person. In the early years of the reign of King James, Alice wrote to her son-in-law about his absence from London: "I must truly and plainly tell your lordship . . . me long experienced in the course and charge of living in London, are of confident opinion that your Lordship, a reasonable fit train, may live at as little expense here for some season of the year as where you do." If Henry chose to remain in the country to save money, Alice called his bluff. And if Henry went to London for the season, Alice could spend more time with Elizabeth, so she ended the letter on a personal point: "I consider the party whose sight and company, I might confess, I affectionately desire is my daughter, but your wife."[33]

Any man who married one of the Stanley coheiresses surely understood the wealth and connections that came with the match, and they may have had some general understanding of the role the Dowager Countess of Derby would play in their lives. But knowing that and living it were two very different things. John Egerton, now Earl of Bridgewater, undoubtedly endured the brunt of it, as Alice was both his mother-in-law and his stepmother, but even Henry, a scion of the ancient earldom of Huntingdon, would not be spared Alice's constant oversight. In February 1614, just a few years after she wrote telling him to do his duty and go to London, Alice orchestrated some adjustments to her daughter's jointure. At that time, she wrote to Henry to thank him for making the adjustments, "I will not be unmindful to have you righted desiring you will be careful for the settling of my daughter's jointure, which I understand from my brother Spencer you are, and for the same do return you many thanks."[34] Elizabeth's uncle may have spoken to Henry man to man to work out the final settlement, but everyone understood that Alice was calling the shots.

Of course, Alice would not think twice about acting on behalf of her son-in-law when he needed her. In May 1609, she wrote to the lord treasurer about a deal for the king to buy forest lands from Henry Hastings because, as she explained, "my son, the Earl of Huntingdon's health [is] not well serving him to attend your Lordship in person." She went on to explain that it had been recently discovered "that these woods have been undervalued to my son" and perhaps they could reach a fairer price for the sale.[35] Regardless of the outcome, she would not sit idly by and let her son-in-law make a bad deal if a more lucrative agreement could be made. That was Alice's core philosophy in every aspect of her life.

CHAPTER SEVEN

CREATING A DYNASTY

"You Have Gained Yourself a Good Report"

Alice's devotion to her family redoubled when she became a grand-mother. In 1603, just as England welcomed a new royal family, Alice and Thomas prepared to welcome a grandchild, as Frances was pregnant. Thomas had grandchildren from the daughter of his first marriage, but this baby would be Alice's first grandchild. Despite the differences in their personalities, Alice and Thomas must have been proud—and a bit relieved—that the dynastic family they had established was about to enter its third generation in just three years. Alice outfitted Frances's first lying-in chamber with a canopy bed furnished in crimson velvet and did all she could to ensure that Frances's pregnancy was safe and comfortable. The child would be born into a rarified world of luxury and refinement, one befitting an infant with Spencer and Stanley bloodlines who would grow up to call the Dowager Countess of Derby "grandmother" and Lord Chancellor Ellesmere "grandfather."

As for all aristocratic mothers of the age, supporting her daughters as they became mothers themselves was among Alice's most important duties. She would likely have been present to accompany Anne, Frances, and Elizabeth in their lying-in chambers and to help deliver their children, just as her own mother had been there for her. Anne had six children, five of whom survived into adulthood. Elizabeth was mother to four children, all of whom survived. Frances, however, would call upon her mother the most, giving birth fifteen times between 1603 and 1623, eleven of the children surviving at least beyond the first year of their lives.

Alice, Thomas, and their extended family welcomed each grandchild, regardless of sex, into the folds of their growing dynasty and household. Nobles at the time maintained multigenerational households with adult children, siblings, extended networks of in-laws, cousins, friends, and grandchildren constantly coming and going from one another's homes, just as Thomas and Alice frequently traveled, often separately, among the estates of their children, kin, and friends. The concept of an aristocratic household was porous, yet because of their blended family lines, the household of Alice and Thomas, as well as that of John and Frances, was particularly interwoven. Preparing for and raising children was also a multigenerational affair, and the family's household accounts are informative. With each of Frances's pregnancies, the joint Egerton family spent lavishly, purchasing new fabrics, furniture, and sundries. During Frances's first pregnancy, they spent £309 (£40,000/$55,000 today) on Frances's birthing chamber and the baby's nursery, as well as a schoolroom.[1] There were also expenses for the baby's christening and the hiring of a wet nurse, since noblewomen did not usually nurse their own children. Typically, a trusted Protestant woman from the local village would assume a temporary role in the household and nourish the infant.[2] For the next twenty years, the family invested in nurses and maids, as well as laces, linens, taffetas, feather beds, silk screens, and other luxurious fixings to keep Frances comfortable and safe, all with the expectation that Alice and Ellesmere's shared grandchildren would know a world only of the finest things.

Unfortunately, during that era, birth and death were closely linked. Just as household receipts reveal the luxurious purchases intended to heal a mother and swaddle a newborn, they contain more somber expenses, such as a "clean board for a coffin," "15 yards of black velvet," and the costs of "laying the coffin in the ground." In 1614, Frances and John Egerton buried their one-year-old daughter, Alice. In 1620 and 1623, they laid two young sons, James and Charles, to rest. As for their births, no expense was spared for their funerals. The Egertons spent close to £30 (£4,000/$5,500 today) to bury their sons. Each boy had been named for his respective godfather, King James and his son Prince Charles (later King Charles I). Despite the ubiquity of childhood mortality, for a family to lose a beloved child was a deeply felt tragedy.

When the family was among the aristocracy, their loss was often expressed in a memorial elegy published by a poet or writer. One writer, Abraham Darcie, published a single-page elegy to the boys in 1623, as Charles's passing left the Bridgewaters without a male heir. Darcie entitled his tract "To Immortalize the Noble Memorie," in the hope that it would do just that for the two boys as honorable members of the Egerton family, descendants of the houses of both Derby and Spencer. He wrote his verse in English and French, concluding with the stanza

> *For the more pleasure that a worthy thing*
> *Unto the mind of any man doth bring,*
> *When thereof one doth the fruition lose,*
> *Grief Stronger is, and tears are more profuse.*[3]

His words may not have done much to ease the family's grief, but it must have comforted them a little to see their children so publicly praised.

In an age when life and death seemed random and unpredictable, many looked to the skies for signs of what the future might hold. Alice, Thomas, Frances, John, or someone else in one of their households practiced astrology alongside religion, and as long as the family conformed to the state-sanctioned Protestant faith, their concepts were not at odds with each other. In fact, moderate Calvinists and other Protestant conformists believed that because God had created the cosmos, the heavens could be read as an indication of his grace. In seventeenth-century Europe, astrology, astronomy, and conventional religious practice were all intertwined.[4] Frances owned a copy of Tycho Brahe's *Astronomicall Conjectur*, as did many of her peers.[5] Brahe, a Danish nobleman, was one of the most famous astronomers of the day, and although his books established numerous leading scientific theories of the time, many people purchased copies because, like Frances and her family, they believed his work was the most accurate for casting horoscopes.[6] At least twice, the family drafted "natal lists," documents that recorded the names of the children, their birth dates and years, plus the day of the week and hour each child had been born.[7] Someone could then correlate the information with the information in books such as those by Brahe to create astrological charts for the children. That was not considered "fortune telling" per se but a way to comb the heavens for signs of providence. The best-case scenario for Alice, Ellesmere, Frances, and John was that the charts would offer hope that the future of their dynasty would be safe and even thrive; the worst-case scenario might help prepare them for the brutal possibilities of loss.

Two horoscopes survive for the Egerton family, one made for an anonymous girl and the other for an anonymous boy, both done by the astrologer Richard Piper, who explained that he did not have enough information, so the charts he had cast were incomplete: "I should have had the place of birth as well as the year, day, and hour: as plus: how far distant north or south from London; and also how far distant east or west from London." But he did the best he could in an attempt to satisfy his wealthy clients, using planetary locations and astrological houses. He foretold a life marred by health problems for the girl: "I conjecture she might be in danger of death about her 9th year of age. . . . About 40 I fear her blood will be distempered with melancholy & superfluous phlegm and will hardly leave her till she leave the world: which if she do at that time it will be happy for her for I find no happy or comfortable direction of the horoscope after those years."[8] All the family could do was hope that their faith and godliness could alter this course or else assume Piper had made a mistake because he had not had all the information he needed to cast an accurate chart. In reality, no horoscope could really prepare Alice, Frances, and their family for the heartache of grief when one of Frances and John's children died; the family, like all others, mourned and continued on, focusing on the hopes they held for their surviving children.

Alice was present when many of her grandchildren entered the world, as she likely was when they departed it. She was also deeply invested in every moment in between, just as she had been with her own daughters. Educating her grandchildren to prepare them for their promising futures was a fundamental part of her life's work. Anne, Frances, and Elizabeth were all educated and literate in English and French. Upper-class children, regardless of gender, were first educated primarily at home. When sons reached their early teens, they were typically sent away to public schools and universities to learn Latin, theology, and law and then to the Inns of Court to continue their professional development, just as Alice's brothers had done years before. When

Alice's daughters became mothers themselves, they were also committed to the education of their offspring. Frances and John hired an array of tutors in French, music, singing, and dancing for their sons and daughters. In 1615, for example, the family paid £4 (£500/$700 today) for four months of French lessons for ten-year-old Arabella Egerton, and £7 (£1,000/$1,400 today) for music lessons for twelve-year-old Frances.[9] With eleven children to educate, the Bridgewaters' home came to resemble an expensive school.

The eldest son of Elizabeth and Henry, named Ferdinando, attended Queen's College, Cambridge, and Alice closely monitored his academic performance. She wrote to him, "You have gained yourself a good report of the wise and learned, for so I hear you have. And, I hope ever well, is the directions of those that take comfort in your well doing be embraced and followed, which out of my love I desire you to do, no less for your own good, than for the great contentment that will give your friends."[10] Ferdinando's education was not just for his own edification but was to provide "great contentment" to those around him. In Alice's world, each family member's performance was a reflection on her entire dynasty.

Whereas older sons were sent off to university, some aristocratic daughters and younger sons were sent to live with well-respected families of their kin to make connections, refine their social skills, and learn the ways of the world from those who had experience. Alice was, of course, primed to assist in the upbringing of several of her grandchildren. In 1626, Elizabeth wrote to her husband after visiting Alice and her own children at Harefield, "I found my mother livy well, I praise God, and my children so merry, weigh in my judgment. Amended since we saw them last, Bess sings very finely; is something fatter which well becomes her."[11] Bess, as Elizabeth was called, spent many years at Harefield, and Alice grew extremely close to her, taking a strong interest in securing a promising future for her protégée. The next year, Elizabeth visited Harefield again and reported to her husband that their daughter's bounty of linens far surpassed the quantity that they had after twenty years of marriage: "God send her a good husband. She hath now a good portion and more linen for a house than we have being twenty year old, my lady desires much that she were married, and 'tis fit for us to take care to seek her a husband, as I know you believe so against assure you my Lady doth not mean ever to part with her but to a husband."[12] Henry did not believe his fifteen-year-old daughter was ready to marry, despite what his formidable mother-in-law thought. Alice ensured that her granddaughter was a cultured young lady, but she was determined to keep her under her own watchful eye to prepare her for the day when it was time for her to marry.

Alice may have been controlling, but she also cared deeply for her daughters and grandchildren. She genuinely wanted to see them thrive in the world, and she knew as well as anyone else how dangerous and unstable that world could be. Her daughters, grandchildren, and sons-in-law came and went from Harefield on a regular basis. The estate was the primary seat of Alice's realm, and they all orbited around her. Alice's love and her need for control were two sides of the same coin. On one occasion, she wrote to her son-in-law Henry, Earl of Huntingdon, "I thank you for the news you sent me of my daughter's well-being, and that of your little daughter is so fine a child. I hope your Lordship shall have much comfort of them all, I pray God bless them." She added a postscript on behalf of Anne, who was visiting: "My daughter Chandos, being present at the sealing of this letter, desires her love might be commended to your lordship and if there be a Parliament this year, the hope you will bring her sister to London."[13] In letters such as that, the fights over land, money, court intrigue, social performance, and royal bloodlines fall away, and it is easy to picture an aging mother at a writing desk in a candlelit room with her eldest daughter at her side sending thoughts of love to her youngest daughter, who had become a mother herself.

◆──────◆──────◆

For the better part of twenty years, Alice was devoted to helping her daughters become mothers and her grandchildren prepare for their own responsibilities. But her sphere of influence extended beyond her immediate family. Proactively building and fostering a political and social network, as well as maintaining the one she had, was also essential to her. She expected each of her daughters to fulfill their duties to their local communities and to exert their influence whenever possible. The men in their lives might have held high political offices, but Alice expected the women to do their part to advance the family's fortunes, just as she had always done.

Anne is the hardest of the Stanley daughters to know, as so few details of her first marriage survive. It seems she spent less time than her sisters did at Harefield or in London, having settled into her life with her husband, Grey Brydges, Lord Chandos, at his ancestral home Sudeley Castle in the bucolic Cotswolds, some hundred miles from Harefield Place. Yet in the months before Ellesmere died, Anne wrote to her stepfather in the hope that he might find an appointment for a young reverend. She thought he would benefit from "any dignity in your Lordships gift" in improving his station, and as a good lady, she wanted to foster the connection. Her mother had taught her well, as she concluded her letter by demurely referring to herself in the third person and stating her potential gratitude: "Your Lordship shall be sure that this which the rest of your many favors shall be bestowed upon her who, though she cannot requite them, yet will ever freely acknowledge them and with them the happiness of continuing in your Lordships good opinion being."[14] Anne, like her mother, wanted to do her part to make fruitful connections among people in her sphere and was proficient in the highly gendered performance of humbling herself to a man in power while expecting him to take her request seriously.

Of all Alice's daughters, Elizabeth, Countess of Huntingdon, was most like her mother in this way. Beyond hosting the family's 1607 celebration at her home of Ashby de la Zouch, Elizabeth was a patron of writers who became famous, including John Donne, and of local poets, including Thomas Pestell, whom few would remember. When Elizabeth married Henry Hastings, heir to the Earl of Huntingdon, she assumed an important place within the local community, just as Alice had when she had married the heir to the Earl of Derby. Both were old noble houses rich in reputation and land but poor in capital. And, like her mother, Elizabeth was as committed to her county as she was to her country.

It was a reciprocal relationship. The city of Leicester, just outside the Hastingses' estate, acknowledged her influence and on numerous occasions sent gifts to the Countess of Huntingdon. The town also seemed to keep tabs on the comings and goings at Ashby and made a point of sending gifts when the earl and countess hosted important visitors, including her mother. In the summer of 1606, Alice went to Ashby for an extended visit because Elizabeth was pregnant with her first child. As a welcome gift, the city sent the two women several bottles of wine and some sugar. The next month, they sent the same gift and later a cake. When Alice returned later that fall to check in on her daughter and her newborn granddaughter, the town sent a book and some horses.[15]

Such gifts were not just tribute or niceties bestowed upon the local elite. Elizabeth and Henry were devoted to their tenants and community and worked hard to fulfill their many duties to them. For example, the couple served as patrons of the Ashby School, a local boys' grammar school that the Hastings family had funded since its founding in 1567.[16] In 1607, John Brinsley, the school's headmaster, dedicated a book to the Countess of Huntingdon. In it, he expressed his admiration for her "unfeigned desire both to observe the fame, and walk in all the ways of the Lord." He also touted Elizabeth's ability to blend her learnedness with her piety: "not to delight the curious with an hour's reading, (which I leave to others) but to help the honest heart that is desirous to learn of our Savior how to pray."[17] Though Brinsley's kind words may have been equal parts gratitude and sycophantism, Elizabeth's relationship with the local school embodied the way she had been taught to do her duty to the community, her spiritual devotion, and her love of learning.

In a way that would have made Alice proud, Elizabeth exerted her political influence beyond her county seat, far exceeding the geographic boundaries of the British Isles. On October 30, 1616, Sir Thomas Roe wrote to her, "Your noble design to do me a courtesy was so free, so undeserved, that I will never forget that I owe your Ladyship more than I am or ever shall be." Alice, Elizabeth, and her sisters were accustomed to receiving gushing thanks from men whose careers they had helped advance, but Roe sent that letter from the Mughal court in India, where he was serving as an ambassador for King James on a mission to negotiate a trade treaty. The details of precisely how Elizabeth helped Roe are unknown, but the fact that he wrote her from India indicates that she had done something significant.

Alice's sister Anne owned stock in the East India Company, and little clues such as this serve as reminders that women such as Elizabeth, her mother, and her sisters were never far removed from the violent exploitation of people and resources Europeans were committing around the world.[18] Roe shared his harsh judgment of the Mughals in his letter to Elizabeth, writing,

"You have all in you, more than the books and religion of these, only they have craft enough to be as wicked as any in our court, and in all the wisdom of the Devil they are excellently learned. So that I may like to profit well."[19] The jewels, gold, silks, sugars, and wine that Alice, Anne, Frances, and Elizabeth adored were all products of the rise of often violent maritime global trade. Although they never saw foreign lands themselves, the political and material lives of those women and their peers extended far beyond the boundaries of their estates. In the 1570s, Alice's parents had dreamed that their daughter might exert some influence in the North of England; nearly forty years later, Alice's own daughter was playing some small role in shaping the English influence at the Mughal court.

Like her mother, Elizabeth understood that her primary responsibility was to her own family. The match between Henry and Elizabeth was in large part fueled by the Hastingses' need for the windfall of cash and rental incomes Elizabeth brought with her to the marriage through the Stanley inheritance settlement, but those did not entirely alleviate the Hastingses' debts, and it became Elizabeth's responsibility in part to continue to seek ways to increase their income. One of their best options was to secure a lucrative match for their son and heir, Ferdinando. On August 7, 1623, the fourteen-year-old Ferdinando wed the ten-year-old Lucy Davies. Lucy's father was Sir John Davies, whose career somewhat mirrored that of Lord Ellesmere. He, too, had humble roots but had found prosperity in practicing law and had risen rapidly through the ranks and accumulated significant personal wealth. He had also been an acclaimed poet in his younger years and had penned Alice and Ellesmere's entertainment at Harefield for Queen Elizabeth twenty-one years earlier.

Though the Hastingses and Alice surely had great respect for Davies, they were dubious about his wife, Lady Eleanor Davies, the daughter of an Englishman with an Irish title. The English aristocracy looked down upon landed families with Irish titles, considering them inferior to their own peerage. Eleanor was also a difficult woman with a penchant for making wild prophecies and religious fanaticism. In the years to come, she would be committed to Bedlam Hospital and imprisoned on several occasions for attempting to predict the death of the king and once for pouring tar over the altar at

Lichfield Cathedral. Getting into the marriage business with Eleanor seemed risky, but Lucy was a lovely girl and the family banked on dealing exclusively with Sir John.

Both families understood that the bride and groom were mere children and far too young to engage in marital relations, let alone establish a household of their own, but neither party wanted to miss the opportunity to lock in such a fine match, as Lucy brought with her a dowry of £6,500 (£855,000/$1.18 million today) and Ferdinando an ancient English title. The couple would be legally married but would commence marital relations only after they had grown up and Lucy began menstruating. Until then, each child would remain in the household of his or her parents. Such an arrangement was not uncommon in aristocratic circles of the time. Just two months after the nuptials, Elizabeth sent a letter to Sir John reassuring him that Ferdinando was fond of receiving letters from his child bride, noting, "I assure you my son is proud of my sweet daughter's lines, I pray God bless them both, as to my own milieu I wish to her all happiness."[20]

Things may have started off smoothly, but it did not take long before the relationship between the two families was tested over mundane problems, such as who would choose the lady to wait upon young Lucy. Sir John wrote to Elizabeth that he had heard rumors that Alice wanted to make the selection, and Elizabeth wrote to assure him, "Upon the offense you took concerning an unkindness offense that you should say upon the general carriage of business would to the like effect as to have write."[21] A bickering match over Lucy's attendants would soon be the least of their problems.

The period of relative amiability ended with the death of Sir John Davies in 1626. Lucy and Ferdinando still lived apart, and Ferdinando said, "He would not lie with his lady till he had my lady's consent." At eighteen, Ferdinando was legally of age, but the younger Lucy was just on the cusp of maturity, and sex was no doubt a scary thing for the young wife. Ferdinando's words demonstrate the compassion, patience, and respect he had for Lucy. Alice, however, seemed to have little concern for the emotional well-being of the young woman and weighed in to remind her daughter that the legality of the marriage could be questioned if the young couple did not consummate it.[22] The union and the hefty monies that came with it were never far from her mind. Nearly thirty years prior, she had written a similar letter to Henry's grandfather, the fourth Earl of Huntingdon, confirming "the solemnization of our desired marriage which now I understand is fully consummated" between her daughter Elizabeth and Henry.[23]

Alice did not need to worry too much about the Hastingses; Elizabeth had learned a great deal from her mother's dealings with inheritance laws. Though Henry refused to leave Leicester, Elizabeth went to London to attend Sir John Davies's funeral and secure Lucy's unpaid marriage portion and the estate of Englefield, the Davieses' home, for her son. From her mother's house in Harefield, Elizabeth wrote to her husband, "I know you will expect a large account of my son's business, but I have had to do with such an irresolute woman that it is impossible to draw certain conclusion from her fantastical a creature as my Sister Davies." The rest of the letter recounts the extravagant cost of Davies's funeral and the widow, Eleanor Davies's, desire to retain possession of Englefield. Lucy also said that she wanted her mother to hold the estate, although the wishes of a teenage girl were of no concern to Elizabeth and her family.[24] The Countess of Huntingdon geared up for a fight for the dowry she felt her son was due and petitioned the courts to decide.

Almost three years later, on October 28, 1629, the King's Bench reached a verdict in the Hastingses' favor.[25] The family received the settlement, and Ferdinando and Lucy moved into Englefield. The Countess of Huntingdon and her family had successfully triumphed in another legal dispute. Two decades before, she had relied on her mother to lead the charge; this time she secured her own child's holdings. Alice must have been beaming with pride as her dynasty added the estate of Englefield to their portfolio. No one but poor Lucy paid any mind to the "fantastical" Eleanor, although Alice and her daughters would continue to face off with Eleanor for the rest of their lives. The most public and vicious of their feuds with her was yet to come.

—◆———◆———◆—

Though Alice could trust that Elizabeth was managing her family affairs as she had taught her to do, she was not as confident about her eldest daughter, Anne. Sometime before 1607, Anne had married Grey Brydges, Lord Chandos, and the couple had resided primarily at Sudeley Castle in Gloucestershire, where they planned to raise their children: two sons and three daughters, plus another son, Robert, who died in infancy. Grey had a glittering reputation as a local patron, "For, having an ample fortune, he expended it in the most generous manner; his house being kept open three days every week for the gentry: and the poor were as constantly fed with the remnants of his hospitable entertainments."[26]

Life at Sudeley took a sudden turn when Grey's health began to decline. In the summer of 1621, at forty years of age, Anne was expecting a baby. Despite his wife's pregnancy, Grey traveled to the town of Spa in the Low Countries (Belgium today) to soak in the mineral-rich natural pools, a popularly prescribed remedy for all sorts of ailments. While he was there, his health continued to deteriorate, and he died on August 10, allegedly "by drinking Spa water; he died in his coach on his way homeward."[27] Though soaking in the spa waters was deemed good for the body, drinking them could cause infections. His body was transported back to Sudeley for burial. Anne entered widowhood with a newborn infant among her other children, all under the age of seven. The newborn son, William, had arrived just days before Grey died. His father never set eyes upon him. The couple's male heir was their one-year-old son, George.

Poets tried to capture Grey's legacy. In an elegy entitled "Tears for the Death of the Truly Honorable, the Lord Chandos," an anonymous poet mourned:

> We dare not love a man, nor pleasure take
> In others' worth for noble Chandos' sake:
> And when we seek the best with Reason's light,
> We fear to wish him longer in our sight.[28]

Everyone in the family shared the grief. Anne had lost her husband, and Alice had lost one of her chosen sons-in-law, selected specifically by her to wed her eldest daughter. Their union had been part of her master plan, and though very few records survive that provide any insights into Grey and Anne's marriage, their life appeared to follow the standard script of their peers: a grand country castle in the Cotswolds, a circle of poets vying for their patronage, and sons and daughters to enhance their expanding network of kin. Grey's death meant that Anne would have to navigate the perils of widowhood by quickly securing custody of her young children and her assets to retain her position in society, as she had watched her mother do years before.

One might have anticipated that Alice would have guided Anne through the emotional and harrowing processes of petitioning the Court of Wards to guarantee control over her children, but that was not the kind of woman Alice was. Instead, she petitioned the Court of Wards to grant *her* the wardship of Anne's eldest son and heir, George. If Alice were named his legal guardian, she would control his inheritance portion and have the authority to arrange his marriage. There are no surviving sources explicitly outlining why Alice took her daughter's son away, nor how Anne may have responded. She did not put up a fight against her mother in court, but the events in the coming years suggest that Alice may not have trusted Anne to make good choices in her widowhood and Alice would not risk her grandson's future. On May 11, 1622, King James granted the Dowager Countess of Derby the wardship of her two-year-old grandson. Though Alice was only after the legal guardianship of the heir, both George and his younger brother, William, were sent to Harefield Place to live with Alice permanently. Anne was granted custody of her three daughters.

The arrangement was unusual, even by the standards of the day. Many grandchildren, both boys and girls, frequently lived for long periods with their wealthy relatives or in the homes of other noble families as a way of increasing their social circles; it was a normal part of their upbringing and education. But in this instance, Alice was not taking in adolescent grandsons for the purpose of overseeing their transformation into adulthood; George and William were just toddlers. Alice, like many of her peers, knew firsthand the tumult created by widowhood. Nearly a lifetime ago, when her beloved Ferdinando had died, she had had to petition the Court of Wards to retain the custody of her own precious daughters. Yet now, nearly thirty years later, she had applied to the court to take her daughter's son from her.

Alice moved her family around like chess pieces on a board; she had now captured a male heir. Yet her estate was secure and she would have been free to name any one of her descendants as her heir, just as she was also free to divide it up as she wished. She did not need legal custody of a boy to protect her legacy or financial future, so it may not have been her own future she was concerned with. Becoming George's guardian also meant that Alice, not Anne or any man Anne might marry, would control George's inheritance. Her decision to secure the wardship of her daughter's eldest son may have seemed tyrannical and cruel; however, a total devotion to the preservation and advancement of her family was essential to her ethos.

Perhaps Anne truly believed that her sons, and thus her legacy and that of her deceased husband, would be better protected in her mother's hands. If Anne felt ill equipped to ensure promising futures for her sons, placing them with Alice would give both of them the most options. Maybe Anne made the painful choice to let go of her sons because she truly believed it was in their best interests. Sadly, that would soon prove to be true.

PART III

CHAPTER EIGHT

SECRETS AND VIOLENCE

"This Monstrous Change of a Father into an Enemy"

When Anne's husband, Grey, died unexpectedly in August 1621, she found herself in a challenging position. Sudden widowhood was tragically common, but what no one likely expected was the meager financial condition in which he left the Chandos estate. Shortly after the couple wed, Anne had been named a Stanley coheiress, securing a portion of the £20,400 (£2.7 million/$3.7 million today) settlement and retaining rental income from the lands she inherited. The English laws of coverture, however, meant that her husband had assumed total control over all her assets. Alice had ensured jointures in the marriage agreements for Frances and Elizabeth, so one assumes that she would have done the same for Anne, although none of the contracts for her marriage agreement survive. But even Alice and her well-positioned daughters could do only so much to ensure financially stable futures since their husbands had to be willing to make good on the marriage agreements and manage the estates responsibly or hire someone to do it. When Grey's estate was settled after his death, Anne was left with £800 per year (£105,000/$145,000 today).[1] Though that sum was far greater than the incomes of most people in the realm, it was paltry in comparison to what she had brought into the marriage. It would certainly not allow her to maintain the life she and her children had known and may have been a contributing factor as to why she allowed her mother to gain the wardship of her eldest son, George, and take in her infant son, William.

It is not clear in the historical record what happened to the wealth Anne had gained through her mother's hard-fought inheritance suit. Aristocrats of the age often struggled to maintain a healthy balance between their lavish lifestyles and the rental incomes intended to support them. The details of the Chandos estate are unknown, but in 1622, there was no question that Anne would need to do something to reestablish her financial stability for herself and her three daughters. Remarrying was her best option, and this time, as a grown woman and a mother, she would find her own husband. She started searching for a husband with the same focus with which people today might search for a new job; aristocratic women approached marriage as a "career."[2]

By 1624, Anne had found a potential husband, but there is no evidence to suggest that anyone else in her family was pleased with the match. If anything, her next husband's reputation would have caused considerable concern among Alice and her wider family, yet as the widow of a well-regarded baron and a mother, Anne was free to make her own choice. Alice probably agreed that her daughter should remarry to stabilize her financial condition, but she did not support Anne's choice of a husband. On July 22, 1624, Anne married Mervyn Touchet, the second Earl of Castlehaven. Both of Castlehaven's parents were English, but his title was Irish. His father, George Touchet, Lord Audley, had been born to humble roots, not unlike Alice's second husband, Thomas Egerton. Whereas Egerton was a lawyer and had risen through the peerage via political service in England, Touchet had elevated his standing through military service in Ireland. He had fought on behalf of the English in several Irish rebellions and been appointed the Governor of Kells, a city that served as an important military outpost in Ireland. That put him on a political trajectory in Ireland rather than England, and in 1613, he served in the Irish House of Lords.[3] Castlehaven's mother, Lucy Mervyn, was the daughter of an English country knight, not unlike Alice, although the Mervyns were not nearly as wealthy as the Spencers.

In a society obsessed with hierarchy, Castlehaven's family was "lower" than Anne's, although it was an age in which many families successfully advanced their stations; Alice's own life certainly reflected that possibility. Castlehaven's first wife, Elizabeth Barnham, had been the daughter of a wealthy London draper, and the couple had had six children.[4] Though he profited from his father's holdings in Ireland, Castlehaven hoped to make a career for himself in England. He studied at Middle Temple, served as a justice of the peace in Dorset, and ultimately sat in the English Parliament, although he showed virtually no interest in or aptitude for either law or politics.[5] When his father died in 1617, Castlehaven inherited his estate, rental incomes in both Ireland and England, and title. He purchased his mother's family estate, Fonthill Gifford in Wiltshire, and made that manor the seat of his local power. When Castlehaven's wife, Elizabeth, died in 1622, his was not among the wealthiest or even most respected families of the day, but he was financially stable. That must have been what appealed to Anne. In turn, she brought an enviable lineage and social network to the marriage.

There was nothing odd about their match, as many aristocrats viewed a successful union as being one that blended financial and social capital. What was peculiar, however, was their significant age difference; Anne was nearly thirteen years his senior. They both had sons and daughters from their first marriages, so neither needed children from their union to perpetuate their lines and legacies. At forty-one years of age, Anne was in search of financial stability and a husband who would not expect any more children. At twenty-nine, Castlehaven understood the benefits deriving from Anne's connections and reputation. It was a marriage of need and opportunity; anything else they might have wanted was irrelevant.

In 1628, Anne and Castlehaven continued to consolidate their interests by marrying her oldest daughter, Elizabeth, to his son and heir, James, Lord Audley. Stepbrother and -sister became husband and wife, and the families became even more entangled. Though it was not the norm for English stepsiblings to marry each other, Anne had watched other women in her family make similar choices in their own later marriages. Alice's older sister Anne had married her son to her third husband's daughter after she had married Robert Sackville. Alice had opted to marry Anne's own sister Frances to their stepbrother John as part of Alice and Thomas's plans for financial and familial stability. Just like her mother and aunt, Anne probably believed that the match would help secure her family's financial interests. Audley was sixteen and Elizabeth was thirteen, but their ages at marriage were not a concern, given their family's social status. They had lived together as stepsiblings for four years, and as the children of aristocratic parents, they surely understood that marriage was primarily a business arrangement. Together, Elizabeth and Audley would inherit Castlehaven's earldom and wealth, along with Anne's lineage. With virtually nothing left of her Stanley inheritance, it seemed to be the best Anne could do for her eldest daughter. At least she would one day be a countess. As Anne and Castlehaven were unlikely to have children together, the hope was also that they would both be more likely to look out for the interests of their future grandchildren, who would share both their bloodlines. It was a strategy for amassing power; the strategy was not the problem; the problem was Castlehaven and his family.

The English aristocracy was unapologetically snobbish and turned up its collective nose at families such as the Touchets, who had made their rise through the Irish peerage and their incomes through Irish rentals. Such close ties to Ireland also prompted constant suspicions that Castlehaven was Catholic. Castlehaven downplayed the rumors, but his younger brother, Ferdinando, flaunted his Catholicism. The whole situation surely provoked in Alice haunting memories of the disaster that the Hesketh Plot had nearly caused in her early married life with her own Ferdinando. In 1630, Castlehaven's brother attempted to travel abroad with false papers. It was presumed that he did so in order to meet with Catholic plotters on the European continent, and the Protestant English state arrested him. To make matters worse, Castlehaven's sister was Eleanor Davies, the "fantastical creature" whom Alice's son-in-law and daughter, the Earl and Countess of Huntingdon, had taken to court when she had refused to pay her daughter's marriage portion. In 1630, as Anne's Castlehaven brother-in-law was being held in prison as a recusant, a pejorative term English Protestants often used to describe subversive Catholics in the realm, her sister Elizabeth was embroiled with Eleanor in the lawsuit to settle Lucy Davies's marriage settlement. Eleanor was also earning a dangerous reputation in the court of King Charles, who had succeeded to his father's throne in 1625, as she ranted incoherent prophecies about the demise of the English kingdom. Castlehaven lacked the political clout to advocate for his siblings. Too many people, both in London and in the earl's own county of Wiltshire, believed him to be a Catholic, and Castlehaven did not refute the accusations, although he also was not as overt with his faith as his brother had been. His reputation suffered as he refused to try to convince the king that he was devoted to the Church of England, indicating that he probably at least leaned toward Catholicism. By marrying Castlehaven and then arranging the match between her daughter and his son, Anne had cast a line from Alice's pristine family into the Touchet quagmire; Alice feared that line would sink them all.

The king and his councillors grew weary of Castlehaven and his trouble-some siblings, and Alice and her other sons-in-law would not, or could not, save Anne's new in-laws. By the end of 1630, the king had stripped Castlehaven of most of his local offices as his family fell further from grace.[6] Though Anne and her daughters were now inextricably linked to a family in a political free fall, Alice showed no intention of stepping in to try to salvage matters. In fact, she wanted to isolate herself from them. In the summer of 1630, she was seventy-one years old and all she desired was to oversee the renovations of a country estate in Ruislip she had leased, just four miles southwest of Harefield.[7] She was growing annoyed at her floundering in-laws and bemoaned her frustrations to her middle daughter, Frances, when she wrote "that if it should please God to call for me, I might have a place to lay my stuff in out of my Lord Castlehaven's fingering."[8] She cringed at the thought of Castlehaven laying claim to anything that belonged to her. At least she could maintain control over Anne's two sons to keep them from their stepfather's reach. The underlying tone of Alice's letter to Frances hints that she may have been exasperated with Anne for making such an unsuitable match for herself, and she makes no mention of trying to do anything to help her eldest daughter. Anne and her teenage daughter, Eliza-beth, were on their own. (There is no mention of either of Anne's two youngest daughters in the historical record from the period.) In truth, Anne and Elizabeth Touchet were already far more vulnerable than even Alice could have imagined.

✦+ ———— ✦ ———— +✦

Just one week into her second marriage, Anne knew she had made an enor-mous mistake when Castlehaven revealed a scandalous desire: he wanted to watch her have sex with other men. When she adamantly refused, he pro-claimed that "her body was his body and what he commanded her to do she ought not but to perform."[9] He insisted that as her husband, he had a right to control every aspect of her life. Patriarchal English culture ensured that Cas-tlehaven was the head of his family, and the laws of coverture entitled him to ownership of all of Anne's assets, but she refused to grant him authority over her very being. She would not give in to his shocking carnal demands. Yet that did not prevent him from continuing to make them.

Castlehaven did not just express an abstract sexual desire; he had specific men in mind whom he wanted Anne to sleep with. Within the household, the earl had garnered a reputation for developing unusually close friendships with some of his male servants and elevating his "favorites" to professional positions that surpassed their rank. Two of Castlehaven's stewards, John Anktill and Henry Skipwith, were among the cohort, as was Anne's footman, Giles Broadway. Ultimately, the earl arranged for Anktill to marry his daughter Lucy and he set the couple up in a small estate of their own. He then focused his attention on Henry Skipwith. Over time, Skipwith began to dine at the same table as the earl and the family, and other servants were instructed to call him "Mister Skipwith." Nobles and other servants were distrustful of close friendships such as that between people of different status within the household because they blurred hierarchical lines, but as the head of his estate, Castlehaven insisted that he had the right to do as he wished. Though English custom firmly placed men at the head of the household, they were expected to adhere to and model a certain set of standards. It was the father's job to ensure order within his estate and demonstrate upright behavior. In reality, however, there was no one to stop him from abusing his patriarchal authority. The best Anne could do was continue to refuse to have sex with the men Castlehaven urged her toward. After all, she would hardly risk the humiliation of telling anyone about her husband's behavior, and no one else in the household was in a position of enough power to stop him without throwing everything into chaos.

Castlehaven's abuse did not stop there. His fondness for Skipwith started to overshadow his relationship with his own son, Audley, which deteriorated to its lowest point when Castlehaven devised a ghastly plot. Perhaps he disliked Audley and wanted to disinherit him, perhaps he felt more of an affinity toward the faithful servant in his employ, or perhaps he was just a sick man. In reality, it was a probably a combination of all those things that ultimately inspired Castlehaven's choices.

One day in 1629, seemingly out of the blue, Castlehaven approached Elizabeth, his teenage stepdaughter/daughter-in-law, to say "that upon his knowledge, her husband [Audley] loved her not." Everyone in the household knew that the young couple did not get along very well, but Elizabeth was devastated by Castlehaven's bluntness and mean-spirited remark. His cruelty continued. He threatened "that he would turn her out of doors, if she did not lie with Skipwith."[10] He may not have been able to convince his wife to play his sexual games, so he instead exploited her daughter. Elizabeth was distraught at the thought that her husband did not love her and terrified that her father-in-law/stepfather would throw her out of the house if she did not do as he commanded. Young and scared, Elizabeth obeyed Castlehaven.

Unbeknown to Elizabeth, the two men schemed that if Elizabeth became pregnant by Skipwith, Castlehaven would name the child his heir, thus securing a place in his lineage for his favorite servant and cutting his son out of his rightful inheritance. Because Elizabeth had become his daughter-in-law, Castlehaven could claim any child she had as his heir, a grotesque abuse of Elizabeth both as his daughter-in-law and as a person. He started sitting in the bedchamber to watch Skipwith have sex with the fourteen-year-old Elizabeth, who was scared and angry, motivated by the belief of the lie Castlehaven had told her that she had been cast aside by her husband. In time, rumors spread throughout the house that Elizabeth and Skipwith were carrying on a not-so-secret affair. In later testimonies, Elizabeth alluded to the idea that she had grown to like the attention of Skipwith, but she was still only fourteen. Elizabeth later told court investigators that her mother had known about the affair and "never persuaded her against it."[11] If that were true, it is easy to judge Anne as a criminally negligent mother, which she may have been. She was also, however, dealing with trauma of her own at Castlehaven's hands.

Once Castlehaven had succeeded in sexually manipulating Elizabeth, he grew hungry for more control over the other woman in his life. He continued to pressure Anne to allow him to watch her have sex with servants, and she continuously refused. At the time, she did not tell anyone about it. She must have been ashamed that her mother had been right to take custody of her sons two years before she had married Castlehaven, and she was probably relieved that they were safely at Harefield. Life at Fonthill Gifford was miserable. Anne had been raised on the grand Tudor estates of the Earls of Derby and had been the wife of a baron and lady of the idyllic Sudeley Castle. She was the eldest of the celebrated Stanley coheiresses. Her second marriage had elevated her from baroness to countess, finally granting her the same status as her mother and two younger sisters, but to get there, she had married a man her powerful mother disliked, a man determined to sexually humiliate her. The

English aristocracy may have mocked Castlehaven's Catholic tendencies and Irish ties, but there had never been gossip about him as any kind of deviant.

Now Anne's household was in disarray, cloaked in tensions and hostilities, and her teenage daughter was openly carrying on an affair with a servant at Castlehaven's urging. Though Elizabeth may have even grown to believe her relationship with Skipwith was consensual, in truth, she had been emotionally and mentally manipulated by both her stepfather and Skipwith. The young woman had no ability to change her situation. She also did not hide her disdain for her husband, Audley, and may have derived some pleasure from making a cuckold of him. The cuckold, a husband whose wife committed adultery, was a popular seventeenth-century archetype and was depicted in woodcuts as a man with horns growing out of his head. The modern term "horny" derives from this image, and the trope was that the horned man could not satisfy his wife's sexual desire, so she humiliated him by taking lovers.

The young Lady Audley was not the only subject of gossip within the estate. Some servants whispered that Anne was unfaithful in her marriage, although such rumors remained vague. And of course, Fonthill Gifford was filled with stories that Castlehaven had an insatiable sexual appetite. The gossip about the earl was quite specific as stories circulated that he frequently had sex with servants and prostitutes. Anne was not naive, and infidelity was common in aristocratic marriages on the parts of both husbands and wives. Lots of lords had sex with their servants. She may not have liked it, but part of being a countess meant ignoring gossip about petty things. After all, most elite unions were about power, not love; her mother's second marriage had certainly taught her that. But things changed when the household rumors turned into stories that Castlehaven was having sex not only with his servants but specifically with a male servant, Lawrence Fitzpatrick.

At this time, English concepts of sexuality differed from modern concepts of sexual identity. The terms *homosexual* and *heterosexual* did not come into existence until the 1890s, and *transsexual* was not used until the beginning of the twentieth century. In fact, in the 1600s, there was a tacit understanding that men might have sexual relations with other men. There were times in men's lives when same-sex relationships were considered a fairly common phase—when they were abroad on the European continent on the Grand

Tour or away at school—and not as a permanent fixed aspect of their core identity.[12] In Anne and Castlehaven's England, as long as married couples produced children to inherit, husbands and wives often maintained separate sexual relationships, so infidelity was not necessarily the problem, nor would it have been inherently a problem if Castlehaven were attracted to other men.

King James himself very publicly had close and often physical relationships with men at court, especially his "favorite," the Duke of Buckingham.[13] When James's son Charles I inherited the throne, however, in 1625, the new king had a dramatically different stance, as he had been appalled by what he considered to be the lascivious nature of his father's court. The court of King Charles was a much less sexualized place, and although Charles carried on affairs of his own, they were with women, never with men. Despite the new king's more prudish attitudes toward sex, English men and women often carried on intimate same-sex relationships that involved sleeping in the same beds, touching, and kissing. Though the religiously devout did not approve, none of that behavior was forbidden by law.

Sodomy, however, was deemed a criminal act because it was sex that involved genital penetration and ejaculation without the possibility of reproduction; it was sex for sheer pleasure, whether anal sex or sex with animals, both referred to as "buggery." That belief conflated sodomy with sexual deviance, and English aristocrats saw men and women who engaged in sodomy as being driven by sexual desire completely devoid of any respect for social order.[14] Legally, the charges of sodomy and bestiality had been defined together in Henry VIII's 1534 Statute on Buggery, "An Act for the Punishment of the Vice of Buggery: For As much as there is not yet sufficient and condign punishment appointed and limited by the due course of the laws of this realm for the detestable and abominable vice of buggery committed with mankind or beast."[15] Before 1534, sodomy was a crime in ecclesiastical, or church, courts. Henry VIII's Reformation included legal reforms, as the monarch seized jurisdiction over certain crimes, such as sodomy/bestiality. Other medieval offenses, such as abandonment (leaving one's spouse) and public drunkenness, remained under the purview of ecclesiastical courts.

The servants at Fonthill Gifford were not just gossiping about the relationship between Castlehaven and Fitzpatrick, they also gossiped about their positions during sex. The rumor was that Castlehaven had allowed Fitzpatrick to penetrate him. English statutes defined sodomy, but beyond the laws, there was a rigid cultural power dynamic that came into play in male same-sex relationships, as there was in virtually all aspects of life. Given the earl's social status, his having sex with male servants would be less transgressive if he penetrated his servants because that was viewed as the position of power; his servants (men of lesser status) were not supposed to penetrate the earl. The mere notion that Castlehaven was sexually submissive to his servant completely reversed the social order. English culture was so regimented and coded that even sexual positions reinforced and protected established hierarchies, and Castlehaven had broken all the rules. Fonthill Gifford was an estate plagued with dangerous secrets. Yet things were about to get even worse.

+—•—+

One autumn evening in 1630 began as any other night at the Castlehaven estate. Anne retired to the bedchamber with her husband, but he insisted that the footman, Giles Broadway, come with them. Broadway was one of the servants Castlehaven had been prodding Anne to have sex with. She remained steadfast that she would not, although by that time Castlehaven had been badgering her for more than six years. She ignored Broadway as he slept at the foot of the couple's bed. Anne was sound asleep at midnight when Castlehaven awoke and demanded that Broadway light him a pipe. Broadway stood up to do as his lord commanded, and Castlehaven saw that he was aroused. That was the moment the violence erupted. Both Anne and Castlehaven would later recount the subsequent events with a similar narrative; however, she would call it rape, and he would call it a husband's prerogative.

Castlehaven pulled Broadway into bed with them as Anne awoke in terror. In a tangle of bed linens, Castlehaven grabbed at Anne's arms and legs as she fought to free herself. Despite her flailing, the two men overpowered her and Castlehaven pinned down both of her hands and one of her legs. Broadway climbed on top of her and "knew her carnally."[16] As soon as the rape was over, Castlehaven released her limbs and Broadway moved from atop her. Anne bolted out of bed and lunged for a knife kept in the bedchamber. She wanted to kill herself, but Broadway jumped up and violently wrestled the knife from her hands, breaking it in the fight. Defenseless and distraught, Anne crumbled.

As the sun rose over Fonthill Gifford the next morning, no one in the household seemed to know what had transpired the night before, and if anyone had heard the attack taking place, he or she did not come forward. But aristocratic estates existed within their own cultural microclimate, and even if no one else knew the details of what had happened, tensions within Fonthill Gifford were reaching a boiling point. By the end of October 1630, Audley could no longer ignore the fact that his young wife, Elizabeth, was having an affair with Skipwith and that his father seemed to have masterminded the entire thing. He grew enraged that his father would favor a servant over his own son and blamed Elizabeth as being a coconspirator against him. Anne must have been horrified that her daughter's life was combusting, yet she continued to keep silent about her own violation. Though the women of the house had every intention of maintaining secrecy, Audley had other plans.

On November 1, 1630, the eighteen-year-old Lord Audley approached the Privy Council with the claim that his father was trying to swindle him out of his rightful inheritance. By that time, King Charles I was on the throne, promoting a court of decorum and virtue—in appearance, at least, in stark contrast to that of his father, James I. Audley knew only that his wife had been sleeping with another man and that his father had orchestrated the affair, and he hoped that the king would step in and return things to their proper order. Audley's claim to the council made no mention of the assault on Anne, and he probably did not know about it. If he had, he likely would never have brought the Privy Council into the situation, as the laws of the time stipulated that if a noble were convicted of criminal charges, the Crown, not his heirs, would inherit his estate. Rape and sodomy were both criminal offenses, whereas inheritance disputes were civil. Though Audley surely hated his father, his focus was on securing his inheritance, which meant charging him with financial misconduct, not accusing him of crimes.

After he reached out to the Privy Council, he wrote a scolding letter to his father, saying "Your own dear branches hang down their heads to see their sap and livelihood conferred upon another in that late scene of you acted. But now at Fonthill, we had all our parts for your shame." He then asserted, "Pardon me, my Lord, if in this monstrous change of a father into an enemy, I stand upon my guard and from you, appeal unto the father of our country, the King Majesty, that hope to find him a father when my own forsakes me." Audley's report to the Privy Council certainly excluded mention of Castlehaven's affair with Fitzpatrick, as buggery was also a criminal offense, but the young lord concluded his remarks to his father with condemnation: "'Tis a fearful judgment to be a prisoner to bestial affection and lust."[17] Even if he had heard nothing about the attack on Anne, he clearly knew more than what he had told the Privy Council, and he was still taking a dangerous gamble by inviting the court into Fonthill Gifford, an estate with so many scandalous secrets. If the full extent of what was going on was discovered, he could lose everything. As a young man, sickened by his father, betrayed by his wife, and at risk of watching his inheritance pass to a servant, Audley was willing to take that chance, or else he was so blinded with rage that he did not care what happened.

◆────────◆────────◆

The Privy Council was accustomed to being dragged into inheritance squabbles, but Castlehaven's family's reputation, combined with his son's claim of estate mismanagement via sexual trysts, seemed particularly bizarre. Members of the Privy Council were also aware that in the decade before all of that, the Dowager Countess of Derby had petitioned the Court of Wards for the guardianship of Anne's, now Countess of Castlehaven's, eldest son. Perhaps initially Alice had wanted to control her grandson's inheritance, but when the members of the Privy Council were called to Fonthill Gifford, they may have viewed Alice's control of George's wardship with new suspicion. If the Dowager Countess of Derby had deemed Castlehaven to be a suitable man, she surely would have acceded to the normal order of things and allowed the young boys to remain in the care of their mother and stepfather until they were of an appropriate age to be properly socialized in someone else's household, probably hers. Why had she preemptively intervened?

The council sent several investigators to Fonthill Gifford to study the situation more closely. Henry Montagu, Earl of Manchester, was one of the lead investigators. Manchester and Alice were old friends, and, in a sense, the investigators who entered Fonthill Gifford were already influenced by

Portrait of Lady Alice and the Angel, ca. 1633

Credit: Lady Huntingdon's Memorial Manuscript, courtesy of the Rt Hon The Earl of Derby

Engraving of Alice, Dowager Countess of Derby, after 1594

Portrait of Ferdinando Stanley,
Lord Strange, later fifth Earl of
Derby. Circle of Marcus Gheeraerts
the Younger, ca. 1590

*Credit: Courtesy of the Rt Hon
The Earl of Derby*

Engraving of
Thomas Egerton,
Lord Chancellor Ellesmere,
ca. 1616

*Credit: The Huntington Library,
Art Museum, and Botanical
Gardens, San Marino, CA*

Portrait of Frances Stanley Egerton, Countess of Bridgewater. Paul van Somer, ca. 1617–20.

Credit: Courtesy of the Rt Hon The Earl of Derby

Engraving of Elizabeth Stanley Hastings, Countess of Huntingdon, ca. 1635

Credit: The Huntington Library, Art Museum, and Botanical Gardens, San Marino, CA

Engraving of Henry Hastings,
Earl of Huntingdon, ca. seventeenth
century

*Credit: The Huntington Library, Art
Museum, and Botanical Gardens,
San Marino, CA*

Engraving of Mervyn
Touchet, Earl of
Castlehaven, ca. 1642

*Credit: The Huntington
Library, Art Museum, and
Botanical Gardens,
San Marino, CA*

Queen Elizabeth I, The Rainbow Portrait. Isaac Oliver, ca. 1565–1617

Engraving of Harefield Place

Drawn from the Monument and Eng.d by W.P. Sherlock.

MONUMENT OF ALICE COUNTESS OF DERBY.

Pub. June 11. 1800. by T. Cadell, Jun.r and W. Davies, Strand.

Engraving of the tomb of Alice Egerton, Dowager Countess of Derby

Credit: The Huntington Library, Art Museum, and Botanical Gardens, San Marino, CA

Alice's earlier suspicions about Castlehaven, as well as the fact that just two years prior, the king had stripped Castlehaven of some of his privileges, arrested his brother, and banished his sister from court. The Privy Council must have known that there was something wrong with the Touchets.

In the first week of December 1630, investigators questioned household servants and family members. As servants divulged all the gossip and rumors that had circulated around the estate for years, it quickly became clear that Castlehaven might have been guilty of far more than trying to make his son a cuckold. Some of the servants claimed that Anne had been having an affair with Skipwith; others recounted salacious details of sexual encounters they had witnessed between servants and the family. They divulged stories of Castlehaven's many lovers, male and female. The investigators received sensational, conflicting, and muddled reports as they questioned people multiple times, trying to tease out the truth.

On December 9, they questioned Elizabeth. She was livid when she learned of the stories that Skipwith had slept with others in the house, and when asked, she insisted that she had been the only one to have sex with him and only because she had been commanded to do so by her terrorizing stepfather. Like other young aristocratic wives, Elizabeth noted how little control she had over her person and the fact that her husband had been cruel to her. Undeniably a victim in that abusive household, she was determined to hold any ground she could, and she wanted revenge. She spewed stories about Castlehaven's sexual deviance, sparing no detail about his relations with his male servants.[18] With the investigators convinced that Castlehaven had perpetrated a dizzying array of sexual crimes, they questioned Anne again, as she had seemingly withheld information during her initial interview. Now that investigators had unearthed so many stories, she was forced to relive the horrible night.

A victim of sexual violence, then as now, often has to endure two ordeals: the experience of the assault itself and the separate torment of an investigation and potential trial. We do not know what Anne felt as she told her story to the men interrogating her, men she knew, men who knew her family, her mother. Did the words pour out easily, fueled by rage, or did she choke on them as she held back tears? She overcame whatever it was that she felt and found her voice. Patriarchal norms may have imbued Castlehaven with authority over her as his wife, but in the hierarchical world of the English aristocracy, she was by far his better. For a brief moment, she may have felt small and fragile, but ultimately, she remembered that she was one of the Stanley coheiresses with royal blood in her veins. She would stand for herself just as her cousin Queen Elizabeth had done, as her mother, the Dowager Countess of Derby, would do.

Anne finally came forward with the story that her husband had assisted their footman, Giles Broadway, to rape her earlier that autumn. She admitted to investigators that although she and Castlehaven had been married for more than six years before the event took place, her husband had always paid little attention to her in their marriage, preferring male company over her own in the bedchamber. Confirming her husband's relations with men was damning, but more so was her acknowledgment that he had allowed himself to be penetrated by servants, subverting both social and household hierarchy. If her reputation was to be destroyed, she would do anything in her power to take her husband down with her. She explained that he had wanted to watch her lie with other men, and when she had repeatedly refused, he had resorted to plotting her rape.

Anne's revelation plunged the estate into a new level of chaos, and things quickly unraveled. That same day, the court sent Elizabeth and her servants away from Fonthill Gifford to reside with Sir William Slingsby, a knight and justice of Middlesex, near Harefield, and his family, who promised to keep her safe while investigators sorted out what was really going on. By December 12, the Earl of Castlehaven was "under restraint by his Majesty's special command."[19] Two days later, Anne was sent to reside with the Bishop of Winchester, some thirty miles south of Fonthill Gifford, for "safe keeping."[20] On December 21, 1630, Castlehaven was formally arrested, and investigators seized temporary control of the entire estate. There was no Christmas for Anne that year, as the investigators continued to dig and question.

Finally, just after New Year's Day, Anne and Audley confirmed the compromising details about Castlehaven's sexual trysts with Lawrence Fitzpatrick and Anne officially accused Broadway of raping her. A rape charge was much murkier for Castlehaven. On the one hand, seventeenth-century English law made no distinction between a rapist and an accomplice, which meant that Castlehaven could be accused of rape. On the other hand, Castlehaven and Anne were husband and wife, and marital rape did not legally exist at the time, nor would it receive full legal recognition as a crime in the United Kingdom until the twentieth century.

The accusations were so egregious that the Privy Council decided it needed to act. London lawyers would sort out the legality of the charges. On January 27, 1631, Castlehaven, Broadway, and Fitzpatrick were sent to the Tower of London to await trial. The week before, Castlehaven submitted a petition to the court of a list of household goods he would pay to have sent to his jail cell, befitting his station, including a "bed of crimson taffeta" with bedding, six sets of sheets (four for himself and two for the servants who were to attend to him in prison), twelve tapestries, a set of dishes, and other sundry goods. He also requested access to funds to continue to pay his staff and settle his debts.[21]

All the while, Elizabeth remained in the custody of Sir Slingsby and Anne remained with the Bishop of Winchester. The Privy Council appointed a steward to continue to collect the rents from tenants, which were used, in part, to cover the costs of living for Anne, Elizabeth, and Audley and to pay their household servants. Anne, Elizabeth, and Audley may all have hated Castlehaven, but by revealing the truth about life at Fonthill Gifford, they had lost control of the estate. Throughout the months to follow, they all separately petitioned the Privy Council to request their belongings and monies to be delivered to them. Anne had fled the estate so quickly that it took two weeks for her to secure a trunk of "necessary provisions for her Ladyship" to be delivered to her.[22]

No one knew what the future held or how long the situation would last. The Privy Council originally intended for Elizabeth to remain in Middlesex for just three or four days, but by February 1631, Sir Slingsby wrote to the Privy Council that Elizabeth "with her servants have been ever since entertained to his great trouble" and that after ten weeks, he "pray[ed] to be released of his charge."[23] Later that same month, the court granted Anne and Audley each £100 (£12,000/$16,000 today) for their maintenance until the trial.[24] Everything was coming undone in a frenzied and harrowing flurry as the members of the Castlehaven family awaited the start of the trial.

◆─────────◆─────────◆

While all of that transpired, Alice, the matriarch who had led her own family through so many challenges and had several of her grandchildren in her care, was uncharacteristically silent throughout the winter of 1630 and early 1631. After a lifetime of writing to powerful courtiers and building her vast patronage network, the dowager countess seemingly did not send a single petition on behalf of her suffering daughter and granddaughter, nor did she offer to take either into her custody or give them any money. Her friend the Earl of Manchester helped to organize the trial and ensure that Anne and Elizabeth were safe in their temporary arrangements, and he must have been keeping Alice informed. But Alice herself appears to have been completely absent from the tumult. Anne's sisters and their husbands were also seemingly removed. In 1616, Thomas Gainsford's dedicatory epistle to the Stanley women had eulogized them: "Yea, such Daughters, and such a Mother, that me thinks you move together like faire Planets in conspicuous Orbs and from whose influence can proceed nothing, but sweet presages."[25] Now one fair planet was in an orbit all her own, lost in a dark void. Where were her sisters and her mother, seemingly with gravitational forces of their own?

Alice deployed a strategy of quiet containment. Rather than taking in her daughter and granddaughter, she isolated them from the rest of the family, especially the Chandos sons, so as to protect the larger family unit from the chaos and horrific scandal of the disgraced Castlehaven household. She left her daughter and granddaughter to suffer their traumas alone in an effort to preserve whatever good name for the others she could. She still had several grandchildren who would need to secure good marriages, and the Earls of Huntingdon and Bridgewater could still rise at court. She had Spencer nieces and nephews who would not want to be associated with the dishonor of the scandal, either. Like other ambitious aristocratic women, Alice saw herself and her family as a holistic unit, not something made up of individual entities, so whatever pain Anne and Elizabeth were suffering was secondary to the protection of her family; their suffering was their own. Anne had not just betrayed Alice by marrying Castlehaven, she had betrayed the dynasty. Alice's behavior was callous, but it was also shrewd. She believed that no good would come from her spending her political capital too early. That did not mean she would never act for Anne and Elizabeth, however. First, she had to remain stoically in command of her family; then, in due course, she could begin to do what she did best: fight to restore order.

CHAPTER NINE

TRIALS AND EXECUTIONS

"B'smeared with Your Sensual Life"

The fact that an earl was charged with buggery, combined with the alleged rape of one of the Stanley coheiresses, sent the English peerage into a frenzy. Though buggery and rape were felonies in English common law, Castlehaven would not be tried in a standard criminal court. As a member of the peerage, even with an Irish title, he was no ordinary defendant and would be tried and judged in the Lord Steward's Court. King Charles put some of his most politically powerful and influential men in charge of the special trial: Sir Richard Weston (Lord Treasurer); Henry Montagu, Earl of Manchester (Lord Privy Seal); Thomas Howard, second Earl of Arundel (Earl Marshal); and William Herbert, third Earl of Pembroke (Lord Chamberlain). Thomas Coventry, first Baron Coventry, would serve as Lord High Steward during the trial. The five men would act as the judges, but as this was no ordinary trial, the king wanted a special council of jurors, demanding "twenty-five, if not twenty-seven," peers of the realm to decide the fate of the Earl of Castlehaven.[1]

The judges appointed jurors they deemed fit to sit in judgment of an earl, one of their peers. The Countess of Castlehaven's own pedigree also complicated matters. She was, after all, the eldest daughter of Ferdinando Stanley and Alice, the Dowager Countess of Derby, and the stepdaughter of the late Thomas Egerton, Lord Chancellor Ellesmere. Her brothers-in-law were the Earls of Bridgewater and Huntingdon, and her sisters were respected countesses. She was mother to the heirs of Lord Chandos, the "King of the Cotswolds." Her great-great-great-grandfather was Henry VII. The jurors were well aware of her lineage, and they could not ignore her impressive family tree, for if they did so, many of them would be ignoring their own. Birth and close family marriages connected Anne and her daughter, Elizabeth, to ten of the jurors. Two of the jurors were Anne's first cousins, one on her mother's side and one on her father's side. Alice's old friend the Earl of Manchester would be sitting on the judges' bench, ensuring that her interests were well represented, and although no correspondence between the two survives, it is impossible to think that they did not speak about what was to happen. Beyond that important alliance, Alice also had friends among the jurors. The Countess of Castlehaven was so well connected throughout the realm that it would have been virtually impossible to find a gentleman of the English peerage without some tie to her or her high-ranking family. In comparison, with his Irish title and modest lineage, Castlehaven's networks could not rival those of his wife. That may not have been fair, but fairness was rarely a factor in the mindset of the English aristocracy.

The court agreed that Fitzpatrick and Castlehaven would face charges of buggery (i.e., sodomy). Though the English aristocracy was scandalized by the thought that an earl would allow his servant to penetrate him, it was legally straightforward for the court to bring the charge of buggery against the two men, as people of the time understood buggery to mean "that self-sin of sodomy," either between two men, a man and a woman, or a man and an animal.[2] Legally, the charge was about anal penetration that resulted in ejaculation. According to the various testimonies given during the investigation at Fonthill Gifford, Fitzpatrick and Castlehaven were both guilty of the crime. The two men would stand trial separately, as Castlehaven's status had earned him a special hearing in the Lord Steward's Court while Fitzpatrick would face a standard criminal proceeding in the common-law Court of King's Bench.

Broadway would stand trial for rape, as Anne had every legal right to accuse him of the crime, although technically the charges had been filed on behalf of the state in criminal matters. Given Anne's social standing, though for her coming forward about the event had been excruciating, legally charging Broadway was easy. Beyond Anne's family lineage and connections, the jurors would have been willing to take Anne more seriously than other seventeenth-century women who brought an accusation of rape to trial. Her age would have been particularly important. In 1631, Anne was fifty years old, and her age, combined with her bloodlines, made her matronly and respectable in the eyes of the jurors. Her peers saw her as an established woman with nothing to gain and everything to lose through a false accusation of rape. The highest-ranking men of England were willing to believe her, whereas they might have been less willing to believe women of lower standing or younger women, who were often deemed to be mischievous and therefore untrustworthy.

Establishing the legality of charging Castlehaven with rape was far less clear. Though the court may have felt a comradery with Anne, they still needed to establish whether Castlehaven could even be accused of "ravishing" his wife. The men who made up the council would certainly have viewed Castlehaven as an unfit husband and deviant outsider with an Irish title and Catholic sympathies, but those were not felonies. The court would need to establish a sound legal argument to charge him with rape because the laws of coverture technically made Anne his property and marital rape did not exist as a crime in the eyes of the law. However, because English law at the time made no distinction between a rapist and an accomplice, the court read that as a potential way to charge Castlehaven with rape; theoretically, to charge Broadway meant it would be possible to charge Castlehaven.

At the same time that the government was preparing its case, Castlehaven was busily conferring with numerous lawyers from his jail cell in the Tower to devise an argument as to why he could not legally be charged with rape. They drafted and submitted a set of questions to the judges in an attempt to demonstrate that the charges made against Castlehaven were confused and extended beyond the boundaries of a responsible interpretation of English law. After careful deliberation, the court answered each one of the earl's questions. The dialectic manuscript survives, outlining Castlehaven's loaded interrogatories and the court's responses that established the legal framework for the trial:

1 **Quere:** Whether may a wife bear witness against her husband?

Ans: In civil causes she cannot, in criminal she may especially where she is the party grieved.

The court ruled that Anne could testify against her husband because she was the victim of the crime. Without Anne's testimony, they could not charge Castlehaven with rape, as she would need to claim that he had been there and assisted Broadway in her attack. She was not advocating for someone else, only for herself. Coverture laws included spousal privilege, which meant that a wife could not be forced to testify against her husband if he committed a crime against someone else, but wives had long been allowed to testify against their husbands when they were the victim, as in cases of abandonment and abduction. Each court had its own procedures (not unlike today), and there was a long history of women testifying in court, depending on the charges. It was not unusual that a woman's testimony would be given; it was, however, unheard of that a wife would testify against her husband in a rape trial.

2 Quere: Whether buggery without penetration be condemned by the Statute?

Ans: It may. The use of the body to spend seed doth is.

Debates about penetration were central to the sodomy and rape charges levied against Castlehaven, Broadway, and Fitzpatrick, but here the earl was arguing specifically against the buggery charge. The earl claimed that Fitzpatrick had not actually penetrated him but had merely rubbed up against him until he ejaculated. Castlehaven therefore contested the argument that he had been sodomized by his servant. The judges' answer redefined the scope of the crime in a surprisingly broad way to be tied to any bodily stimulus or rubbing that resulted in a male sexual partner "spending seed," meaning ejaculating. That language is not in Henry VIII's statute on buggery, but the interpretation would not set any legal precedent because Castlehaven would be facing a special council of judges in his trial. The court interpreted the law this way specifically for and only in regard to the Castlehaven trials.

3 Quere: Whether one can ravish a woman of ill fame or no?

Ans: A whore may be ravished & it is felony to do it.

Throughout his imprisonment, Castlehaven contended that his wife and son had plotted his demise and trumped up the absurd charges. He argued that a wife and son who acted against the head of the family were a threat to social order and therefore their words could not be trusted, thus attempting to cast Anne as a "woman of ill fame." Castlehaven was also suggesting to the court that Anne had been unfaithful in their marriage and therefore was untrustworthy. He tried to argue that because his wife was of poor moral character, sexually taking her against her will did not constitute rape, but the court's response to the interrogatory confirmed that Anne was not the one on trial. The court's answer dismissed Castlehaven's claim as irrelevant to the charge, as it would be a felony to "ravish" even a "whore," let alone a countess with a royal bloodline, whether she was faithful in her marriage or not. The court reiterated that any woman sexually taken against her will was legally entitled to bring a charge against her assailant or assailants. That reading of the law was not new; whether a court would believe her was a different matter entirely.

4 Quere: Whether there be a necessity of occasion for a ravishing in convenient time?

Ans: In an indictment, there is not. In an appeal, there is.

Castlehaven tried to suggest that his wife's charge exceeded the statute of limitations because she did not initially bring the rape charge until Audley made his accusation that his father was squandering his inheritance. Castlehaven tried to argue that too much time had lapsed between the night of Anne's alleged rape and when the court had charged him with the felony. That claim was the best legal option he had to discredit the charges. In fact, members of the court may have seen Anne's reluctance to reveal her assault as a signal of her honorability because in their minds, a virtuous woman would not have wanted to be at the center of such a debate. Though legally any statute of limitations was not contingent upon the victim's virtue, it mattered to the men sitting on the bench. And regardless of their feelings, the law allowed for the court to bring an indictment at any point in time.

5 Quere: Whether men of nonworth shall be sufficient proof against a Baron?

Ans: In case of felony any man is sufficient.[3]

Because of his rank, Castlehaven was scheduled to stand trial separately from Broadway and Fitzpatrick, and both servants were slated to testify against him. It was bad enough that his wife was permitted to offer testimony, but Castlehaven and his lawyers tried to argue that permitting two servants to testify against their master would lead to a total unraveling of the social order. As Anne was accusing her husband and Broadway of the same crime, and because rape was a felony charge, the court saw no reason that Broadway should not be called to testify. If the court was going to charge the earl with rape, it had to permit Anne's and Broadway's testimonies; otherwise there would be no one to make the charge. The court also allowed Fitzpatrick's testimony in the buggery charge because buggery, too, was a felony.

✦━━━●━━━✦

The Earl of Castlehaven's trial was scheduled to take place in Westminster on Monday, April 25, 1631. In the days before the trial, the judges decided that it would be best if Anne did not appear in person at court but that her sworn testimony should be read on her behalf. That was done to try to spare her the embarrassment of having to address the court in person and to help her preserve as much dignity as possible. It also worked to Anne's advantage because her testimony was likely to be far less distracting to the jurors if it was read aloud by a man. In fact, King Charles issued a royal proclamation forbidding women and children from attending the trial, even as spectators, "upon pain of ever after being reputed to have forfeited their modesty."[4] If even attending the trial could destroy a woman's reputation, what hope did Anne and Elizabeth have of making it through the ordeal intact? Ever since the Privy Council had seized control of Fonthill Gifford in December 1630, the lives of mother and daughter had been thrown into uncertainty, and on the eve of the trial, all they could do was wait.

On the night before his trial, from his prison cell in the Tower of London, the Earl of Castlehaven wrote to his younger brother, Ferdinando Touchet, in a desperate attempt to settle his affairs. He asked Ferdinando to look after his children. He made specific requests for his daughter and each of his two sons, convinced that regardless of the outcome, their stepmother would never care for them. He informed his brother that he had set aside £2,000 (£245,000/$338,000 today) as a marriage portion for his daughter, Frances. He left his younger son, George, in his steward's care, as "there must a rough hand be hold on him for [George] is of a harsh nature." On the night before he faced judgment, he also made a shockingly compassionate plea for his son and heir, whose letters to the Privy Council had brought the glaring light to shine on Castlehaven and his crimes. He wrote to his brother, "I pray you comfort my son, Audley, although he hath undone his house, preserve him and impact it rather to youth and ill council than an inbred wickedness. If you look not to him, he will be lost."[5] As a desperate prisoner, Castlehaven feared for the future of his children: an unwed daughter who would need a husband who would be willing to look beyond the stain of her family's reputation; an unkind younger son who would need to learn to be a good man; and an heir whom Castlehaven worried would be consumed by guilt and led astray by a wicked stepmother. In his darkest moment, as he sat alone in a jail cell in the Tower of London on the eve of his trial, he succumbed to the mindset that nothing mattered more than the security of his estate and the continuation of the family line.

The next day, he stood trial for rape and sodomy. As the charges made against him were so appalling, King Charles and his legal counselors carefully constructed the procedures that the specially appointed court would follow. The judges and jury would be expected to adhere to the established confines of the existing legal system, and because of the extremely unusual nature of the trial, any deviations in the court's legal interpretations would not establish any new legal precedents that could be applied in future trials unrelated to the Castlehaven affairs. As was customary, the king would not attend the trial himself.

Criminal trials in seventeenth-century England functioned quite differently than they do today. In most criminal proceedings, the prosecution did not necessarily need to prove to the jurors that the defendant was guilty beyond a reasonable doubt. Rather, the trial was an opportunity for jurors to make the determination as to what they understood to be the truth based on the evidence, although they were expected to interpret the evidence reasonably, based on the established laws of the realm. The burden rested on the defendant to convince the court that the charges were untrue. Defendants were not guaranteed counsel in court, although Castlehaven had been permitted to confer with solicitors while in prison. On the other side, the prosecution might be argued by multiple attorneys before the judges and jury. And the team of presiding judges was permitted to offer a vote of guilt or innocence along with the jurors.

Spectators, all men, packed the courtroom in the chamber at Westminster. They removed their hats as Lord Coventry and the other four judges, including Alice's friend the Earl of Manchester, the Lord Privy Seal, entered the chamber and took their seats at tables draped in green fabric. Then the twenty-two jurors entered the room according to their rank within the peerage. Every formality and hierarchical protocol was to be followed. The jurors sat along two tables that flanked the base of the judges' platform. The assembled twenty-seven noblemen gathered at the head of the courtroom made up a body of the most respected jurists and peers in the realm, a stern and commanding sight. Lord Coventry held the staff of the Lord High Steward the way a reigning monarch held a scepter.

Lord Coventry commanded the "peers of the realm and privy councilors" to put their hats back on and then called for the prisoner.[6] Castlehaven was brought in from a small chamber near the court and escorted to a "pew lined with green," although he remained standing. Lord Coventry addressed the earl by his lesser title: "My Lord Audley, the king hath understood both by report and by the verdict of diverse gentlemen of quality in your county, that you stand impeached of divers great and heinous crimes." He continued to outline the will of King Charles that Castlehaven should stand trial by "your peers and who have as much justice in their hearts as noble blood in their veins" and concluded that "God will put into the hearts of these noble persons to find it out that which is just."[7]

Castlehaven then humbly addressed the court: "My Lord High Steward, I have been a close prisoner this six months without friend, without council, and am but of weak speech at the best. And, herefore, I desire to have the liberty of having counsel to speak for me." Lord Coventry coldly responded, "For your imprisonment, My Lord, so long, it hath been to you a special favor, for you have had time enough, and more than ever man had, that hath been committed for such offences, and more favor then ever any that came to this bar, and you shall demand nothing that the law can allow you."[8] Coventry then put the question to the judges to interpret the law and determine whether Castlehaven was permitted to have an appointed counselor speak on his behalf, which they ruled was in violation of the criminal proceedings. Castlehaven would have to stand and speak for himself. The clerk of the court then asked the defendant to enter his plea, to which Castlehaven responded, "Not guilty."

The judges knew they had to immediately establish the legitimacy of allowing Anne's testimony to be read on her behalf. They opened with a debate, addressing the fact that Anne had not immediately come forward about her rape and that several months had lapsed before Castlehaven was officially charged with the crime. The court quickly established that Anne's charge was not beyond any statute of limitations. The court determined:

> *Whether it is adjudged a rape, when the woman complaineth not presently? And, whether there be a necessity of accusation within a convenient time, as within twenty-four hours?*
>
> *The judges resolved, that insomuch as she was forced against her will, and then showed her dislike, she was not limited to any time for her complaint.*[9]

With that ruling established, the king's three attorneys, Sir Robert Heath (Attorney General), Sir Richard Sheldon (Solicitor General), and Sir Thomas Crewe (King's Sergeant), took turns recounting aspects of life at Fonthill Gifford. Castlehaven, barred from having a single lawyer present, would have to wait to respond as the king's three lawyers laid out the claims before the judges and jurors. They included every rumor of Castlehaven's inappropriate relationship with John Anktill, Henry Skipwith, Giles Broadway, and Lawrence Fitzpatrick and his desire to watch those men have sex with his wife and the young women in the house. Though Skipwith never stood trial for anything, the court spent considerable time recounting the details of his relationship with the young Elizabeth, Lady Audley, and how Castlehaven wished him to impregnate his son's wife. According to one lawyer, Castlehaven was so "bawdy to his own wife if she loved him, she must love Henry Skipwith whom he loved above all, and not in an honest love, but in a dishonest." The attorneys implored the jury to consider "how a noble man of his quality should fall into such abominable sins," and they offered a possible explanation: "that he was constant in no religion but in the morning would be a papist, and in the afternoon a Protestant."[10] The prosecution's argument was not based solely on the acts that Castlehaven had been charged with. His dubious faith and inability to keep an orderly household were both factors that they argued demonstrated what an unfit man he was. They also argued that the sexual relationship between Skipwith and Elizabeth was relevant to the trial because a good lord of the manor would never tolerate, let alone orchestrate, such dishonor in his home.[11]

A judge then stood and read aloud the Countess of Castlehaven's testimony. The first part recounted her husband's desire to watch her have sex with other men, casting doubt on the fitness of her husband as a man and a peer of the realm. Her statement then described the night her husband and Broadway had raped her: "That one night, being a-bed with her at Fonthill, he called for his man, Broadway, and commanded him to lie at his bed's feet; and about midnight (she being asleep) called him to light a pipe of tobacco. Broadway rose in his shirt, and my Lord pulled him into Bed to him and her, and made him lie next to her." Once Broadway climbed into her bed, "Broadway lay with her, and knew her carnally, whilst she made resistance, and the lord held both her hands, and one of her legs the while." After the assault, "as soon as she was free, she would have killed herself with a knife, but that Broadway forcibly took the knife from her and broke it."[12] When Broadway was called to testify in person, he supported the countess's account in every way except one: he claimed that he had not penetrated her but had rubbed against her and ejaculated on her. It would be up to the jury to take a side.

The court also read aloud a statement prepared by Anne's daughter, Elizabeth. Her testimony did not pertain to either the rape or the sodomy charge. Rather, she told of how "she was first tempted to lie with Skipwith by the earl's allurements." She claimed that the earl was not satisfied knowing that the two were having an affair, but he "himself saw her and Skipwith lie together divers times; and nine servants of the house had also seen it." In her statement, she pleaded to the court that she had not wanted to sleep with Skipwith but that her father-in-law/stepfather had manipulated her.[13] Traditional court rules would not have allowed for an earl's stepdaughter to serve as a character witness against him, but none of the traditional rules were being applied. Elizabeth may have been abused, or even assaulted, by Skipwith at Castlehaven's urging, but she had never made a formal accusation of rape the way her mother had, and Skipwith was never charged with anything. Elizabeth's read testimony served only to enhance the court's understanding of Castlehaven's sexual depravity and to demonstrate that he was an unfit husband and father, which in the eyes of the English peerage meant he was also an unfit nobleman. Anne surely wanted to spare her daughter the humiliation and shame that would come with making a public and formal rape accusation, but Elizabeth's testimony was essential to exposing the depths of Castlehaven's inadequacies.

Lawrence Fitzpatrick, Henry Skipwith, and Giles Broadway were all examined in person by the court. They provided conflicting accounts, as Fitzpatrick claimed that Skipwith had affairs with Anne and her daughter, whereas Skipwith contended that he had had sex only with Elizabeth at the earl's urging. In addressing the sodomy charge, Fitzpatrick stated that "the Lord made him lie with him" multiple times but that he had "juice on the body and spent his seed but did not penetrate his body, and that he hears he did so with others," implying that he had heard Castlehaven had sex with full penetration with other men.[14]

The earl adamantly contested the statements made by his wife and servant, yet he said nothing in court about Elizabeth's statement. He also accused Audley of conspiring with Anne and Broadway. Castlehaven's son did not testify against him in court, although he had been the one to initiate the investigation in the first place. Castlehaven yelled at the court and "objected against the incompetency of the witnesses, as the one his wife, the other his servant; and they drawn to this by his son's practice, who sought his life: and desired to know, if there were not a statute against the incompetency of witnesses?" The earl then reraised the issue of whether rape without penetration could truly be a rape. He "desired to be resolved, whether because Broadway doth not depose any penetration, but only that he emitted upon her belly while the earl held her, that should be judged felony as for a rape?" The judges again coolly reiterated their acceptance of the rape charge and their view that it was "so consequently to be felony."[15] After the judges ruled against every objection the earl made, it was time for the court to offer its judgment. Lord Coventry called for a vote on the rape charge first. He asked each judge and juror, and one by one the men called out their verdict. Twenty-six men voted guilty, only one juror voting not guilty.

That verdict alone ensured the Earl of Castlehaven's execution, but the court still had to rule on the buggery charge. Although Castlehaven's fate had been sealed with the rape verdict, the sodomy charge served to further destroy his reputation. This court was not just out for justice; it was after vengeance against a man who had sadistically disrespected one of their own and subverted the class order. Anne's testimony had said nothing about her husband's sexual relationships with other men, and the court was solely dependent on Fitzpatrick's testimony to the charge, despite the fact that he, too, would soon stand trial for the same crime. Though the jurors were willing to publicly humiliate Castlehaven with the charge, they were less willing to convict him of it. When Lord Coventry repeated the roll call for the buggery charge, Castlehaven was found guilty by only one vote: 14–13. The earl was immediately taken back to his cell. The court would notify the king of the verdicts, and Charles I would decide the sentence.

⁕────⊹────⁕

No historical sources survive that reveal where Anne, Elizabeth, Alice, and their family were during the trial. We do not know if they were alone in different locations or faced the hours of uncertainty together. They left no record about the chaotic pendulum of emotions, fear, shame, guilt, rage, and exhaustion they must have experienced while waiting for word of the verdicts. Were they gathered in a room, a female space, filled with deafening silence periodically broken by the sound of uncomfortable fidgeting in heavy velvet dresses? The Earls of Bridgewater and Huntingdon may have been in the courtroom, watching their brother-in-law wilt under the heat of the radiating judgments passed by their friends and kinsmen. Regardless of where each member of the family was, the guilty verdicts must have brought a flood of relief, soon to be replaced by the desperate desire to find a way forward.

The trial brought a day of reckoning for Anne, Elizabeth, and Lord Audley. The court had reached its verdict condemning the Earl of Castlehaven, and it was time for Alice to step out from the shadows. The verdict demolished the Castlehaven family, and only Alice could now help her daughter and granddaughter rebuild their lives. She was also determined to continue isolating the rest of the family from the crisis and prevent it from soiling their reputations. Alice petitioned the king directly, asking if she might now take custody of her daughter, meaning that Anne be allowed to move to Harefield Place, a request the king granted. Though Anne was not a prisoner, the Privy Council had placed her in the home of the Bishop of Winchester, and Alice knew how important it would be to remain humble in the eyes of King Charles; she was not about to send for her daughter without the king's blessing. Though she was grateful for the permission, she wanted to proceed with caution, as she knew Broadway and Fitzpatrick were still to stand trial. Since the earl had been found guilty, it was hard to imagine that the two servants would not also receive the same judgment. Alice wanted to begin planning for a future when the entire ordeal was behind them. She wrote to her close friend Dudley Carleton, Viscount Dorchester, the king's secretary of state, who had served as one of the jurors, to seek his help in executing her plans. First she asked for his support to "further the reconcilement of the Lord Audley and his lady, who I hope will hereafter know a virtuous good and loving wife to him." Much as she had worked nearly twenty years ago to reconcile the marriage between her sister Anne and Robert Sackville, it was imperative to her sense of order that her granddaughter and Lord Audley resume their marriage, regardless of what had transpired.

Alice then expressed her hope "that neither my daughter nor [grand-daughter] will ever offend either God or his Majesty again by their wicked courses, but redeem what is past, by their reformation and newness of life." She pleaded with Dorchester to help them achieve that dream by "your lordship's favor that where you think the time draws near for obtaining their pardons (which as yet you say cannot be granted) you will not be unmindful when you see it stand with the conveniences of time to be a humble suitor to his Majesty from me in soliciting him for it."[16] Anne and Elizabeth had both been victims of sexual violence, and whatever Alice, as a mother, felt about that, she would have believed that they, too, were guilty of crimes against the social order of the English aristocracy. Throughout her life, she had demonstrated her own strict adherence to the belief that the people in her family, regardless of their gender, were expected to always present the best, most honorable, most virtuous versions of themselves. Though she found Castlehaven to be abhorrent, she also blamed Anne for putting herself and her family in their current position and Elizabeth for her willingness to carry on an affair with Skipwith, regardless of the power her stepfather had held over her. That was victim shaming, to be sure, but that did not matter to Alice. She was adamant that each of them would need a royal pardon to be cleansed of their involvement in such a horrific series of events; the king would decide what specific offenses the pardons would be for, since neither woman had been charged with a crime. The pardons would serve as evidence of royal forgiveness, which was essential if Anne and Elizabeth were to be forgiven by anyone else—including Alice.

Alice was not the only family member to petition the king in the aftermath of the trial. Three of the earl's siblings—Amy Blount, Elizabeth Griffen, and Christian Mervyn—sent a petition to the king in which they "pray him to examine those persons upon whose testimonies the Earl has been adjudged to die."[17] Like the Earl of Castlehaven, they believed that Anne and Audley had conspired against their brother and that the king should declare a mistrial, as a wife and servant should not have been permitted to testify against an earl. On May 7, 1631, Charles I responded with a decree that the verdict would be upheld. He did, however, conclude that owing to Castlehaven's noble ancestry, the earl could have his head cut off in lieu of being hanged.[18] Dying would be less painful that way. On May 10, the earl's brother-in-law Sir Archibald Douglas again pleaded with the king to reconsider the earl's sentence. Douglas also argued that Anne was untrustworthy and had conspired against her husband.[19] His pleas did nothing to change the situation.

In the final days of the Earl of Castlehaven's life, his son Audley wrote to him after petitioning both the king and several friends to try to stay the execution. Lord Audley had only wanted to secure his inheritance, not see his father executed. But in the final days, he knew the situation was completely out of his hands. He thanked his father for forgiving him but also explained, "I can with a safe conscience wash my hands from your blood which to my grief, your lordship and others, thereby have lately imprinted unto me and my care shall be to give you and the world, satisfaction of the integrity of my intention, and do most willingly and heartily forgive you as I desire of my god to be forgiven." With those words, Audley hoped to relieve his guilty conscience by forgiving his father. He also expressed solidarity with his father, explaining, "I never kept any witness against you, but only against my wife. You shall not need to entreat me to remove your accuser."[20] Audley may have forgiven Castlehaven, but he would never forgive Elizabeth for her affair with Skipwith and the testimony she had provided at his father's trial. He intended to cast her from his home; they would remain married in name only. Alice's desire that the young couple reconcile seemed increasingly unlikely.

On May 14, 1631, the Earl of Castlehaven was beheaded on Tower Green. As he stood on the scaffold above the crowd, he spoke out: "I must confess before you all myself to be a most vile wretched and miserable sinner worthy of death . . . but for the two accusations for which I stand here condemned and ready to suffer death, as I hope for remission of my sins, I am in no ways guilty of them." He then condemned the rumors of his Catholicism and spoke of his devotion to the Protestant Church of England. Just before he knelt and placed his head on the block, he said, "Now lastly, I beseech you all when you shall preview the ax falling to separate my head and body that you will accompany my soul with prayers unto the kingdom of heaven where I hope to rest forever."[21] As with the trial, there is no record of where Anne, Elizabeth, Alice, and the rest of their family were that day, but whether they were near Tower Hill or Harefield, their prayers had certainly been answered.

Alice waited a week before she took up her cause again, writing to the king on May 21, 1631, that she would not accept her daughter or granddaughter into her home until they received royal pardons. She wrote, "It is my heart's grief that by the languishing and continual sorrow I have suffered for my daughter Castlehaven and grandchild Audley, who have infinitely offended God, and next your excellent Majesty by their lewd and wicked crimes, and much perplexed me. And as I have ever since humbly upon my knees begged of the Almighty to remit and pardon their offense, so I now do the same unto your Majesty." She was particularly upset at Audley and Elizabeth's refusal to reconcile, as she explained to the king: "I did upon her disobedience to my command (when I advised her to go live with her husband) deeply protest and vow never to receive her to dwell in my house."[22] In June, a deal was reached: Lord Audley would pay Elizabeth £300 (£37,000/$51,000 today) "per annum for her life, in respect he is not willing to cohabit with her." Alice and Anne each also agreed to pay her £200 per year (£25,000/$35,000 today). The couple remained married, but they would never live together again, nor would Alice receive Elizabeth into her home.[23] She would, however, continue to push for royal pardons.

◆————◆————◆

The joint trial of Giles Broadway and Lawrence Fitzpatrick was held on June 27, 1631, before the King's Bench. No special counsel was appointed for the two servants, and King Charles did not issue a proclamation forbidding women from attending. As Castlehaven had already been executed, there was no doubt that the two men would also be convicted. The outcome might have been preordained, but there was still one major surprise to come in the courtroom. In a shocking scene, Anne appeared in person at the trial. After she took her place at the witness stand, the lord chief justice started by asking her "whether the evidence she had formerly given at her Lord's arraignment was true; and the full matter of charge she had then to deliver against the prisoner?" She responded that her former testimony had been completely true. When asked to confirm that Broadway had indeed penetrated her, "she testified he lay with her by force, her meaning was, that he had known her carnally, and that he did enter her body." She would not offer any more details, nor would the court ask her to.

Anne then made a dramatic request: "she wished to look on the prisoner," which the court granted. As she looked at Broadway, she spoke to the court, with every eye fixed upon her. She explained that "although she could not look on him but with a kind of indignation, and with shame, in regard of that which had been offered unto her, and she suffered by him, yet she had so much charity in her, and such respect to God and his truth, that she had delivered nothing for malice." Those were the only words Anne ever publicly spoke about the affair. On the sobering and public stage of an English courtroom, that noblewoman looked at her assailant and defended her honor and dignity. In desiring to confront Broadway, she also played the cards she had been dealt by making it clear (in both trials) that she was the victim, despite the claims her disgraced husband had made. But at Broadway's trial, she also demonstrated a magnanimous attitude toward her assailant, reminding jurors of her noble heritage and honorable character. She concluded by saying that she "hoped that her oath and evidence thereupon should be credited: and so desired to be believed and dismissed. Which being granted, she departed with as much privacy as might be into her coach."[24]

After Anne left the chamber, the judges called for the verdict. The jurors found both Broadway and Fitzpatrick guilty. The two were hanged on July 6, 1631. The trials were over, but the ordeal was far from done.

Alice continued her efforts to help secure whatever favor she could for her daughter and granddaughter. One month after Broadway and Fitzpatrick's execution, she again wrote to Secretary Dorchester, begging him to ask the king to grant the two women pardons. She explained that "they are left most miserable indeed, destitute of all other means to maintain either of them." Because Castlehaven had been convicted as a felon, the Crown seized control of all his assets, leaving Alice and Anne, as well as Lord Audley, desperate to convince the king to return some of their claims to lands and rents. Alice, of course, was too smart to come right out and ask for the king to act. Instead, she placed the blame completely on the Earl of Castlehaven and her daughter for "wasting the estate she had from the Lord Chandos her former husband." Alice continued to argue that a royal pardon was the only way to fully restore their honor, making them then worthy of the restoration of some of their properties.[25] Throughout the summer, Lord Audley, Alice, and Elizabeth continued to work with the king and his magistrates to settle Castlehaven's debts and sort out control of his lands, which ultimately happened.[26] Three years later, in April 1634, in her own act of magnanimous favor, Alice granted Anne the use of Ruislip, the estate near Harefield she had hoped to keep from the Earl of Castlehaven's "fingering."[27]

Finally, on November 14, 1631, Anne received a royal pardon for the crimes of adultery, fornication, and incontinency (lack of control), suggesting that the king believed she had had extramarital affairs. Elizabeth's pardon for the same offenses came sixteen days later.[28] At Alice's urging, the king had exonerated the two women. That grand act of institutionalized victim shaming served to cleanse their reputations and allow order to be restored. Should anyone have attempted to use the nightmare to reflect on Anne, Elizabeth, Alice, or any other member of their family, they could remind their adversaries that the king himself had said it was over and the women were officially freed from any negative light. Of course, no one was that naive, and Anne, Elizabeth, Alice, and the rest of the family braced themselves to face yet another jury, this time in the court of public opinion.

+———◆———+

News of the Castlehaven trials traveled across England and even reached the European continent. From the moment of Castlehaven's arrest, people of all social ranks were mortified, though also eager to recount to one another the details as rumors circulated. An English aristocrat had not been tried for a felony in a century, and an earl facing both rape and sodomy charges was unheard of.[29] While Alice, Anne, and their family desperately navigated the realities of the ordeal, the broader public consumed the trials and executions as entertainment. Sir John Scudamore was serving as a justice of the peace in Herefordshire, 140 miles northwest of London, so he hired John Flower, a London clerk, to send him several newsletters a month to keep up on international news and court gossip while he was away from the capital. In his December 17, 1630, letter Flower reported Castlehaven's arrest before the earl had even been transported to the Tower of London. Nine days before Castlehaven's trial, Flower's newsletter laid out the charges "against the Earl of Castlehaven, the one for a rape and the other for a fouler offence."[30] Subsequent letters included updates on both trials and all three executions.[31] Spectators at the trials took notes on the proceedings, and the literate community wildly copied and shared them in the manner of premodern tabloids. Someone even went to the trouble to translate the full proceedings into French so courtiers and scandal-loving hordes across the English Channel could be astounded by the spectacle of an English countess successfully accusing her lascivious husband of rape.[32]

It might be easy to understand why many seventeenth-century husbands and peers would have disliked a wife who charged her husband with rape and testified against him, but threatened aristocratic men were not Anne's most notorious public antagonists; that role fell to Eleanor Touchet Davies Douglas, the earl's older sister. Eleanor had already scuffled with Anne's youngest sister and brother-in-law, the Earl and Countess of Huntingdon, when she had refused to pay the marriage portion of her daughter Lucy, who had married their son Ferdinando. In the end, the Huntingdons had triumphed in the suit against Eleanor and seized control of her estate of Englefield for their son and heir. Since then, Eleanor had remarried Sir Archibald Douglas, who had petitioned the king to overturn the Earl of Castlehaven's order of execution, to no avail. Eleanor had an ugly history with Alice and her daughters, and her brother's demise and execution renewed her fanatical quest for vengeance. The Stanley women may have been more skilled at wielding the law than Eleanor was, but her weapon of choice was the printing press.

In the seventeenth century, "cheap print" flooded the streets of London and people of all classes devoured the inexpensive, ephemeral pamphlets. A rag might contain a sermon, a eulogy for an esteemed peer, or a naughty poem mocking a less-than-esteemed peer. Over the course of her life, Eleanor would publish nearly seventy-five distinct titles, ranging from dense hyperbolic prophecies to scathing libels. In 1633, to mark the two-year anniversary of her brother's execution, she published "Woe to the House," meaning the House of Stanley. In it, she called the Countess of Castlehaven a Jezebel and a "Lye Satann," which was meant to be an anagram of her name, "Ane Stanly."[33] Alice and Anne had ardently worked that year to move beyond the horrors of the trials, but Eleanor would do all in her power to keep Anne and her family trapped in the nightmare. Although it was a court of English peers that had convicted her brother, Eleanor believed that Anne was his true murderer and deserved a painful death:

Hast thou killed, and also taken possession, in the place, etc. and the dogs shall eat Jezebel by the walls of Israel. . . . And when Jehu was come to

Israel, Jezebel heard of it, and she painted her face, and tired her head,
and looked out of a window, etc. And he trod her under foot.[34]

Eleanor took the name Jezebel from the Book of Revelation. The biblical Jezebel had enticed servants to perform wretched acts, reminiscent of a servant accused of raping his mistress. Jezebel had also seduced people into eating sacred food, much as Eve was said to have tempted Adam to eat the apple, thus getting them cast out of the Garden of Eden. In her scathing pamphlet, Eleanor conflated Anne, Jezebel, and Eve to claim that Anne had corruptly convinced a jury to condemn the earl as a social outcast. Eve is blamed for mankind's expulsion from Paradise; Jezebel is blamed for encouraging wrongful acts; and Eleanor blamed Anne for the loss of the Castlehaven estates and the earl's execution.

Eleanor's second attack on Anne and her family came in 1644 with the publication of "The Word of God to the Citie of London." By then Anne was living in almost complete seclusion in Ruislip, just outside Harefield. In 1642, a London publisher had printed a transcript of the Earl of Castlehaven's arraignment, probably as an effort to make quick money, thus returning the scandal to public memory.[35] The publication reignited Eleanor's fury, and she could not resist flooding London with her own account of the trial. She wrote on her brother's behalf, "affirming for that fact whereof the Earl of Castlehaven was accused by his wife (such a wicked woman). . . . And how the Lord slew them both."[36] Eleanor argued that the countess's accusation of rape had misrepresented reality: the countess was the "whore." Eleanor, like her brother, contended that Anne had had sex with her servant, not that he had raped her. Eleanor slayed Anne with the long-standing trope that the Countess of Castlehaven was sexually promiscuous as a way of publicly shaming her and dismissing her pain. Anne had no recourse but to stand silently behind her royal pardon.

Beyond Eleanor's scathing pamphlets, other anonymous authors published an array of libelous poems about the Castlehaven trials. Most depicted Anne in the same light as Eleanor's pamphlets: as a ruinous whore, not a victim. One popular libel was written in the voice of the Earl of Castlehaven, depicting him not as an assailant but as a cuckold:

I need no trophies, to adorn my hearse

my wife, exalts my horns in every verse:
and paste them hath, so fully on my tomb
that for my arms, there is no vacant room.
Who will take such a Countess to his bed
that first gives horns, and then cuts off his head.[37]

Not everyone saw the countess that way. An unknown author published a poetic response to the lines above:

Blame not thy wife, for what thyself hath wrought
Thou caused thy horns in forcing me to naught
For hadst thou been but human, not a beast
Thy arms had been supporters to thy crest
Nor needst you yet have had a tomb, or hearse
Besmear'd with your sensual life in verse
Who then would take such a Lord unto her bed
That to gain horns himself, would lose his head.[38]

By marrying Anne, the Earl of Castlehaven had been offered a place in an old and noble circle and choosing to marry his son to her daughter had only strengthened that potential alliance. She had offered her coat of arms to support his crest, and it had been his actions, not hers, that had devastated their lives. In the end, they had all been left "besmear'd."

◆———◆———◆

Elite families were accustomed to the rise and fall from grace that came with aristocratic life, but no other family of the age endured a trauma on the scale of the Castlehaven trials. Alice and her daughters' families not only survived but emerged intact. There are no records of the personal feelings of Anne or her daughter Elizabeth, but if they saw themselves as part of a greater whole, they may have at least taken comfort that their dynasty would survive, certainly not under the name Castlehaven but as the heirs of Spencer, Derby, Chandos, Bridgewater, and Huntingdon. Alice, her daughters, her sons-in-law, and her grandchildren helped see to that. After a flood of petitions, pleas, and negotiations, Anne and Elizabeth could be free enough to live comfortably, albeit quietly, and perhaps to try to heal.

Though the family may have been resting high on their well-earned laurels of unprecedented legal success, life would not continue without some conflict. Eleanor Davies Douglas remained an in-law. In July 1635, word reached Alice that her grandson Ferdinando and his wife, Lucy, had invited Eleanor, Lucy's mother, to live with them; Alice would not hear of it. She insisted that her granddaughter, Ferdinando's sister, who was also named Alice, write a letter to the Earl of Huntingdon, their father, to put a stop to the arrangements. The young Alice begged her father on behalf of herself and her grandmother, coyly claiming that the request had come from "your noble friends and myself, your poor obedient child, one that prays to God for advancement of honor to yourself." By insisting that the letter be in the voice of Alice the younger, Alice the elder continued to direct family dynamics at every level. That power move also allowed her to put extra pressure on Huntingdon, as both his daunting mother-in-law and sweet daughter were asking for his intervention. The young Alice cautioned her father that he would face "ruin and decay" if he were "harboring upon your own estate and means a woman of such conviction, which when I call to mind the dishonest and abuses, she most wickedly spared."[39] Eleanor Davies Douglas would not divide them any more than she and her monstrous family already had.

The Earl of Huntingdon put a stop to things, probably to the discomfort of Ferdinando and Lucy but to the delight of Alice and her granddaughter. A few weeks after Lady Eleanor had been cast out of the Huntingdon estates, Alice again insisted that her granddaughter write to the Earl of Huntingdon, politely reminding him that Alice, "well liking that she, Lady Douglas, had not other entertainment at your Lordship's house." Though the subtext of the letter demonstrated Alice's continued command over her family, niceties were never to be ignored, so the letter concluded with a gentle pat on the head: "Her ladyship gives you many thanks."[40] The seventy-six-year-old Alice continued to dictate to her family whom they were permitted to receive into their homes, as she had nearly her entire life. She had never misguided them, and so her family continued to listen.

CHAPTER TEN

FINAL CELEBRATIONS

"Such a Rural Queen"

After the horror and chaos of the Castlehaven trials, Alice and her family needed to find a way to move on and reaffirm their place in society, reclaim their sense of themselves. Alice might have operated in the shadows until the trial was over, but the family knew that the firm wall of judges and jurors Castlehaven had faced was due in large part to the web of powerful alliances Alice had spent her life building and maintaining. The royal pardons and the financial settlements Alice had negotiated helped cauterize the wounds, but they were not enough; the wounds needed to be dressed and wrapped in glittering bandages that might even distract from the pain and ugliness underneath. In 1607, after the private act of Parliament that had settled their hard-fought Stanley inheritance suit, the family had gathered at Ashby de la Zouch, the home of the Earl and Countess of Huntingdon, for hunting, feasts, dancing, and a masque entertainment. What better way for the family to show their best selves than with another spectacular gathering?

The event was held at Harefield Place, Alice's seat of power, sometime in 1632 or 1633.[1] The entire entertainment celebrated Alice and the way she once again had led the family to victory, just as the gathering at Ashby twenty-five years earlier had. It was also the second time the tiny village of Harefield served as the stage for a grand performance. The first was when Alice and her second husband, Thomas Egerton, had hosted Queen Elizabeth, the last Tudor monarch, on her final summer progress in 1602. Harefield had been the site of an entertainment for a monarch; now it was the site of an entertainment for a matriarch, fashioning the seventy-three-year-old Alice as a queen.

In the thirty-plus years since Alice and Thomas had hosted Queen Elizabeth, aristocratic culture had changed. The Stuart kings and queens preferred an updated style for court masques, a term derived from masquerade, as the participants wore decorative masks over their faces, lending an aura of splendor, playfulness, and mystery. Tudor monarchs had hosted masques where courtiers in festive costumes would dance together. Although those parties had often included short theatrical interludes of courtiers dramatically reciting lines set to music, the backdrops and props had tended to be sparse and the scripts fairly light. The Stuarts had ushered in new styles of entertainment revolving around more sophisticated allegorical literary productions with elaborate scripts, sets, and costumes. Courtiers still danced into the wee hours of the night wearing resplendent attire, but the structured performances were a more central part of the gatherings. In the first two decades of the seventeenth century, King James's wife, Anna of Denmark, and their son Prince Henry had all championed this highly learned style of masque.[2] Queen Anna's premier author of the courtly genre had been Ben Jonson, whom she had most probably first met at Althorp in 1603, when the Spencer family had commissioned Jonson to write the masque in honor of her and Prince Henry's visit there.[3] Though Alice had certainly not been responsible for the cultural movement, she and her family had played a role in making the critical connections for Jonson and introducing the new queen to England's poets and artists.

When it came to entertainments, Alice and her family were always right on trend, if not aspiring to set the bar slightly higher than their peers'. It is therefore no wonder that when the family began planning their post-Castlehaven entertainment in 1632, they opted for a courtly style masque that would be more than a mere feast with minstrels and dancing. They would celebrate Alice with literature and invite all their peers, many of whom had likely witnessed the Castlehaven trials or even served on the jury. And what better way to mark Alice's place at the head of the multigenerational dynasty than to have her grandchildren act as the players? They ranged in age from early adolescence to early twenties, so the script would have to be light enough to be age appropriate for the rather inexperienced troupe of performers.

To navigate the pass between literary masque and young performers, the family hired a clerk who worked for the Earl of Bridgewater but was showing promise as a writer: John Milton, who would go on to become the celebrated author of epic poems such as *Paradise Lost*. But that would be thirty-five years in the future. Now the inexperienced poet was in his midtwenties when the family charged him with writing a masque that would delight, amuse, and honor Alice, Dowager Countess of Derby. The result was *Arcades*, in which Milton transformed Harefield into the mythical realm of Arcadia and populated the enchanted land with nymphs, shepherds, gods, fantastical characters, and dancing tree spirits. Alice sat at the end of the Great Hall in Harefield Place, looking out over her fairy-tale kingdom as the costumed children and young adults danced and sang:

> *Mark what radiant State she spreads,*
> *In circle round her shining throne*
> *Shooting her beams like silver threads:*
> *This, this is she alone,*
> *Sitting like a goddess bright*
> *In the center of her light.*[4]

Each verse of the song ended with the simple but poignant lines

> *Such a rural Queen*
> *All Arcadia hath not seen.*

Alice was the "rural Queen" and Harefield her kingdom. Her daughters, sons-in-law, grandchildren, and other kin and friends in attendance were her subjects. Alice's Arcadia was a place of escape, respite, and even jubilation.

At least, that was what the family wanted people to think; perhaps it was even what they thought themselves. No historical records provide insight into the interior perspectives of any member of Alice's family, but it is reasonable to assume that each understood that his or her own place as a member of a strong dynasty required falling into line with Alice. They had been raised from birth to share her devotion and duty to family; the entire aristocratic culture lauded those as virtues, and its survival depended on strict adherence to them. Every member of the family likely felt a responsibility to embody those qualities as best they could, not necessarily for Alice but because they, too, saw themselves as part of a larger whole and aspired to rise within it. They surely each felt jealousy, annoyance, frustration, or even resentment at times, but their entire society operated on the belief that a person was merely a single thread woven into a tapestry. In her own eyes and those of her family, Alice's thread may have been luminous silver, but she was still just one thread. Each thread provides a unique color or texture, but a clear image could emerge only when they came together.

✦────●────✦

The family was so delighted by the performance that two years later, in 1634, they again commissioned Milton to write them another entertainment: *A Masque at Ludlow Castle*, which is today more commonly known as *Comus*. Just as before, the family gathered to mark a triumph. This time, Alice's son-in-law the Earl of Bridgewater was the guest of honor. King Charles had appointed Bridgewater to the esteemed post of the President of the Marches of Wales, making him the king's royal representative in the region. It was an enormous honor and a sizable job and also meant that Bridgewater acquired Ludlow Castle on the English-Welsh border. Charles I had made the appointment on July 8, 1631, just two days after Broadway and Fitzpatrick, the two servants found guilty in the Castlehaven trials, had been executed.[5] The timing of the appointment had surely been intended to signify the king's unwavering support of Bridgewater and his family, despite their unfortunate ties to the Earl of Castlehaven. In the aftermath of the scandals, the Earl of Bridgewater waited three years to take office in 1634 so the family could properly resolve the crisis.

At the end of September 1634, the family finally gathered at Ludlow Castle, a medieval stronghold nestled in a lush forest on a hilltop above the Thames. The event coincided with Michaelmas, an important festival day that predated England's break with the Roman Catholic Church a hundred years earlier. English courts continued to use the pre-Reformation calendar to break the year up into four quarter sessions, with each session beginning on a religious holiday that coincided with the natural seasons. March 25 (spring) was Lady Day, celebrated as the day of the Annunciation, when the Archangel Gabriel had revealed to the Virgin Mary that she was with child. The date also marked when Mary had been churched, or purified, after giving birth. June 24 (summer) marked Midsummer, which aligned with the feast day of St. John the Baptist. September 29 (autumn) was Michaelmas, the feast day of St. Michael. And December 25 (winter) was Christmas, or Christ's mass. Some judicial courts rotated on quarter days, local towns held festivals and markets, and rents were typically due. The English year revolved around those days, so holding Bridgewater's family celebration and his installation as the President of the Marches of Wales on Michaelmas also signified the beginning of a new era for the family.

Everyone traveled to the castle in the center of the wilds along the English-Welsh border to watch three of Frances's and John's children, named Alice, Thomas, and John, playing the leading roles in Milton's masque, just as the children had performed in *Arcades* for their grandmother. Alice was eighteen; John, the Bridgewater heir, was just eleven; and Thomas was not yet ten. The children's music teacher, Henry Lawes, composed the score and performed in the masque as well, probably playing the part of Comus. The young performers were, of course, outfitted in new gloves, shoes, and strings of pearls for the occasion.[6]

Milton referenced Bridgewater's new appointment and esteemed political stature to frame the opening scene of the masque:

> *A noble peer of mickle trust, and power*
> *Has in his charge, with tempered awe to guide*
> *An old, and haughty nation proud in arms:*
> *Where his fair offspring nursed in 'Princely lore*
> *Are coming to attend their father's State,*
> *And new-entrusted scepter, but their way*
> *Lies through the perplexed paths of this dreary wood.*

The masque opens with young Alice and her two brothers going for a walk in Ludlow Forest. Alice is separated from her brothers and meets Comus, an evil demon who takes her back to his lair. Comus then tries to seduce her and steal her virtue. She ardently resists and defends herself against him. Guided by a good attendant spirit, her brothers find her just in time, and the three escape, unscathed, and return safely home. Upon seeing their mother and father, the spirit sings:

Noble Lord, and Lady bright,
I have brought ye new delight,
Here behold so goodly grown
Three fair branches of your own,
Heaven hath timely tried their youth
Their faith, their patience, and their truth,
And sent them here through hard assays
With a crown of deathless Praise,
To triumph in victorious dance
O'er sensual Folly, and Intemperance.[7]

Milton's masque captured an idealized version of Alice's noble family, one that had endured hardship and separation, only to reunite as an unwavering pillar of honor. Over the decades, there had been countless times when the family could easily have crumbled: the arrest of Ferdinando's mother, the Hesketh Plot, Ferdinando's sudden death, the perilous inheritance suit, Alice's sister who refused to live with her husband, Alice and Ellesmere's tumultuous marriage, and the hellfires of the Castlehaven trials. They had overcome all manner of tribulations, and they marked the successes together with a literary spectacle that allowed Alice and her kin to see themselves as triumphant, never acknowledging any price that had been paid to get there or any pain felt along the way. Gathered on that dark September night at Ludlow, the family embarked on the next chapter of their lives.

It would be the last time Alice would attend a performance like that hosted by her family. The fields of Althorp and the grandeur of Lathom Hall may have seemed far away as she watched her grandchildren dance before her, but she was a woman who carried every experience with her to guide not only her own life but the lives of those she held most dear. When she had married Ferdinando as a bride of twenty, she had assumed the aspirations of the Spencers, taking them on as her own. Becoming a mother and then a countess had been natural steps in her progress toward fully embodying the person she and her family needed her to be. Ferdinando's death and the subsequent inheritance suit had tested her and proved that she was capable of fully executing her role within the turbulent English peerage. From that point on, and over the course of three different monarchs' reigns, she had remained remarkably unchanged in her laserlike ambition for herself and her family. Her world did not value personal evolution. In fact, Alice and those around her could be extremely distrustful of people whose personalities changed dramatically over the arc of their life. They respected fortitude and constancy as honorable means by which to navigate an inherently unstable world. Alice's unwavering devotion to her family and their station would have been read by her peers as an ability to hold steadfastly to that which was most important, even if she was demanding at times. Bathed in the golden candlelight at Ludlow, amused by music, dance, and poetry, surrounded by her family as they celebrated Bridgewater's political ascent, Alice must have felt that she had accomplished exactly what she had been meant to do in her life.

✦———————✦———————✦

Alice never cared for anyone more than she did her three daughters. Even when her words and actions were cruel, the well-being of Anne, Elizabeth, and Frances was at the center of every decision she made. As rewarding as the performance at Ludlow Castle was in the autumn of 1634, the family surely also felt the pain of absence. Elizabeth, Countess of Huntingdon, had died the year before. Her health had been failing for some time. On July 7, 1632, she had written to her husband while conducting business in London on his behalf, "I am not very well. Since Thursday in the night, I have had much pain in my back and foot, but my back is well, and all my pain is now in my feet. Sir John Stanhope [and] Doctor Turner was with me this morning, and tomorrow intends to give me a purge. It is a feverish humor and wind comes from my spleen and I hope in God within a few days I shall be well."[8] She wrote again to the earl five days later, telling him that she had been bled and that it seemed to "settle the wind in my bowels [and] spleen. . . . I am a little weak having eaten almost nothing till this night since Thursday."[9] Despite her physical suffering, and perhaps even to the detriment of her health, she had continued to travel between Leicester and London regularly in the final year of her life, ever determined to improve her family's financial holdings and her husband's reputation and to see her mother.

She died on January 20, 1633, in Whitefriars, at the London home of her sister Frances, Countess of Bridgewater.[10] Peter Chamberlain, doctor of physics, issued a certificate testifying that "the causes of her death was the infection of the mother or place of conception," meaning that she had uterine cancer. The doctor explained that he had not suspected the disease because he had "never perceived anything to come from those parts of any offensive smell." In the final days of her life, Elizabeth began to complain of abdominal pain, so the doctors bled her near her intestines. He described a "bloody flux or looseness" that was dislodged as a result of the purge, "from which being freed, she received her last hours with as much ease as slumber to a quiet mind and labored body."[11] A peaceful passing was viewed as a sign of God's grace, so Elizabeth's gentle death must have brought some comfort to her mother and sisters, who were likely with her at the end. The Countess of Huntingdon's body was then "laid into a chariot adorned with echelons and her Ladyship's coronet belonging to her estate and a black velvet cushion carried before her by two Officers of Arms in their Coates."[12] The two heralds accompanied her body home to Ashby de la Zouch, where her funeral was held on February 9, 1633, and she was buried there.

Because she was survived by her husband, the Countess of Huntingdon did not leave a will. The only surviving records of her death are a heraldic death certificate and the sermon preached at her funeral, which was published three times in the 1630s, signifying how well respected she was. The unknown author praised the Countess of Huntingdon for her humility in spite of her noble Stanley bloodline and her honorable marriage into the Hastings family when he said, "It were easy for me to name many noble names like unto these, to prove that nobility by which she esteemed herself principally honored."[13] The sermon also praised her as a mother by noting that "She made the fruit of her body, to become the fruit of the spirit." It also hailed the countess's piety and intelligence: "And as she had the knowledge of truth to give light unto her Religion, so she had the truth of Religion to give life unto her knowledge." In the final passage, the author recounted that "the day of her dissolution, I coming to her, she professed, that whatsoever her sufferings were, yet she did nothing but clasp herself about her sweet Savior."[14] The sermon also celebrated an aspect of Elizabeth's life that would surely have made Alice proud: "Her understanding was of great perspicacity, and as she failed not to imply the same for the comprehending of such occasions and affairs, as might well advantage and sustain the estate of her house, and procure and reinforce the content and comfort of her noble Lord."[15]

Elizabeth's tireless efforts to ensure her family's financial security had become an integral part of the way she was to be remembered. Not only was she a noble wife by birth and motherhood, but her actions also displayed her nobility as she strove to preserve and protect her family's status, just as her mother had taught her.

This printed sermon was intended for a broad audience and meant to pay tribute to Elizabeth's virtues in the hope that it would inspire others to emulate her. Though it surely made Alice proud, it may have been of little comfort to her. After all, she had had a special relationship with Elizabeth, and no eulogy could ever capture what that truly meant. In 1635, a London-based writer and artist, Abraham Darcie and Thomas St. Leger, created a lavishly decorated illuminated manuscript specifically for Alice to memorialize her daughter. The manuscript contains painted emblems, pages of heraldry, poems, and acrostic verses. It also includes a full-page painting of Alice wearing black mourning clothes, seated at a table with a book in her hands and a blond angel standing behind her. Alice was in her midseventies when her daughter died, but she looks young and earnestly devout in the portrait, which is followed by forty-two pages of verse that celebrate the lives of both Alice and her daughter. In one place, Darcie and St. Leger wrote:

> *Blessed you are, that still your life apply*
> *To die, that you may live eternally*
> *Make virtue to be your monument*
> *For it will keep you, when your life is spent.*[16]

The manuscript was devoted to depicting Elizabeth as Alice's daughter, not as her husband's wife or mother of her own children. That was an extremely unconventional way to pay tribute to an adult woman at the time but somehow seems appropriate for Alice and her youngest daughter, who shared so many of her values. The volume also includes one drawing of Elizabeth's two surviving sisters weeping over her sarcophagus. The memorial manuscript captures Alice's relationship with and influence over her daughters, exactly as she would have wanted.

Alice lost her second daughter, Frances, Countess of Bridgewater, just three years later, on March 11, 1636, at Bridgewater House in the Barbican of London. Little is known about the cause of her death, although her funeral sermon alludes to a sickness. Her body was transported to the Church of St. Peter and St. Paul in Little Gaddesden in Hertfordshire.[17] The small stone chapel was just a few miles away from Ashridge, the Egertons' primary country seat. Her funeral was held there, and her body was laid to rest in a humble monument. Since her interment there, the small church has become the primary resting place of descendants of the Egerton family.[18] Frances's funeral sermon survived, although it never circulated in print. In it, the preacher noted, "'Twas a greater honor to her that she maintained the dignity of her birth; and lived and died in that honor she was born to . . . but the greatest honor the world can give her is this: she continued the line in well doing . . . the body of her bodility consisted in her blood, but the soul of it, in the eminency of her virtues."[19] Over the course of her life, Frances gave birth fifteen times, with eleven children surviving into adulthood. She spent far more time in a birthing chamber than any other woman in her family. She also built an impressive library. Her younger sister, Elizabeth, inherited their mother's aptitude for the law and politics, while Frances perpetuated the bloodline and maintained the family's literary patronage. Her funeral sermon celebrated her piety as manifested in her role as a mother:

> she lives in her children, they are her walking images, her living pictures: She lives in her virtues; her works praise her in the gate: She lives in her happy memory; every hearth is a monument, more durable than this costly marble: every tongue an epitaph to speak her praise . . . she desired not pompam funeris, and I endeavored not pompam orationis: 'tis a little pile that I have erected, not a mausoleum tomb.[20]

After Frances's death, the writer Robert Codrington penned a private verse, dedicated to Alice:

> These tears on blessed Bridgewaters death, we do
> Illustrious Lady consecrate to you,
> In whom the honors of great Spencers line
> And Stanley glories do unclouded shine,
> Not to be dimmed to Death, while tears we pyre
> On your blest Daughters honored hearse, this hour.[21]

The private manuscripts created for Alice upon the death of her two daughters perfectly capture all that Alice held most precious: her Spencer roots, her Stanley bloodlines, and her beloved and honorable daughters.

Anne, Alice's eldest daughter, outlived both her sisters and her mother. She died in October 1647, and no one eulogized her virtue or honor. In 1635, Frances, one of her daughters, got married, and Anne signed the marriage contract, into which she also put a £2,000 (£245,000/$338,000 today) marriage portion for her daughter, as well as arranging for her to have a jointure.[22] That is the last-known document executed by the Dowager Countess of Castlehaven. Anne had withdrawn from the world after the Castlehaven trials, but she used her highest title for the duration of her life; Castlehaven was a pariah's name, but a countess outranked her previous role as baroness, and for Anne, like all others of her society, rank mattered more. Whether Alice ordered her into the shadows or Anne chose to retreat quietly is not clear, nor is any aspect of the relationship between Alice and Anne in those later years. Anne had had no control over bringing her monstrous second husband to trial, yet throughout the Castlehaven ordeal, she had showed unrelenting courage followed by a seeming willingness to step back and let Alice say what she needed to about her and Elizabeth in order to secure royal pardons to clear their names. She lived out her days at Haydon Hall, her mother's estate near Ruislip, under Alice's protection and later that of her own sons, whom Alice had raised. When she died, she was buried in Ruislip, although the exact site of her grave is unknown.

✦·————   ————·✦

Alice's death was as well orchestrated and elaborate as her life. She initially wrote her will on December 24, 1636, while she was still "in good health," but her health took a turn in a month's time and she added an additional schedule on January 24, 1637.[23] She died at Harefield Place just two days later at the age of seventy-seven. Unsurprisingly to anyone who knew her, Alice left detailed instructions in her will for her burial, bequests, and all other aspects of her estate. Her will afforded her the final opportunity to construct her legacy and leave her dynasty in the best possible position.

Under the darkness of night, two days after her last breath, her body was transported "to be laid in the tomb which [she] lately made in the upper chancel of the parish church of Harefield."[24] The upper chancel was the prime spot in the small chapel, ensuring that parishioners would always be looking at the splendor and artistry of her commanding funeral monument, which remains in place to this day. Her effigy lies on a carved black curtain, decorated with the crests of the Spencers, the Stanleys, and the families of her three sons-in-law. (There is, of course, no marker for the Earl of Castlehaven.) With her hands in a prayerful position, her recumbent figure gazes up into a dome shrouded in carved stone painted to look like green-and-gold curtains. Her carved figure is swathed in a red gown, matching the dresses of the figures of her three daughters kneeling below her. Two sides of the canopy are enclosed with black tablets with gold lettering. The first reads:

> *This is the monument of Alice Countesse Dowager of Derby, one of the daughters of Sir John Spencer of Althorp in the county of Northampton Knight: and wife of the right Honorable Ferdinando Earl of Derby, by whom she had issue 3 daughters. His daughters & coheiress Anne the eldest married to Grey, Lord Chandos, Frances the second to John Earl of Bridgewater, Elizabeth the third to Henry Earl of Huntingdon. This Countess died the 26 of Jan. 1636* & her aforsaid Honorable Lord & Husband who died before her lieth buried in the Parish church of Ormeskerke with his ancestors whose souls remain in everlasting joy.*

The second tablet simply reads:

> *This Noble Lady's second husband was my Lord Chancellor Egerton whose only daughter was mother to Julian Lady Newdigate.***

---

* The date on the tablet reflects the old style of dates, when England took March 25 to be the date to advance the calendar year. In our modern calendar, Alice died the 26th of January, 1637.

** Julian Leigh, Egerton's granddaughter, married Lord Richard Newdigate on February 2, 1632, five years before Alice's death. In the later seventeenth and eighteenth centuries, the Newdigates became influential residents of Harefield, and this tablet helps to contextualize the tomb as Newdigate markers increased in the church over time. It is possible to speculate that the tablet may not have originally been part of the tomb but may have been added by a later Newdigate at some point after Alice's death, as it seems unlikely that she would have bothered to make mention of that distant family line.

Each of the four corners at the top of the tomb is marked with a crowned griffin, a symbol of the Spencer family. At the top is a banner that reads DIEU DEFENDE LE DROIT (God defend the right), the Spencer family motto. A stag, the symbol of the Stanley family, and a griffin stand perched above the banner, serving as the supporters of her large coat of arms. Beyond the heraldic reference in her shield, there is just one small impalement at the bottom of her tomb signifying her second marriage, which is partially obstructed by another tomb. Alice's human remains are concealed inside the base of her tomb.

Though most aristocratic widows chose to be buried with their first husband or the father of their children, Alice decided to remain alone in Harefield. She was likely disinclined to attempt to negotiate with her estranged brother-in-law William, sixth Earl of Derby, to be interred with Ferdinando in the Stanley family chapel in Ormskirk, Lancashire. She had no interest in spending eternity next to Thomas Egerton, especially as he had been buried alongside his first wife in Cheshire. Instead, she opted to remain in Harefield, the village that had been her home for nearly forty years. She would remain its "rural Queen" for eternity.

Alice may have erected her tomb to last the ages, but she choreographed a somber funeral procession for those she left behind in her own time. Her will specified that twenty poor women from Harefield, twenty poor women from Colham, Hollingdon, and Uxbridge (collectively), all her household servants at Harefield Place, her surviving daughter, Anne, her grandsons George and William Brydges, and her granddaughter Alice Hastings should all receive "blacks," expensive mourning clothes.[25] She wanted to create a band of mourners for her funeral, for which she left instructions in her will: "I desire that mine own servants within two days and two nights next after my descent may carry [my body] to my said tomb in the night time there to be interred in decent and Christian manner, only with forty torches."[26]

In the seventeenth century, the aristocracy practiced two styles of funerals: heraldic funerals and night funerals. Heraldic funerals followed a tightly scripted state-sanctioned service replete with pomp and circumstance. Alice commissioned a tomb that was dripping with heraldry and she received a death certificate from the College of Arms, yet she did not want a heraldic funeral.[27] By requesting a night funeral, she ensured that her funeral would be outside the regimented jurisdiction of the College of Arms and thus the state. Night funerals were increasingly popular among noblemen and -women who wanted their funerals to reflect their personal wealth, authority, and social rank. (Many seventeenth-century women also opted for night funerals because it avoided the embalming required for a heraldic funeral.[28]) Alice would not share her interment with the state or a well-ordered herald. Those most beholden and devoted to her would escort her lifeless body in a slow funeral march, with only the stars and forty torches to illuminate their path, as they laid her to rest in the monument she had built for herself. Her personal chaplain, John Prichard, gave the funeral service. Alice insisted on leaving this world the same way she had lived every moment of her adult life: at the center of her family's orbit.

+———————+———————+

Beyond the instructions for her funeral, Alice outlined a series of projects and distributions in her will. If aristocratic marriage and motherhood could be business ventures, so, too, could death. Alice called for the construction of almshouses in her will and requested that her executors and the parish appoint "a Master of the said hospital" who would select six poor women of the parish to reside in the almshouses. The master was "to read twice service or some other godly prayers daily to the said six poor women."[29] The brick houses had an H-shaped plan, and eight narrow chimneys rose from the roof. Two stone reliefs of crowned griffins were set above the windows flanking the front door, again highlighting the Spencers. Alice stipulated in her will that each widow was to receive £5 (£610/$840 today) per annum maintenance for life, as was the master of the hospital. She left £1 (£120/$165 today) per annum for the physical upkeep of the building. She also requested that a year after her death, her executors purchase lands valued at £36 (£4,400/$6,000 today) per annum for the use of the master and widows. That was all very generous, yet she never missed a chance to incorporate her heraldic symbols, so she went so far as to "appoint them my seal of arms engraven in silver and made lozenge-wise to be their common seal."[30] Alice wanted the various heraldic family symbols she'd amassed in her life to be configured in a diamond, or lozenge, shape. That was the standard shape for an unmarried woman's coat of arms, whether she be a widow or never married, and Alice's desire for the symbol to be the seal of her almshouses signified the power she found in widowhood. She would remain a patroness to Harefield's widows, and they would use her heraldic seal as their own.

Alice's charity did not end there. Upon her death, she also called for £50 (£6,100/$8,400 today) to be distributed "to the poorest inhabitants of Harefield" and another £50 to be distributed "to the poorest inhabitants of Colham, Hollingdon, and Uxbridge," neighboring communities where she owned property.[31] By that time, some of Alice's peers would have deemed the tradition of leaving doles to the poor as superstitious and outmoded.[32] Before the Reformation, Catholics in England had used doles to pay people to say prayers for their souls in the hope that the continued displays of devotion would minimize their soul's stint in Purgatory. After the English Reformation, however, some Protestants grew leery of doles, and the state-sanctioned *Book of Common Prayer*, the central prayer book for the Protestant Church of England adopted in the sixteenth century, made no mention of doles at all. On the other hand, devout Calvinists or "Puritans," the pejorative term used by the English, believed that charity was a sign of providence.[33] Alice was neither a Catholic nor a more fanatical Calvinist, as she was much more spiritually moderate without any hint of subversion. Conformists such as Alice and many of her aristocratic peers viewed charity as the secular responsibility of local elites.[34] Leaving hefty doles to the local poor of the parishes where she had held considerable properties furthered her legacy as a local patron and "rural Queen." The bequeathal also helped counterbalance the grandeur of her tomb and her extravagant lifestyle. The hope was that her tenants would remember her as a virtuous noblewoman.

‹––•––›

Once Alice outlined her charitable disbursements, she turned to the distribution of wealth across her family. Alice named her grandson and ward George Brydges, Lord Chandos, as her heir. George was Anne's eldest son, and he was seventeen when Alice died, but she had raised him and his younger brother, William, in large part to keep them out of the Earl of Castlehaven's clutches. As her heir, George inherited Harefield Place and all of Alice's leases in Harefield and in the neighboring villages, ensuring him a hefty rental income to last his lifetime. George also received all her other "goods, chattels, leases, plate, household stuff, game of swans, and jewels" that she did not bequeath to specific family members.[35] The landed wealth, however, came with strings attached, as Alice expected to continue to call the shots, even from beyond the grave. She had debts to pay, and her heir would help her do just that.

Alice also used her will to secure her now wealthy young heir a bride. It was her dying wish that George should wed "Lady Susanna Montagu, one of the daughters of the said Earl of Manchester, as a fit wife for my said grandchild." To sweeten the deal, Alice set aside a string of pearls for Lady Susanna if the marriage were to go forward. Susanna's father, the Earl of Manchester, Lord Privy Seal, had been a lifelong friend of Alice. She also named him one of the executors of her estate and left him a token worth £50 (£6,100/$8,400 today), as well as a silver gilt memento for his wife worth £5 (£610/$840 today). By the time of her death, Alice had spent almost sixty years at the center of England's ruling class and she had many powerful friends, but the Earl of Manchester was no ordinary ally. Although no sources survive outlining a specific plan, it is not too far-fetched to suspect that Alice and Manchester, one of the presiding judges at the Earl of Castlehaven's trial, had reached some kind of agreement that would benefit the younger generations of each of their families while Manchester was organizing the procedures for the unprecedented legal case. Behind the scenes, Alice may have used her entire estate as an incentive for Manchester to ensure that the trial played out the way it did. Though her petitions to the king may have secured a settlement at the end of the Castlehaven trials, Alice's will paid her final debt. George and Susanna married that December.

Alice also ensured that her sole surviving daughter, Anne, would be well provided for. Her will instructed Anne to live out her life at Haydon Hall near Ruislip, just five miles from Harefield. Alice also left Anne eleven necklaces, a black chain with gold, a new coach, two coach horses, six milk cows, and a "competent number" of pigs and poultry.[36] Her previous arrangement with the king had already outlined the money Alice would leave Anne for her maintenance throughout her life. Alice had watched her daughter suffer incredible horrors and had tried to secure what favor she could for her. But she also never publicly defended Anne, instead chastising her and pleading with the king to grant her daughter forgiveness for marrying a man such as Castlehaven. Alice had championed the institutionalized victim-shaming Anne had endured, and none of her peers would have expected her to do otherwise. Only after Alice had ensured that the family's reputation would remain intact had she begun to offer security and respite for Anne.

There is no record of Alice ever mentioning Elizabeth, Lady Audley, after the trials, and her resentment probably stemmed from Elizabeth and Lord Audley's refusal to reconcile. Despite all that had happened, upon her death Alice provided Anne a quiet and comfortable life, and Anne accepted it.

The rest of Alice's will was an extravagant inventory of her colossal estate. She doled out jewels, tapestries, gold, and other lavish belongings to her granddaughters Alice and Elizabeth Hastings, even leaving a considerable marriage portion for Alice, with whom she was particularly close. She also left tokens of affection to their brother, Ferdinando Hastings. Alice also remembered her Bridgewater grandchildren with bequests. Though her daughters Frances and Elizabeth were gone, she left tokens to both her sons-in-law, who had served her well: to her "noble son-in-law, the said Henry Earl of Huntingdon, one gilt cup of £40 [£4,900/$6,750 today] value; to my noble son-in-law, the said John Earl of Bridgewater, one other gilt cup of £40 and two dozen of gold buttons beset with diamonds in each of them."[37] Bridgewater received other rental incomes and financial disbursements because, after all, he had been her stepson, too; the properties Thomas had passed to her were now to go to Bridgewater and then to their shared grandchildren. The plan she and Thomas had devised so long before had come to fruition, as most of her plans usually did.

━━━◆━━━◆━━━◆━━━

Three years after Alice's death, Robert Codrington, the minor poet who had written the dedicatory poem for Alice upon Frances's death, wrote another elegy, this time honoring the Dowager Countess of Derby. He presented it to her beloved granddaughter Alice Hastings:

> *All shall improve themselves by her, and try*
> *As blessed like to her to live, as blessed to die,*
> *Religion shall rejoice, and Heaven shall smile*

To see their pious troupes increased, the while
The grateful World shall holy trophies raise,
To Spencers honors, and high Stanleys praise.[38]

The verse articulated all Alice had hoped would continue after her death. She devoted her entire life to the elevation of the "Spencer honors" through "high Stanley praise." She expected her three daughters, their children, and anyone else in her sphere of influence to continue the rise. Of course, Codrington and Alice both ignored the harsher realities of those ambitions. To succeed in Alice's world meant defining yourself by the way others saw you; it meant always choosing power over peace. Throughout her adult life, Alice had overpowered the people in her family who did not share her intense and narrow determination. Whether dealing with her second husband, her brothers-in-law, her sons-in-law, her grandchildren, or even one of her beloved daughters, she cared far more about collective upward mobility achieved through calculated maneuvering than she did about any personal needs or pains. With his elegy, Codrington held Alice up as a model to her granddaughter to aspire to perpetuate that lineage of noble advancement. Nothing would have made Alice happier.

EPILOGUE

If you are in central London, you can hop onto the Metropolitan line at the Euston Square Underground station and take the Tube to the end of the line at Uxbridge. You will emerge in the center of a bustling shopping center on Uxbridge High Street, replete with Primark, Tesco, and Marks & Spencer. You then take bus 331 for the twenty-minute ride to Harefield. Though the village today reflects the norms of modern life, Alice would recognize the lush hills, the densely packed tree line that runs along the perimeter of the pastures, and the gentle curves along the banks of the Colne River. She might scan the landscape in search of her estate, Harefield Place, but she would not find it. Her beloved country seat, where she raised her grandchildren and entertained Queen Elizabeth and which Milton transformed into her Arcadia, was destroyed in the eighteenth century and replaced with another, larger estate, which went on to serve as a hospital and was later again renovated and updated. Today, the building and most of the lands surrounding the old estate are part of a golf club. At the edge of town, a newer construction of luxury condominiums now bears the name Harefield Place.

From the green at the center of town, you can walk south, where Rickmansworth Road turns into Church Hill, and you'll pass a small modern residential street called Countess Close, named after the Dowager Countess of Derby. A few yards farther south and on the opposite side of the street, you come to the seventeenth-century almshouses Alice commissioned in her will. Today, the building is fitted with two renovated apartments rather than the original six rooms Alice envisioned, although one heavy dark beam runs across the central interior ceiling line as a remainder of the original structure. Above one of the exterior doors, set into the dark red bricks, is a carved relief of Alice's coat of arms in the lozenge shape, denoting the arms of a widow, supported by the Stanley stag and the Spencer griffin with the countess's coronet suspended at the top. The almshouses still serve as a home to two widows from the community and are protected by Harefield Parochial Charities.

As you continue south down Church Hill, you quickly arrive at St. Mary the Virgin Church. In front of the structure, white markers sprout up from the verdant earth, the tombstones of the Australian Cemetery, the final resting place of members of Australian military corps treated at the hospital during the First and Second World Wars. Every year on April 25, the village honors the Australian and Kiwi soldiers in its annual Anzac Day celebration. Alice probably had no knowledge of the existence of Australia, and it is both remarkable and jarring the way centuries of world history converge on a small plot of hallowed land on the periphery of greater London. Once you step into the church itself, you are visually bombarded by centuries of monuments and markers on every wall and in the floor, yet it does not take long for your eyes to home in on the colossal structure in the upper chancel. Alice's remains lie entombed within its base, just as she commanded in her will.

A street, almshouses, and a vibrant tomb are far more than most seventeenth-century people have to remind us that they inhabited this world, especially when that person was a woman. In a sense, however, these structures are the most ephemeral markers of Alice's life; they pay homage to her, or they depict the self-fashioned legacy she chose. They tell us that she was born a Spencer and became a Stanley countess, the wife of the lord chancellor, and a mother, but they tell us nothing about how any of that happened, how she experienced it, or what it might have meant to her. And of course, she intentionally erased any connection between herself and those she loved and the Earl of Castlehaven.

Markers such as this may have brought peace and pride to Alice and her family, and they are portals to the communal past for the people of Harefield. But Alice, her daughters, her husbands, and other kin left far more behind. It is understandable why Alice, Anne, and their families wanted everyone to forget about the Castlehaven trials, but after nearly four hundred years, their experiences, strategies, bravery, and humanity can offer us a gut-wrenching history of sexual violence, as well as a history of women and their allies fighting back. Because the Earl of Castlehaven faced a special trial at the request of the king, the outcome did not establish any legal precedent, but that does not mean it was an anomaly. It was, however, exceptional and invites us to consider a more complex experience for women in the past as people who were never solely reduced to their gender alone. The class status, reputations, and personal connections of Alice, Anne, and those around them all impacted the way their peers saw them and the options they had. Alice may not have wanted her family to be known for that ordeal, but with time, it is now possible to see it and still see so much more.

Reading about the Castlehaven trials and the family celebrations that followed provides an opportunity to consider Alice and women like her more wholly. Her skill at navigating perilous legal moments was remarkable, even admirable. Her masterful aptitude for survival and advancement, however, came at an enormous expense to those she cared about the most. To be part of Alice's dynasty meant to endure the bite of her staunch and steadfast views of propriety. Her long-suffering second husband knew that well, but Anne and Anne's daughter Elizabeth probably suffered the most pain from it, as Alice blamed them for having been the victims of sexual violence and actively isolated them from the rest of their family. Alice eventually brought Anne back into the folds of her protection for the rest of both of their lives. Details about her granddaughter Elizabeth's life are, frustratingly, lost, a fate she shares with most women of the age.

Examining the arc of Alice's life is not meant to valorize her but to encourage us to think with more care and complexity about the lives of women in the past. Alice is emblematic of the myriad options aristocratic women had when navigating a patriarchal legal system if they had the right allies and knew how to work with them. Her choice to remain a widow or remarry not only allows us to see the nuance and agency wealthy women had in these decisions but reminds us that marriage in the past was not a static institution, nor was it always a safety net; each marriage was different. Of all the roles Alice had, she was most devoted to her responsibilities as a mother, although she had a unique relationship with each of her daughters and then with her grandchildren. She did not always act with kindness toward her family, but she always acted with love.

Through the lives of Alice and her family, we are able to see this compelling age in even finer detail. Some of Spenser's poems and Milton's *Comus* exist because Alice and her family existed. Their lives are captured in legal documents, manorial records, dedications, household receipts, contracts, and correspondence, printed black-and-white pages or sepia-toned manuscripts. This abundance of sources comes together like the multicolored facets of a kaleidoscope through which we can see their world in luminous color and profound dimensionality. Despite what she may have dictated or desired, this glimpse into a vibrant past is Alice's most notable legacy.

ACKNOWLEDGMENTS

I first encountered Alice and her daughters when I was in graduate school and they have been an enormous part of my life since then. Tom Cogswell introduced me to them and taught me how to tell their stories. My first stop on this journey of research was Cynthia Herrup's work and I appreciate her for giving students and historians so much to engage with.

If graduate school made me a historian, Grainne Fox made me an author. She is more than just an agent; she is a mentor, thinking partner, and advisor. This book would not exist without her.

Peter Borland brought wisdom, clarity, and humanity to my work, and I am a stronger writer because of him. I cannot imagine a finer editor and consider myself lucky to have had this chance to work with him and learn from him.

Libby McGuire, Sarah Wright, Gena Lanzi, Katelyn Phillips, and Sean Delone at Atria and Kelly Karczewski at Fletcher & Co. have also all left their mark on this work and helped me navigate the world of publishing.

Claire Baldwin, Lisa Cody, John Guy, and Julia Fox offered close readings and sagacious notes that refined this book in ways I never could have done on my own.

I chased Alice across two continents and am indebted to the librarians, archivists, and reading room staff at many repositories. It would be impossible to do historical work without these esteemed professionals and I'm proud to call them my colleagues.

It takes not just time but also financial resources to pursue this kind of research and I'm grateful to the University of California, Riverside (especially the History Department and Women's Studies Department), the American Philosophical Society, and the Huntington Library for support that made this research possible.

The Huntington has been my intellectual home since I was in graduate school. When I paged my first manuscript about the Castlehaven trials to the reading room, I had no idea that someday I would be the curator for that collection. Mary Robertson taught me how to read these manuscripts, and it is my great honor to follow in her footsteps as the steward for these materials, many of which populate the endnotes in this book. My colleagues at the Huntington, especially the Curatorial Department, are endlessly supportive, creative, and intellectually evocative. I must thank especially Jenny Watts, Stephen Tabor, Karla Nielsen, Joel Klein, Dan Lewis, Krystle Satrum, Sandra Brooke, David Zeidberg, Stephanie Arias, Manuel Flores, Susan Turner-Lowe, Kevin Durkin, Steve Hindle, Emily Goldblatt, Pamela Hearn, and Cris Lutz.

Over the years, scholars whom I admire have morphed into my friends and I could not have written this book without the conversations we've had in seminars, conferences, and over lunches, coffees, and drinks. My deepest gratitude goes to Catherine Allgor, Roy Ritchie, Peter Mancall, Amy Braden, Tawny Paul, Lindsay O'Neill, Rosemary O'Day, James Knowles, Norm Jones, Heidi Braymen, David Cressy, Lori Anne Ferrell, Kathy Feeley, and Isaac Stephens.

This list of smart and generous people who have shaped this book is long and I also wish to thank the NACBS and PCCBS, editors and readers at *Historical Research Journal,* and Sara Austin and Jean Patterson at the *Huntington Library Quarterly*, Lord and Lady Derby, Stephen Lloyd, Christopher Foley, Edward Town, and Jemma Field. John Ross from the Harefield Parochial Charities and his wife, along with the two women who live in Alice's almshouses, opened their homes to me, giving me one of the most memorable days of my life.

I wrote this book during a pandemic, an era of racial reckoning, a contested election, and a political insurrection. It was a time when everyone had every reason to retreat into their own lives and yet my friends had the generosity to offer me unending support, enthusiasm, and even much-needed distraction. There are many to thank, but I am particularly grateful to: Nami Van Elk, Teal Conroy, Shelley Applegate-Moresette, Liz Codispoti, Andrea Haynes, Sandy Flynn, Sarah Frid, Jules Chenowith, Sarah Redmond, Kathleen McGuire, Kim Korinke, and Shannon Orsini. Your texts and love kept me going more than you could ever know.

Gratitude does not even begin to express my thanks to my family. Debbie Wilkie, John Wilkie, Jenn Hancock, Scarlett Hancock-Wilkie, Vienna Hancock-Wilkie, Tim and Tracey Garvin, and Bob and Kathy Osmond, have championed me and celebrated this project even when I wanted to throw my computer out the window.

Matt Osmond has lived with Alice almost as long as he's lived with me. He has read pages, made me go for walks, fed me, listened to me drone on about enclosure laws, entertained me, offered insightful perspective, and given me pep talks that would make professional athletes jealous, reminding me that writing a book is a marathon, not a sprint. I simply could not have done this, or anything else, without him.

Atari, my dog, slept at my feet while I wrote every word of this book . . . and he did not care about any of this.

LIST OF
ABBREVIATIONS

Add MS	Additional MSS Collection, British Library, London
BL	British Library, London
CP	Cecil Papers Online
CSP	*Calendar of State Papers*
DNB	*Dictionary of National Biography*
E(B)	Ellesmere (Brackley) Collection, Northamptonshire Record Office
EL	Ellesmere MSS, Henry E. Huntington Library, San Marino, CA
HA	Hastings MSS, Henry E. Huntington Library, San Marino, CA
HEH	Henry E. Huntington Library, San Marino, CA
HMC	Historical Manuscript Commission
LMA	London Metropolitan Archive
NRO	Northamptonshire Record Office, Northampton
ROL	Record Office for Leicestershire, Leicester and Rutland
SPD	State Papers: Domestic Online
PC	Privy Council (State Papers Online)
TNA	National Archives, Kew
UoN	University of Nottingham, Special Collections, Nottingham

NOTES

CHAPTER 1: SPENCERS ON THE RISE

1. Lawrence Stone, *The Crisis of the Aristocracy, 1558–1641* (Oxford, UK: Oxford University Press, 1965).

2. Briony McDonagh and Stephen Daniels, "Enclosure Stories: Narratives from Northamptonshire," *Cultural Geographies* 19, no. 1 (January 2012): 110.

3. For more about jointures and marriage contracts, see Amy Erickson, *Women and Property in Early Modern England* (London: Routledge, 1993).

4. Althorp Papers, Add MS 75309, vol. 9, BL. [Documents are foldered but unnumbered in a single box.]

5. Ibid.

6. Ibid.

7. Mary Finch, *The Wealth of Five Northamptonshire Families: 1540–1640* (Oxford, UK: Oxford University Press, 1956), 45.

8. Katharine Walker, "The Widowhood of Alice Spencer, Countess Dowager of Derby, 1594–1636," *Transactions of the Historic Society of Lancashire and Cheshire* 149 (2000): 1–17.

9. Christopher Haigh, *Reformation and Resistance in Tudor Lancashire* (Cambridge, UK: Cambridge University Press, 1975), 104–06.

10. J. R. Dickinson, *The Lordship of Man Under the Stanleys: Government and Economy in the Isle of Man, 1580–1704* (Manchester, UK: Published for the Chetham Society by Carnegie Publishing, 1996), 1–8.

11. French Fogle, "'Such a Rural Queen': The Countess Dowager of Derby as Patron," in *Patronage in Late Renaissance England: Papers Read at a Clark Library Seminar, 14 May 1977*, ed. French Fogle and Louis Knafla (Los Angeles: William Andrews Clark Memorial Library, University of California, 1983), 9–10.

12. All details about the traditional noble wedding ceremony in that period come from David Cressy, *Birth, Marriage, and Death: Ritual, Religion, and the Life-*

Cycle in Tudor and Stuart England (Oxford, UK: Oxford University Press, 1997), 338–76.

13. R. F. to unknown, [1584], SP 15/28, f. 151.

CHAPTER 2: MARRIAGE AND MOTHERHOOD

1. Alice Egerton to Robert Cecil, November 1594, CP 170/16.

2. French Fogle, "'Such a Rural Queen': The Countess Dowager of Derby as Patron," in *Patronage in Late Renaissance England: Papers Read at a Clark Library Seminar, 14 May 1977*, ed. French Fogle and Louis Knafla (Los Angeles: William Andrews Clark Memorial Library, University of California, 1983), 10–11.

3. Mark Girouard, *Life in the English Country House* (New Haven, CT: Yale University Press, 1978), 85.

4. Ibid., 82.

5. Ibid.; see also Regulations of c. 1603 for household of Sir Thomas Egerton, c. 1603, EL 1179 and EL 1180, HEH.

6. All details about traditional noblewomen's experience with pregnancy and childbirth in this period come from Sara Mendelson and Patricia Crawford, *Women in Early Modern England, 1550–1720* (Oxford, UK: Clarendon Press, 1998), 26–28 and 148–153, and Merry Wiesner-Hanks, *Women and Gender in Early Modern Europe* (Cambridge, UK: Cambridge University Press, 2008), 56–60, 65–66, and 83–85.

7. Notes on the births of the Stanley coheiresses, undated, EL 996, HEH.

8. Calculating infant mortality rates, meaning death in the first year of life, is extremely complicated, so this number is given as an informed estimate. See Lynda Payne, "Health in England (16th–18th c.)," Children & Youth in History, https://chnm.gmu.edu/cyh/teaching-modules/166.html. See also R. Schofield, "Comment on Infant Mortality," *Local Population Studies* no. 9 (1972), 49.

9. Notes on the ages of Lady Anne Stanley, Lady Frances Egerton, and Lady Elizabeth Huntingdon, daughters of Ferdinand [sic], Earl of Derby, [1637?], EL 996, HEH.

10. A Copy of Lady Alice's Jointure, February 1, 1582, E(B) 27, NRO.

11. Ibid.

12. Margaret, Lady Strange, to William Cecil, July [18?], 1567, SP 15/13, f. 175.

13. *Calendar of State Papers, Spain (Simancas)*, ed. Martin A. S. Hume, vol. 2, *1568–1579* (London, 1894), 692.

14. Ibid., 693.

15. J. E. Neale, *Elizabeth I and Her Parliaments, 1559–1581* (London: Jonathan Cape, 1953), 393.

16. Burghley's Notes on the State of Lancashire and Cheshire, [1571], CP 159/15.

17. Richard Spencer to William Cecil, August 30, 1581, SP 99/1, f. 5.

18. Sir George Carey to William Cecil, November 13, 1583, CP 12/92.

19. List of Knaves, Papists, and Harboureres of Priests, 1586, SP 12/195, f. 184.

20. Anthony Tyrell's Fourth Declaration, September 1, 1586, SP 53/19, f. 81.

21. Nicholas Burden to Thomas Phillips, [March ?] 1586, SP 12/195, f. 135.

22. Removal of the Queen of Scots' Body from Fotheringay, August 1, 1587, SP 53/21, f. 80.

23. F. R. Raines, ed., *The Stanley Papers,* Part 2: *The Derby Household Books* (Lancashire: Chetham Society, 1853), 157.

24. Framing for aspects of Ferdinando and Alice's theatrical and literary patronage comes from Lawrence Manley and Sally-Beth MacLean, *Lord Strange's Men and Their Plays* (New Haven, CT: Yale University Press, 2014), and Fogle, "'Such a Rural Queen.'"

25. Edmund Spenser, "Tears of the Muses," in *Complaints: Containing Sundrie Small Poems of the Worlds Vanitie* (London, 1591).

26. Spenser claimed to be a blood relative of the Spencers of Althorp, but no such relationship has ever been established. See Thomas Heywood, *The Earls of Derby and the Verse Writers and Poets of the Sixteenth and Seventeenth Centuries* (Manchester, UK: Robinson and Bent, 1825), 37.

27. Barnabe Barnes, *Parthenophil and Parthenophe* (1593).

28. Manley and MacLean, *Lord Strange's Men and Their Plays*, 3; Jennifer Andersen, "Nashe's Poem for Ferdinando Stanley, Lord Strange," *ANQ: A Quarterly Journal of Short Articles, Notes and Reviews* 27, no. 3 (2014): 1–9.

29. See Yoshiko Kawachi, *Calendar of English Renaissance Drama, 1558–1642* (New York: Garland Publishing, 1986); Philip Henslowe, *Henslowe's Diary*, ed. R. A. Foakes and R. T. Rickert (Cambridge, UK: Cambridge University Press, 1961); and Philip Henslowe, *Henslowe Papers: Being Documents Supplementary to Henslowe's Diary*, ed. Walter Greg (Folcroft, UK: Folcroft Press, 1969).

30. William Shakespeare, *Titus Andronicus* (London, 1594), STC 22328, Folger Shakespeare Library.

31. Manley and MacLean, *Lord Strange's Men and Their Plays.* See also J. J. Bagley, *The Earls of Derby, 1485–1985* (London: Sidgwick & Jackson, 1985), 73; E. A. J. Honigmann, *Shakespeare: The "Lost Years"* (Manchester, UK: Manchester University Press, 1985), 63; Peter Ackroyd, *Shakespeare: The Biography* (New York: Doubleday, 2005), 139.

32. Raines, *The Stanley Papers*, Part 2: *The Derby Household Books.*

33. Manley and MacLean, *Lord Strange's Men and Their Plays*, 1.

CHAPTER 3: TREASON AND MURDER

1. Ferdinando Stanley to Sir Robert Cecil, September 21, 1593, CP 23/60.

2. William Goldsmith to Robert Cecil, July 11, 1593, CP 169/102.

3. Robert Parsons, *A Conference About the Next Succession to the Crowne of Ingland* (Antwerp, 1594), 266.

4. *HMC: Salisbury MSS*, Part 4, 9, 461.

5. [Captain Duffield] to ——, November 9, 1593, CP 203/150.

6. Confession of Richard Hesketh, 1594, CP 29/74.

7. A prayer of the right honorable Ferdinando, Lord Strange, 1588, EL 9, HEH.

8. Ferdinando Stanley to Robert Cecil, November 1593, CP 24/32.

9. *HMC: Salisbury MSS*, Part 4, 9, 461.

10. Confession of Richard Hesketh, 1594, CP 29/74.

11. Ferdinando Stanley to Robert Cecil, November 1593, CP 24/32.

12. Ferdinando Stanley to Robert Cecil, November 9, 1593, CP 170/72.

13. Alice Egerton to Robert Cecil, November 1594, CP 170/16.

14. *HMC: Salisbury MSS*, Part 4, 9, 421–22.

15. Lawrence Manley and Sally-Beth MacLean. *Lord Strange's Men and Their Plays* (New Haven, CT: Yale University Press, 2014), 322.

16. Account book for the funeral of Henry Stanley, fourth Earl of Derby, private collection of Lord and Lady Derby, Knowsley Hall.

17. "Note of such reasons and conjectures which caused many to suppose his honor to be bewitched," Talbot Papers MS 3199 f. 715, Lambeth Palace Library. The following account of Ferdinando Stanley's illness and death is based on the details from this manuscript, along with "An unsigned note upon the manner of death of

the Earl of Derby, with a brief of the reasons for suspecting the use of witchcraft," April 1594, Talbot Papers MS 3119, ff. 713–15, Lambath Palace Library; John Stow, *Annals of England* (London, 1600), 1275–77; Judith Bonzol, "The Death of the Fifth Earl of Derby: Cunning Folk and Medicine in Early Modern England," *Renaissance and Reformation* 33, no. 4 (2010): 73–100.

18. Talbot Papers, MS 3199, f. 713, Lambeth Palace Library.

19. Alice Egerton to Robert Cecil, April 11, 1594, CP 170/136.

20. Barry Coward, *The Stanleys, Lords Stanley, and Earls of Derby, 1385–1672: The Origins, Wealth, and Power of a Landowning Family* (Manchester, UK: Manchester University Press, 1983).

21. Talbot Papers, MS 3199, f. 713.

22. Ibid., ff. 713–15.

23. Ibid., f. 713.

24. Stow, *Annals of England*, 1275–77.

25. Sir George Carey to Sir Thomas Heneage and Sir Robert Cecil, April 28, 1594, CP 26/43.

26. Alice Egerton to Robert Cecil, April 11, 1594, CP 170/136.

27. Alice Egerton to the Earl of Shrewsbury, June 27, 1594, Talbot Papers, MS 3203, item 14, Lambeth Palace Library.

CHAPTER 4: AN UNRELENTING LAWSUIT

1. Lawrence Manley and Sally-Beth MacLean, *Lord Strange's Men and Their Plays* (New Haven, CT: Yale University Press, 2014), 322.

2. Elizabeth I's Tilbury Speech, July 1588, Harley 6798 f. 87, BL. There is also a large quantity of scholarly literature dedicated to Elizabeth I's gendered power.

3. Edmund Spenser, *Colin Clouts Come Home Againe* (London, 1595). See also French Fogle, "'Such a Rural Queen': The Countess Dowager of Derby as Patron," in *Patronage in Late Renaissance England: Papers Read at a Clark Library Seminar, 14 May 1977*, ed. French Fogle and Louis Knafla (Los Angeles: William Andrews Clark Memorial Library, University of California, 1983),15–18; Daniel Quinlan and Jean Shackelford, "Economy and English Families, 1500–1850," *Journal of Interdisciplinary History* 24, no. 3 (Winter 1994), 195; F. R. Raines, ed., *The Stanley Papers,* Part 1: *The Derby Household Books* (Lancashire: Chetham Society, 1853), 32–35.

4.   Ferdinando Stanley is listed as one of the contributing authors in the table of contents of the 1610 publication *Belvedére, or the Garden of the Muses*, in Raines, *The Stanley Papers*, 35. See also Steven May, "Spenser's 'Amyntas': Three Poems by Ferdinando Stanley, Lord Strange, Fifth Earl of Derby," *Modern Philology* 70, no. 1 (August 1972): 49–52.

5.   Just as Spenser had dedicated works to Alice prior to *Colin Clout*, that was not his first encounter with Lady Compton and Lady Hunsdon. He dedicated his "Mother Hubberd's Tale" to Lady Compton. To Lady Hunsdon, he dedicated his *Muiopotmos*, as well as a sonnet in *The Faerie Queene*. See also Fogle, "'Such a Rural Queen,'" 16–17; A. C. Hamilton, *The Spenser Encyclopedia* (Toronto: University of Toronto Press, 1997), 174; Raines, *The Stanley Papers*, 38; William Shepard Walsh, *Heroes and Heroines of Fiction* (Philadelphia: J. B. Lippincott, 1914), 93.

6.   Spenser, *Colin Clouts Come Home Againe*.

7.   This is probably a play on "nudcock," a term no longer in use that means "fool" or "simpleton"; see *Oxford English Dictionary*; Manley and MacLean, *Lord Strange's Men and Their Plays*, 326.

8.   For an overview of women and early modern law, see Maria Cioni, *Women and the Law in Elizabethan England with Particular Reference to the Court of Chancery* (Cambridge, UK: Cambridge University Press, 1982); Alice Clark, *Working Life of Women in the Seventeenth Century* (London: Routledge, 1982); Amy Erickson, *Women and Property in Early Modern England* (London: Routledge, 1993); Laura Gowing, *Domestic Dangers: Women, Words, and Sex in Early Modern London* (Oxford, UK: Clarendon Press, 1996); Lynne Greenberg, *Essential Works for the Study of Early Modern Women*, Part 1, vol. 1, *Legal Treatises*, ed. Betty Travitsky and Anne Lake Prescott (Aldershot, UK: Ashgate, 2005), x–xii; Eileen Spring, *Law, Land, and Family: Aristocratic Inheritance in England, 1300–1800* (Chapel Hill: University of North Carolina Press, 1993); Tim Stretton, *Women Waging Law in Elizabethan England* (Cambridge, UK: Cambridge University Press, 1998); Barbara Todd, "Freebench and Free Enterprise: Widows and Their Property in Two Berkshire Villages," in *English Rural Society 1500–1800: Essays in Honour of John Thirsk*, ed. John Chartres and David Hey (Cambridge, UK: Cambridge University Press, 1990), 175–200; and Nancy Wright, Margaret Ferguson, and A. R. Buck, eds., *Women, Property, and the Letters of the Law in Early Modern England* (Toronto: University of Toronto Press, 2004).

9. The last will and testament of Ferdinando Stanley, fifth Earl of Derby, Prob/11/84, TNA.

10. Erickson, *Women and Property in Early Modern England*, 171.

11. The last will and testament of Ferdinando Stanley, fifth Earl of Derby.

12. Barry Coward, *The Stanleys, Lords Stanley, and Earls of Derby, 1385–1672: The Origins, Wealth, and Power of a Landowning Family* (Manchester, UK: Manchester University Press, 1983), 44. Many of the details regarding the series of lawsuits between A. E. and William Stanley are based on Coward's work unless otherwise noted. See also Barry Coward, "Disputed Inheritances: Some Difficulties of the Nobility in the Late Sixteenth and Early Seventeenth Centuries," *Bulletin of the Institute of Historical Research* 44, no. 110 (1971): 194–215.

13. Memorandum confirming the delivery of a trunk of evidence to Sir Thomas Egerton, Master of the Rolls, October 30, 1594, EL 773, HEH.

14. Alice Egerton to Robert Cecil, May 9 [1593], CP 170/142.

15. Thomas Heywood, *The Earls of Derby and the Verse Writers and Poets of the Sixteenth and Seventeenth Centuries* (Manchester, UK: Robinson and Bent, 1825), 28.

16. Documents pertaining to the lawsuit between the coheiresses of Ferdinando Stanley and William Stanley, sixth Earl of Derby, EL 781–848, specifically: A book containing copies of documents relating to the affairs of Ferdinando, Earl of Derby, and the arrangements made after his decease, EL 784, HEH. See also Coward, *The Stanleys, Lords Stanley, and Earls of Derby*, 44.

17. J. R. Dickinson, *The Lordship of Man Under the Stanleys: Government and Economy in the Isle of Man, 1580–1704* (Manchester, UK: Published for the Chetham Society by Carnegie Publishing, 1996), 15, 18.

18. Petition on behalf of the inhabitants of the Isle of Man, August 31, 1594, EL 972, HEH.

19. "The tytle of the Lady Strange Lady Frances & Lady Elizabeth Stanley daughters and heires of the right honourable Ferdinando late Earle of Derbie deceased to the Ile of Manne," EL 782, HEH.

20. Grant from Queen Elizabeth to Alice Egerton for an annuity assigned by the Court of Wards and Liveries, March 15, 1597, EL 6748/20, HEH.

21. Alice Egerton to Robert Cecil, August 9, 1597, CP 175/105.

22. Surrender from the Queen of the wardships of E.S.H. and F.E. to A.E., January 14, 1698, EL 776, HEH.

23. Sir Thomas Egerton to Thomas Egerton, Lord Chancellor Ellesmere, August 1599, EL 77, HEH.

24. Thomas Egerton, "A short abstract of the wrytings & assurances" regarding Alice Egerton's jointure, [1599–1617], EL 226, HEH.

25. Queen Elizabeth to the Emperor of Muscovy, [September 11, 1601], CP 88/35.

26. J. J. Bagley, *The Earls of Derby, 1485–1985* (London: Sidgwick & Jackson, 1985), 69.

27. Coward, *The Stanleys, Lords Stanley, and Earls of Derby*, 48.

28. Minutes from the meeting before the judges at Serjeants' Inn regarding the Isle of Man, [November 22, 1602], EL 976, HEH.

29. Coward, *The Stanleys, Lords Stanley, and Earls of Derby*, 49.

30. Ibid., 63.

31. John Chamberlain, *The Letters of John Chamberlain*, vol. 1, ed. N. E. McClure (Philadelphia: American Philosophical Society, 1938), 190.

32. Alice Egerton to the fourth Earl of Huntingdon, February 4, 1601, HA 2507, HEH.

33. Marriage Settlement for Elizabeth Stanley Hastings and Henry Hastings, 1603, HA Personal Papers 14(3), HEH.

34. Act of Parliament, 1607, E(B) 53, NRO.

CHAPTER 5: A RENAISSANCE FAMILY

1. Ross Duffin, "Framing a Ditty for Elizabeth: Thoughts on Music for the 1602 Summer Progress," *Early Music History* 39 (2020): 115.

2. A brief of things that were bought at Harefield, [July 31–August 2, 1602], EL 122, HEH; entertainment of Queen Elizabeth at Harefield and repairs made to Harefield church, [1602], CR 136/B/2411–2510, Warwickshire Record Office.

3. Gabriel Heaton, "Elizabethan Entertainments in Manuscript: The Harefield Festivities (1602) and the Dynamics of Exchange," in *The Progresses, Pageants, and Entertainments of Queen Elizabeth*, ed. Jayne Elisabeth Archer, Elizabeth Goldring, and Sarah Knight (Oxford, UK: Oxford University Press, 2007), see footnote 26 on p. 237.

4. Duffin, "Framing a Ditty for Elizabeth," 118.

5. Ibid., 131.

6. Ibid., 129–131.

7. Ibid., 116.

8. Heaton, "Elizabethan Entertainments in Manuscript," 239.

9. Mary Erler, "Sir John Davies and the Rainbow Portrait of Queen Elizabeth," *Modern Philology* 8, no. 4 (May 1987), 359–71; Heaton, "Elizabethan Entertainments in Manuscript," 239.

10. Egerton Papers, EL 122; Heaton, "Elizabethan Entertainments in Manuscript," fn. 26.

11. Duffin, "Framing a Ditty for Elizabeth," 118; the Earl of Worcester to the Earl of Shrewsbury, September 19, 1602, Lambeth Palace, MS 3203, f. 18r, Lambeth Palace Library.

12. John Chamberlain to Dudley Carleton, Elizabeth I, vol. 285, December 23, 1602, London, item 13.

13. Robert Cecil to Thomas Egerton, April 17, 1603, EL 131, HEH.

14. It is unknown for certain that Thomas and Alice acted as host and hostess, but scholars have argued that there is a likelihood of this. See Leeds Barroll, *Anna of Denmark, Queen of England: A Cultural Biography* (Philadelphia: University of Pennsylvania Press, 2001), 63–64.

15. Ben Jonson, "The Entertainment at Althorp," in *The Progresses, Processions, and Magnificent Festivities, of King James the First, His Royal Consort, Family, and Court*, ed. John Nichols (London: J. B. Nichols, 1828), 176–87.

16. Nichols, *The Progresses, Processions, and Magnificent Festivities*, 195.

17. James Stuart, King of England, *The True Lawe of Free Monarchies* (Edinburgh: Robert Waldegrave, 1598); James Stuart, King of England, *Basilikon Doron* (Edinburgh: Robert Waldegrave, 1599).

18. Thomas Egerton, "Some Notes and Observations upon the Statute of Magna Carta," HM 57342, 1615/1616, HEH.

19. "The Ellesmere Chaucer," EL 26, C 9, HEH.

20. Manuscript by John Donne, EL 6893, HEH.

21. Heidi Brayman Hackel, "The Countess of Bridgewater's London Library," in *Books and Readers in Early Modern England*, ed. Jennifer Andersen and Elizabeth Sauer (Philadelphia: Pennsylvania University Press, 2002).

22. John Norden, *A Progresse of Pietie* (London, 1600), copy at Knowsley Hall in the private collection of Lord and Lady Derby.

23. William Jewell, trans., *The Golden Cabinet of True Treasure: Containing the Summe of Morall Philosophie* (London, 1612).

24. John Davies, *The Holy Roode, or Christs Crosse* (London, 1609).

25. Thomas Gainsford, *The Historie of Trebizond, in Foure Bookes* (London, 1616).

26. Monies distributed for Henry Hastings, September 23, 1606–October 12, 1607, HA Finance 6(4), HEH.

27. Presumed guest list based on the script for the lottery tipped into the back of EL 34, B 9, HEH. Anne's name does not appear on this list. The birth dates of several of her children are unknown, so pregnancy may have been the reason she did not attend.

28. Microfilm Series I/3, Chamberlain's Accounts, 1606–1607, pp. 26–27, ROL.

29. Presentation copy of *The Entertainment at Ashby* made by John Marston for Alice, Countess Dowager of Derby, EL 34, B 9, HEH. There is another contemporary manuscript copy of *The Entertainment at Ashby*, Sloane 848, BL, ll, 149–156, 270–272.

30. EL 34, B 9, HEH, ll, 299–300.

31. Vanessa Wilkie, "The Context for the Text: The Masque Entertainments of the Egerton-Hastings Family," *Huntington Library Quarterly* 83, no. 2 (Spring 2020), 291–304.

32. Lottery in EL 34, B 9; James Knowles, "Marston, Skipwith and *The Entertainment at Ashby*," *English Manuscript Studies 1100–1700* 3 (1992): 137–92.

CHAPTER 6: A WOMAN IN CONTROL

1. Lord Burkhurst to the Earl of Salisbury, November 24, 1607, CP 195/121.

2. Ibid.

3. Ibid.

4. Sir Thomas Lake to the Earl of Salisbury, December 6, 1607, CP 123/94.

5. Sir Thomas Lake to the Earl of Salisbury, December 8, 1607, CP 194/30.

6. Archbishop Bancroft and Lord Chancellor Ellesmere to the Earl of Dorset, December 27, 1608, SP 14/38, f. 117.

7. Earl of Dorset to Archbishop Bancroft and Lord Chancellor Ellesmere, December 31, 1608, SP 14/37, f. 120.

8. Last will and testament of Robert Sackville, Earl of Dorset, February 10, 1609, Prob 11/113/239, TNA.

9. Estimate of annual household expenses, ca. 1600, EL 284, HEH.

10. List of members of the household in attendance on Thomas Egerton and his wife, January 5, 1615, EL 296, HEH.

11. Account of disbursements at York House since January 12, 1606/07, March 23, 1607, EL 172, HEH.

12. Lord Spencer's speech, May 8, 1621, CP 130/39.

13. Appointment of Anthony Watson by Alice as her personal chaplain, HA Personal Papers 15(11), HEH. This was not Anthony Watson, the Bishop of Chichester.

14. Last will and testament of Alice Egerton, Prob/11/174, TNA.

15. Lady Elizabeth Russell to Thomas Egerton, [1595–1604], EL 46, HEH.

16. Thomas Egerton, "Some Notes and Remembrances for Preserving & Continu-yinge of Quietnes Between my Wyffe and my Sonne, After my Death," August 25, 1610, EL 214, HEH.

17. Ibid.

18. Thomas Egerton, "An Unpleasant Declaration of Things Passed, Between the Countesse of Derby, & Me," EL 213, HEH.

19. Last will and testament of Thomas Egerton, Baron Ellesmere, August 16, 1615, EL 720, HEH.

20. Ibid.

21. "Special Probate of the Will of Sir Thomas Egerton, Lord Chancellor, Granted to John Earl of Bridgewater," February 7, 1617, EL 726, HEH.

22. J. Milling, "Kynaston, Edward (bap. 1643, d. 1712?)," in *Oxford Dictionary of National Biography*, ed. H. C. G. Matthew and Brian Harrison (Oxford, UK: Oxford University Press, 2004).

23. Egerton, "Some Notes and Remembrances for Preserving & Continuyinge of Quietnes Between my Wyffe and my Sonne, After my Death," EL 214.

24. "Copy of the Lady of Derby's Bill" (concerning suit with Sir Edward Kynaston), EL 6649, HEH.

25. Ibid.

26. "Answer of Sir Edward Kynaston, Edward Kynaston, and John Ball, Three of the Defendants, to the Bill of Alice, Dowager Countess of Derby,

Plaintiff, Concerning Park Humphrey in Northwood," July 8, 1617, EL 6650, HEH.

27. Ibid.

28. Briefs concerning the suit between Alice Egerton and Kynaston, AH 937 and AH 938, Hertfordshire Archives and Local Studies.

29. "Petition (draft) Alice, Dowager Countess of Derby, to Sir Francis Bacon, Lord Chancellor, Against Sir Edward Kynaston of Oatly Salop Being Put in the Commission of the Peace," November 12, 1618, AH 940, Hertfordshire Archives and Local Studies.

30. It is unclear if Kynaston received the appointment. The name appears on a list of justices of the peace; however, the document is undated and the Edward Kynston listed could have been one of his descendants. See "Names of the Justices of the Peace and Deputy Lieutenants of Shropshire," [c. 1675], E6/1/5, National Library of Wales, transcribed in W. J. Smith, ed., *Herbert Correspondence* (Cardiff: University of Wales Press, 1963), doc. 345.

31. Draft of indenture between Frances Egerton, John Egerton, Alice Egerton, and Edward Kynaston, December 6, 1627, EL 6652, HEH.

32. Alice Egerton to Sir Julius Caesar, February 7, 1603/4, Add 12506/185, BL.

33. Alice Egerton to Henry Hastings, [1604–1617], HA 2511, HEH.

34. Alice Egerton to Henry Hastings, February 18, 1613/14, HA 2513, HEH.

35. Alice Egerton to Lord Treasurer, May 1609, CP 127/57, 25.

CHAPTER 7: CREATING A DYNASTY

1. Accounts for a nursery, April 24, 1604, EL 149, HEH.

2. Merry Wiesner-Hanks, *Women and Gender in Early Modern Europe* (Cambridge, UK: Cambridge University Press, 2008), 91–92.

3. Abraham Darcie, *To Immortalize the Noble Memorie of the Right Honourable Young Lords Iames and Charles Egerton . . .* (London, 1623?).

4. Bernard Capp, *English Almanacs 1500–1800: Astrology and the Popular Press* (Ithaca, NY: Cornell University Press, 1979), 143.

5. "A Catalogue of my Ladies Bookes at London, taken Oct. 27th 1627," EL 6495, HEH.

6. Thomas Kuhn, *The Copernican Revolution: Planetary Astronomy in the Development of Western Thought* (Cambridge, MA: Harvard University Press, 1957), 93.

7. Nativities of the Bridgewater children, EL 6846 and EL 6847, HEH.

8. "A Horoscope About an Unnamed Man and Woman Done by Richard Piper," EL 6451, HEH.

9. Receipts, October 26, 1615, EL 259; November 13, 1615, EL 263, HEH.

10. Alice Egerton to Ferdinando, Lord Hastings, [1601], HA 2508, HEH.

11. Elizabeth Stanley Hastings to Henry Hastings, [1626], HA 4838, HEH.

12. Elizabeth Stanley Hastings to Henry Hastings, January 18, 1626/27, HA 4839, HEH.

13. Alice Egerton to Henry Hastings, [1607–1618], HA 2512, HEH.

14. Anne Stanley to Thomas Egerton, [November 1616–March 1617], EL 416, HEH.

15. Chamberlain accounts, 1608–1609, MF Series I/3 (98), ROL.

16. John Morgan, "Brinsley, John (fl. 1581–1624)," in *Oxford Dictionary of National Biography*, ed. H. C. G. Matthew and Brian Harrison (Oxford, UK: Oxford University Press, 2004).

17. John Brinsley, *The Second Part of the True Watch, Containing the Perfect Rule and Summe of Prayer* (London, 1607).

18. Last will and testament of Anne Sackville, Dowager Duchess of Dorset, July 24, 1616, Prob 11/132/298, TNA.

19. Sir Thomas Roe to Elizabeth Stanley Hastings, October 30, 1616, HA 10561, HEH.

20. Elizabeth Stanley Hastings to Sir John Davies, October 28, 1623, HA 4828, HEH.

21. Elizabeth Stanley Hastings to Sir John Davies, [August–December] [1623–1626], HA 4830, HEH.

22. Henry Hastings to [Roby], [1627], HA 10543, HEH.

23. Alice Egerton to George Hastings fourth Earl of Huntingdon, February 4, 1600/01, HA 2507, HEH.

24. Elizabeth Stanley Hastings to Henry Hastings, [1627], HA 4840, HEH.

25. Journal of David Evans (steward of Lord Bridgewater), 1629–1632, EL 6477, HEH.

26. *Speeches Delivered to Queen Elizabeth, on Her Visit to Giles Brydges, Lord Chandos, at Sudeley Castle, in Gloucestershire*, ed. Sir Egerton Brydges, Bart., M.P., K.J. (printed at the Private Press of Lee Priory by Johnson and Warwick, 1815), 45–46.

27. Lucy, Countess of Bedford, to Dudley Carleton, August 30, 1621, SP 14/122, f. 156.

28. *Speeches Delivered to Queen Elizabeth*, 46.

CHAPTER 8: SECRETS AND VIOLENCE

1. Cynthia Herrup, *A House in Gross Disorder: Sex, Law, and the 2nd Earl of Castlehaven* (Oxford, UK: Oxford University Press, 1999), 13. Much of the framing and many of the details pertaining to the Castlehaven Trials are based on Herrup's work.

2. Barbara Harris, *English Aristocratic Women, 1450–1550: Marriage and Family, Property and Careers* (Oxford, UK: Oxford University Press, 2002), 5–6.

3. G. E. Cokayne, ed., *The Complete Peerage*, vol. 3 (London: St. Catherine Press, 1916), 86.

4. Herrup, *A House in Gross Disorder*, 12.

5. John Ferris and Paul Hunneyball, "Audley, Sir Mervyn," in *The History of Parliament: The House of Commons, 1604–1629*, eds. Andrew Thrush and John Ferris (Cambridge, UK: Cambridge University Press, 2010).

6. Ferris and Hunneyball, "Audley, Sir Mervyn"; Herrup, *A House in Gross Disorder*, 15, 22–23.

7. Lease of Ruislip for twenty-one years, April 28, 1623, ACC/0312/173, LMA.

8. Alice Egerton to Frances Egerton, June 14, 1630, EL 6481, HEH.

9. Herrup, *A House in Gross Disorder*, 61.

10. "The Trial of Mervin Lord Audley," in T. B. Howell, ed., *A Complete Collection of State Trials and Proceedings for High-Treason, and Other Crimes and Misdemeanors: From the Reign of King Richard II to the Reign of King George II* (London, 1816–1828), 393. There are numerous manuscripts that recount the Castlehaven trials, e.g., IL 3339, NRO, and PwV86, UoN. These accounts are very similar, both to each other and to the published account in *A Complete Collection of State Trials*.

11. Herrup, *A House in Gross Disorder*, 44.

12. Alan Bray, *Homosexuality in Renaissance England* (London: Gay Men's Press, 1982); Alexandra Shepard, *Meanings of Manhood in Early Modern England* (Oxford, UK: Oxford University Press, 2003).

13. The literature about this is vast. See, e.g., Michael Young, *James VI and I and the History of Homosexuality* (Basingstoke, UK: Macmillan, 1999).

14. Herrup, *A House in Gross Disorder*, 142–54. See also Ian Moulton, *Before Pornography: Erotic Writing in Early Modern England* (Oxford, UK: Oxford University Press, 2000).

15. Henry VIII, King of England, *The Statutes of the Realme*, 1533–1534, chaps. 4–6, 441.

16. "The Trial of Mervin Lord Audley," in Howell, *A Complete Collection of State Trials*, 392.

17. James Lord Audley to the Earl of Castlehaven, November 1, 1630, SP 16/175, f. 2.

18. Herrup, *A House in Gross Disorder*, 44.

19. Privy Council to the Lord Bishop of Sarum and the Lord Gorges, December 12, 1630, PC 2/40, f. 225.

20. Privy Council to the Lord Bishop of Winchester, December 14, 1630, PC 2/40, f. 225.

21. Meeting at Whitehall, December 20, 1630, PC 2/40, f. 241.

22. Privy Council to the Lord Gorges and the Lord Bishop of Sarum, December 31, 1630, PC 2/40, f. 265.

23. Petition of Sir William Slingsby to the Lords Committees for the cause of the Earl of Castlehaven, February 1631, SP 16/185, f. 124.

24. Meeting at Whitehall, February 23, 1632, PC 2/40, f. 361.

25. Thomas Gainsford, *The Historie of Trebizond, in Foure Bookes* (London, 1616).

CHAPTER 9: TRIALS AND EXECUTIONS

1. Lord Keeper Coventry to Sec. Dorchester, April 23, 1631, SP 16/189, f. 38.

2. David Lindsay, *Ane Dialog Betuix Experience and Ane Courteour of the Miserabyll Estait of the Warld*, I. 3473 (1554). See also "Buggery," *Oxford English Dictionary*.

3. Castlehaven documents, HA Legal 5 (2), HEH.

4. Royal Proclamation, Charles I, 1631, SP 14/105/96, f. 30v.

5. Castlehaven to Sir Ferdinando Audley, April 24, 1631, SP 16/189, f. 66.

6. "The Arraignment of Merven Lord Audley, Earl of Castlehaven," I.L. 3339, f. 2, [c. 1631], NRO.

7. Ibid., ff. 2–3.

8. Ibid., ff. 3–4.

9. "The Trial of Mervin Lord Audley," in T. B. Howell, ed., *A Complete Collection of State Trials and Proceedings for High-Treason, and Other Crimes and Misdemeanors:*

From the Reign of King Richard II to the reign of King George II (London, 1816–1828), 393.

10.   "The Arraignment of Merven Lord Audley, Earl of Castlehaven," f. 7.

11.   Cynthia Herrup, *A House in Gross Disorder: Sex, Law, and the 2nd Earl of Castlehaven* (Oxford, UK: Oxford University Press, 1999), 144–52.

12.   "The Trial of Mervin Lord Audley," 392.

13.   Ibid., 393.

14.   "The Arraignment of Merven Lord Audley, Earl of Castlehaven," f. 10.

15.   "The Trial of Mervin Lord Audley," 393.

16.   Alice Egerton to Sec. Dorchester, April 1631, SP 16/189, f. 140.

17.   Petition of the Ladies Amy Blount, Elizabeth Griffen, and Christian Mervyn, sisters of the condemned Earl of Castlehaven, to the King, [April] 1631, SP 16/189, f. 139.

18.   Charles I to Attorney General Heath, May 7, 1631, SP 16/190, f. 74.

19.   Information of Sir Archibald Douglas, addressed to the king with the view of saving the life of the Earl of Castlehaven, [May 10], 1631, SP 16/190, f. 119.

20.   James Lord Audley to the Earl of Castlehaven, [May 10], 1631, SP 16/190, f. 131.

21.   Harleian MS 791/51–52, BL.

22.   Alice Egerton to Charles I, May 21, 1631, SP 16/192, f. 13.

23.   Minute of the King's directions to Attorney General Heath, [June] 1631, SP 16/195, f. 100.

24.   "The Trial of Lawrence Fitz-Patrick and Giles Broadway," in Howell, *A Complete Collection of State Trials*, 396.

25.   Alice Egerton to Sec. Dorchester, August 6, 1631, SP 16/198, f. 26.

26.   Petition of William Belou to Lord Treasurer Weston, [May] 1631, SP 16/192, f. 148; untitled document [June 29] 1631 PC 2/41, f. 65; Petition of Elizabeth Lady Audley to the Commissioners for the business of the Earl of Castlehaven, [April] 1631, SP 16/189, f. 143; Petition of Elizabeth Lady Audley to the Commissioners for the business of the Earl of Castlehaven, [April] 1631, SP 16/189, f. 141.

27.   Document between William Brydges and Anne, Countess of Castlehaven, pertaining to messuage of lands of Ruislip, April 21, 1634, ACC/0085/571, LMA.

28. Pardons for the Dowager Countess of Castlehaven and Lady Audley, November 30, 1631, SP 16/203, f. 53.

29. Herrup, *A House in Gross Disorder*, 25.

30. John Flower to Viscount Scudamore, April 16, 1631, C115/105/8133, TNA.

31. Newsletters from John Flower to Viscount Scudamore: April 25, 1631, C115/104/8079; July 2, 1631, C115/104/8081; July 9, 1631, C115/104/8082.

32. The Earl of Castlehaven's Execution Speech, May 14, 1631, Harleian 791/51-52, BL; Account in French of the Castlehaven testimonies, undated, Harleian 1330/61v-62v, BL.

33. Eleanor Davies, "Woe to the House," in *Prophetic Writings of Lady Eleanor Davies*, ed. Esther S. Cope (Oxford, UK: Oxford University Press, 1995), 57.

34. Ibid., 58.

35. *The Arraignment and Conviction of Mervin, Lord Audley, Earl of Castlehaven, (Who Was by 26. Peers of the Realm Found Guilty for Committing Rapine and Sodomy) at Westminster, on Monday, April 25, 1631* (London, 1642).

36. Eleanor Davies, *The Word of God to the Citie of London* (1644), 6–7.

37. "I neade noe Trophies, to adorne my hearse." See Herrup, *A House in Gross Disorder*, 120–23 and 160–64. See also Early Stuart Libels online (earlystuartlibels .net); HM 116, p. 122, HEH.

38. "The Ladyes Answere," in Herrup, *A House in Gross Disorder*, 121.

39. Alice Hastings Clifton to Henry Hastings, July 12, 1635, HA 1470, HEH.

40. Alice Hastings Clifton to Henry Hastings, August 1, 1635, HA 1471, HEH.

CHAPTER 10: FINAL CELEBRATIONS

1. Vanessa Wilkie, "The Context for the Text: The Masque Entertainments of the Egerton-Hastings Family," *Huntington Library Quarterly* 83, no. 2 (Spring 2020), 299.

2. Roy Strong, *Henry, Prince of Wales, and England's Lost Renaissance* (London: Thames and Hudson, 1986); Leeds Barroll, *Anna of Denmark, Queen of England: A Cultural Biography* (Philadelphia: University of Pennsylvania Press, 2001).

3. Rosalind Miles, *Ben Jonson: His Craft and Art* (London: Routledge, 1990). Barroll disagreed with Miles, arguing that Anna of Denmark was probably not impressed with the Althorp masque because she did not ask Jonson to write her first masque. See Barroll, *Anna of Denmark*, 65–66.

4. John Milton, *Arcades: With Introduction, Notes and Indexes,* ed. A. W. Verity (Cambridge, UK, 1908), 3.

5. Appointment of John Egerton to the post of President of the Marches of Wales, July 8, 1631, SPD 16/196, f. 25.

6. Receipt, July 14, 1634, EL 6677, HEH.

7. John Milton, *A Mask of the Same Author Presented at Ludlow Castle, 1634* (London, 1645), 2.

8. Elizabeth Stanley Hastings to Henry Hastings, July 7, 1632, HA 4852, HEH.

9. Elizabeth Stanley Hastings to Henry Hastings, July 11, 1632, HA 4853, HEH.

10. Thomas Cogswell, *Home Divisions: Aristocracy, the State and Provincial Conflict* (Manchester, UK: Manchester University Press, 1998), 210.

11. Peter Chamberlaine, account of cause of death of Elizabeth Stanley Hastings, 1633, EL 6840, HEH.

12. Funeral certificate of Elizabeth Stanley Hastings, 1633, HA Personal Papers 18(6), HEH.

13. I. F., *A Sermon Preached at Ashby de-la-Zouch in the Countie of Leicester* (London, 1635), 33.

14. Ibid., 42.

15. Ibid., 34–35. See also Cogswell, *Home Divisions,* 207–08.

16. Lady Huntingdon's memorial manuscripts, PDF 47, private collection of Lord and Lady Derby, Knowsley Hall.

17. Death certificate of the Countess of Bridgewater, 1636, EL 6841, HEH.

18. *The Church of St. Peter & St. Paul Little Gaddesden: An Historical Note* (Little Gaddesden, UK: Hemel Copyprint, 1995), 8.

19. Funeral sermon for the Countess of Bridgewater, 1636, EL 6883, p. 17, HEH.

20. EL 6883, pp. 28–29, HEH.

21. Verses on the Countess of Bridgewater's death by Robert Codrington, EL 6850, HEH.

22. Marriage contract of Frances and Edmund Fortescue, May 14, 1635, EL 6524, HEH.

23. Last will and testament of Alice Egerton, January 24, 1637, Prob/11/174, TNA.

24. Ibid.

25. Ibid.

26. Ibid.

27. Death certificate of the Dowager Countess of Derby, January 1637, EL 1019,

HEH; death certificate of the Dowager Countess of Derby, January 1637, I8, f. 53v, College of Arms.

28. Gittings, Clare, *Death, Burial, and the Individual in Early Modern England* (London: Croom Helm, 1984), 188–190, 196; Ralph Houlbrooke, *Death, Religion, and the Family in England, 1480–1750* (Oxford, UK: Clarendon Press, 1988), 272; Peter Marshall, *Beliefs and the Dead in Reformation England* (Oxford, UK: Oxford University Press, 2002), 153. Marshall argued that some people opted for night funerals because they believed the Church of England to be "irredeemably corrupt," but this argument is too extreme in Alice's case.

29. Last will and testament of Alice Egerton.

30. Ibid.

31. Ibid.

32. See, e.g., Vanessa Harding, "Choices and Changes: Death, Burial, and the English Reformation," in *The Archaeology of Reformation 1480–1580*, eds. David Gaimster and Roberta Gilchrist (London: Routledge, 2003), 393; Steve Hindle, *On the Parish?: The Micro-Politics of Poor Relief in Rural England c. 1550–1750* (Oxford, UK: Oxford University Press, 2004), 121–22; Peter Jupp and Clare Gittings, eds., *Death in England: An Illustrated History* (New Brunswick, NJ: Rutgers University Press, 2000), 191–92; Peter Marshall, *Beliefs and the Dead in Reformation England*, 167–68; Keith Thomas, *Religion and the Decline of Magic: Studies in Popular Beliefs in Sixteenth- and Seventeenth-Century England* (Oxford, UK: Oxford University Press, 1971), 66. Thomas also argued that in very few instances, people left doles to nullify a curse, but there is no evidence to indicate that this interpretation has any bearing here.

33. Ilana Krausman Ben-Amos, "'Good Works' and Social Ties: Helping the Migrant Poor in Early Modern England," in *Protestant Identities: Religion, Society, and Self-Fashioning in Post-Reformation England*, eds. Muriel C. McClendon, Joseph P. Ward, and Michael MacDonald (Stanford, CA: Stanford University Press, 1999), 135; Clare Gittings, "Urban Funerals in Late Medieval and Reformation England," in *Death in Towns: Urban Responses to the Dying and the Dead, 100–1600*, ed. Steven Bassett (Leicester, UK: Leicester University Press, 1992), 173; Thomas, *Religion and the Decline of Magic*, 601.

34. Ben-Amos, "'Good Works' and Social Ties," 125–40; Claire Schen, "Strategies

of Poor Aged Women and Widows in Sixteenth-Century London," in *Women and Ageing in British Society Since 1500*, eds. Lynn Botelho and Pat Thane (London: Routledge, 2001), 13–30; Paul Slack, *From Reformation to Improvement: Public Welfare in Early Modern England* (Oxford UK: Oxford University Press, 1999).

35. Last will and testament of Alice Egerton.

36. Ibid.

37. Ibid.

38. Robert Codrington, "Elegy for Alice, Dowager Countess of Derby," C6715MI/E38, Clark Library.

SELECT BIBLIOGRAPHY

MANUSCRIPT SOURCES

British Library, London (BL)

      Additional MSS (Add MS)

      Egerton MSS

      Harley MSS

      Sloane MSS

Cecil Papers Online (CP)

College of Arms, London

      Stanley, Earls of Derby, D 8490

      Funeral Certificates, I8 and FC

      Dethick's Funerals of Nobility, DF2

Henry E. Huntington Library, San Marino, CA (HEH)

      Ellesmere MSS (EL)

      Hastings MSS (HA)

      Huntington MSS (HM)

Hertfordshire Archives and Local Studies, Hertford

      Ashridge II Collection (AH)

Knowsley Hall, Lancashire

      Private Collection of Lord and Lady Derby

Lambeth Palace Library, London

      Talbot MSS

London Metropolitan Archives, London

      St. Mary the Virgin, Harefield, DRO/080

      Newdigate Family, ACC/1085

      Swakeley's Estate, Ickenham, ACC/0085

      Sussex Archaeological Society, ACC/0250

      Tarleton-Harefield Collection, ACC/0312

      Westminster Sessions of the Peace (WJ)

National Archives, Kew

 Chancery: Six Clerks' Office, C6

 Chancery: Copies of Private Acts of Parliament, C89

 Chancery: Petty Bag Office, C212

 Chancery: Minster's Exhibits, C115 (Scudomore Letters)

 Chancery: Inquisitions Post Mortem, C142

 King's Bench, KB9

 Probate records, Prob 11

 Court of Wards and Liveries (Ward)

Northamptonshire Record Office, Northampton (NRO)

 Ellesmere (Brackley) Collection (E(B))

 Finch Hatton (Kerby) MSS (FH)

 Isham Lamport MSS (IL)

Record Office for Leicestershire, Leicester and Rutland (ROL)

 Chamberlain's Accounts, MF Series I/3–I/4

 Hall Book, BRII/I

State Papers: Domestic Online (SP)

 Elizabeth I

 James I

 Charles I

University of Nottingham, Special Collections, Nottingham (UoN)

 Portland MSS (PwV)

 Warwickshire County Record Office, Warwick

 Newdigate of Arbury, CR 136

William Andrews Clark Library, Los Angeles, CA

 Robert Codrington, *An Elegie Sacred to . . . Alice Countess Dowager of Derby* (C6715MI/E38)

PRINTED PRIMARY SOURCES

Anyan, Thomas. *A Sermon Preached at S. Maries Church in Oxford, the 12 of July 1612.* London, 1612.

The Arraignment and Conviction of Mervin, Lord Audley, Earl of Castlehaven, (Who Was by 26. Peers of the Realm Found Guilty for Committing Rapine and Sodomy) at Westminster, on Monday, April 25, 1631. London, 1642.

Barnes, Barnabe. *Parthenophil and Parthenophe.* 1593.

Brinsley, John. *The Second Part of the True Watch, Containing the Perfect Rule and Summe of Prayer.* London, 1607.

Brydges, Sir Egerton, ed. *Speeches Delivered to Queen Elizabeth, on Her Visit to Giles Brydges, Lord Chandos, at Sudeley Castle, in Gloucestershire.* Printed at the Private Press of Lee Priory by Johnson and Warwick, 1815.

The Calendar of State Papers, Domestic, Charles I. Edited by John Bruce, W. D. Hamilton, and S. C. Lomas. 28 vols. London, 1858–1897.

The Calendar of State Papers, Spain (Simancas), vol. 2, *1568–1579.* Originally published by Her Majesty's Stationery Office, London, 1894.

Chamberlain, John. *The Letters of John Chamberlain,* vol. 1. Edited by N. E. McClure. Philadelphia: American Philosophical Society, 1938.

Codrington, Robert. *An Elegie Sacred to . . . Alice Countess Dowager of Derby.* 1637.

———. *A Treatise of the Knowledge of God . . .* London, 1634.

Davies, John of Hereford. *The Scourge of Folly.* 1611.

Davies, Sir John. *The Holy Roode, or Christs Crosse.* London, 1609.

Davies Douglas, Eleanor. *The Crying Charge.* 1649.

———. *The Restitution of Prophecy; That Buried Talent to Be Revived.* 1651.

———. *The Word of God to the Citie of London.* 1644.

———. [Bound volume of pamphlets by Eleanor Davies Douglas made for her daughter Lucy Hastings with manuscript notes]. D2010, Folger Shakespeare Library.

Gainsford, Thomas. *The Historie of Trebizond, in Foure Bookes.* London, 1616.

Henry VIII, King of England. *The Statutes of the Realme.* 1533–1534.

Henslowe, Philip. *Henslowe Papers: Being Documents Supplementary to Henslowe's Diary.* Edited by Walter Greg. Folcroft, UK: Folcroft Press, 1969.

———. *Henslowe's Diary.* Edited by R. A. Foakes and R. T. Rickert. Cambridge, UK: Cambridge University Press, 1961.

Hill, Robert. *The Pathway to Prayer and Pietie.* London, 1613.

Howell, T. B., ed. *A Complete Collection of State Trials and Proceedings for High-Treason, and Other Crimes and Misdemeanors: From the Reign of King Richard II to the Reign of King George II.* London, 1816–1828.

I. F. *A Sermon Preached at Ashby de-la-Zouch in the Countie of Leicester.* London, 1635.

Jewell, William, trans. *The Golden Cabinet of True Treasure: Containing the Summe of Morall Philosophie.* London, 1612.

Jonson, Ben. *A Particular Entertainment of the Queen and Prince Their Highnesse at Althorpe.* London, 1604.

Milton, John. *Arcades: With Introduction, Notes and Indexes.* Edited by A. W. Verity. Cambridge, UK, 1908.

———, *A Mask of the Same Author Presented at Ludlow Castle, 1634 (Comus).* London, 1645.

Nichols, John. *The Progresses, Processions, and Magnificent Festivities, of King James the First, His Royal Consort, Family, and Court.* London: J. B. Nichols, 1828.

Parsons, Robert. *A Conference About the Next Succession to the Crowne of Ingland.* Antwerp, 1594.

Pestell, Thomas. *The Poems of Thomas Pestell: Edited with an Account of His Life and Work by Hannah Buchan.* Oxford: Basil Blackwell, 1940.

Queen Elizabeth's Progresses: The Queen's Entertainment by the Countess of Derby, at Harefield Place, Middlesex, in July 1602 . . . London: Printed by and for John Nichols and Sons, 1821.

Shakespeare, William. *Titus Andronicus.* London, 1594.

Spenser, Edmund. *Colin Clouts Come Home Againe.* London, 1595.

———. "Tears of the Muses." In *Complaints: Containing Sundrie Small Poems of the Worlds Vanitie.* London, 1591.

Stow, John. *Annals of England.* London, 1600.

Stuart, James, King of England. *Basilikon Doron.* Edinburgh: Robert Waldegrave, 1599.

———. *The True Lawe of Free Monarchies.* Edinburgh: Robert Waldegrave, 1598.

The Trial of the Lord Audley, Earl of Castlehaven, for Inhumanely Causing His Own Wife to Be Ravished and for Buggery. London, 1679.

Vives, Juan Luis. *Instruction of a Christian Woman.* Translated by Richard Hyrde. London, c. 1529.

Whalley, John. *Gods Plentie, Feeding True Pietie.* London, 1615.

SECONDARY SOURCES

Ackroyd, Peter. *Shakespeare: The Biography.* New York: Doubleday, 2005.

Adams, Michael. "Specular Rape: Reflections on Early Modern Reflections of the Present Day." *Centennial Review* 41, no. 2 (1997): 217–50.

Amussen, Susan Dwyer. *An Ordered Society: Gender and Class in Early Modern England.* Oxford, UK: Basil Blackwell, 1988.

Andersen, Jennifer. "Nashe's Poem for Ferdinando Stanley, Lord Strange." *ANQ: A Quarterly Journal of Short Articles, Notes and Reviews* 27, no. 3 (2014): 1–9.

Archer, Jayne Elisabeth, Elizabeth Goldring, and Sarah Knight, eds. *The Progresses, Pageants, and Entertainments of Queen Elizabeth I.* Oxford, UK: Oxford University Press, 2007.

Ariès, Philippe. *Centuries of Childhood: A Social History of Family Life.* Translated by Robert Baldick. New York: Vintage Books, 1962.

Bagley, J. J. *The Earls of Derby, 1485–1985.* London: Sidgwick & Jackson, 1985.

Baines, Barbara J. "Effacing Rape in Early Modern Representation." *ELH* 65, no. 1 (1998): 69–98.

———. *Representing Rape in the English Early Modern Period.* Lewiston, UK: Edwin Mellen Press, 2003.

Barker, Helen. *Rape in Early Modern England: Law, History, and Criticism.* London: Palgrave Macmillan, 2021.

Barroll, Leeds. *Anna of Denmark, Queen of England: A Cultural Biography.* Philadelphia: University of Pennsylvania Press, 2001.

Bashar, Nazife. "Rape in England Between 1550 and 1700." In *The Sexual Dynamics of History*, edited by the London Feminist Group. London: Pluto Press, 1983.

Bassett, Steve, ed. *Death in Towns: Urban Responses to the Dying and the Dead, 100–1600.* Leicester, UK: Leicester University Press, 1992.

Becker, Lucinda. *Death and the Early Modern Englishwoman.* Aldershot, UK: Ashgate, 2003.

Bergeron, David. *Textual Patronage in English Drama, 1570–1640.* Aldershot, UK: Ashgate, 2006.

Berry, Helen, and Elizabeth Foyster, eds. *The Family in Early Modern England.* Cambridge, UK: Cambridge University Press, 2007.

Bonzol, Judith. "The Death of the Fifth Earl of Derby: Cunning Folk and Medicine in Early Modern England." *Renaissance and Reformation* 33, no. 4 (2010): 73–100.

Botelho, Lynn, and Pat Thane, eds. *Women and Ageing in British Society Since 1500.* London: Routledge, 2001.

Bray, Alan. *Homosexuality in Renaissance England.* London: Gay Men's Press, 1982.

Breasted, Barbara. "*Comus* and the Castlehaven Scandal." *Milton Studies* 3 (1971): 201–24.

Brewer, J. Norris. *London and Middlesex: Or, an Historical, Commercial, & Descriptive Survey of the Metropolis of Great-Britain: Including Skeches of Its Environs, and All Topographical Account of the Most Remarkable Places in the Above County*, vol. 4. London, 1816.

Brown, Cedric. *John Milton's Aristocratic Entertainments.* Cambridge, UK: Cambridge University Press, 1985.

Brydges, Sir Egerton. *Memoirs of the Peers of England.* London: Printed for John White, Fleet Street, by Nichols and Sons, Red Lion Passage, 1802.

Burke, Peter, Brian Harrison, and Paul Slack, eds. *Civil Histories: Essays Presented to Sir Keith Thomas.* Oxford, UK: Oxford University Press, 2000.

Butler, Martin. *The Stuart Court Masque and Political Culture.* Cambridge, UK: Cambridge University Press, 2008.

Camino, Mercedes Maroto. *"The Stage Am I": Raping Lucrece in Early Modern England.* Lewiston, UK: Edwin Mellen, 1995.

Capp, Bernard. *English Almanacs, 1500–1800: Astrology and the Popular Press.* Ithaca, NY: Cornell University Press, 1979.

Carter, John. *Rape in Medieval England: An Historical and Sociological Study.* Lanham, MD: University Press of America, 1985.

Catty, Jocelyn. *Writing Rape, Writing Women in Early Modern England: Unbridled Speech.* New York: St. Martin's Press, 1999.

Cavallo, Sandra, and Lyndan Warner, eds. *Widowhood in Medieval and Early Modern Europe.* Essex, UK: Longman, 1999.

Charlton, Kenneth. *Women, Religion and Education in Early Modern England.* London: Routledge, 1999.

Chartres, John, and David Hey, eds. *English Rural Society, 1500–1800: Essays in Honour of Joan Thirsk.* Cambridge, UK: Cambridge University Press, 1990.

Chaytor, Miranda. "Husband(ry): Narratives of Rape in the Seventeenth Century." *Gender and History* 7, no. 3 (November 1995): 378–407.

The Church of St. Peter & St. Paul Little Gaddesden: An Historical Note. Little Gaddesden, UK: Hemel Copyprint, 1995.

Cioni, Maria. *Women and the Law in Elizabethan England with Particular Reference to the Court of Chancery.* Cambridge, UK: Cambridge University Press, 1982.

Clark, Alice. *Working Life of Women in the Seventeenth Century.* London: Routledge, 1982.

Clark, Anna. "Rewriting the History of Rape." *New Society* no. 1235 (August 1986): 12–13.

Cochran, H. S. *St. Mary's, Harefield. Description of the Monuments, Etc.* 3rd ed. Rickmansworth, UK: 1936.

Cogswell, Thomas. *Home Divisions: Aristocracy, the State and Provincial Conflict.* Manchester, UK: Manchester University Press, 1998.

Cokayne, G. E., ed. *The Complete Peerage.* London: St. Catherine Press, 1916.

Cole, Mary Hill. *The Portable Queen: Elizabeth I and the Politics of Ceremony.* Amherst: University of Massachusetts Press, 1999.

Coles, Kimberly. *Religion, Reform, and Women's Writing in Early Modern England.* Cambridge, UK: Cambridge University Press, 2008.

Collier, J. Payne, ed. *Royal Historical Society, London Publications.* Camden Series 12: *The Egerton Papers.* London: John Bowyer Nichols and Sons, 1840.

Collins, Stephen. "British Stepfamily Relationships, 1500–1800." *Journal of Family History* 16, no. 4 (1991): 331–44.

———. "'Reason, Nature and Order': The Stepfamily in English Renaissance Thought." *Renaissance Studies* 13, no. 3 (September 1999): 312–24.

Comensoli, Viviana. *"Household Business": Domestic Plays of Early Modern England.* Toronto: University of Toronto Press, 1996.

Cooper, Nicholas. *Houses of the Gentry, 1480–1680.* New Haven, CT: Yale University Press, 1999.

Cope, Esther S. *Handmaid of the Holy Spirit: Dame Eleanor Davis, Never Soe Mad a Ladie.* Ann Arbor: University of Michigan Press, 1992.

———, ed. *Prophetic Writings of Lady Eleanor Davies.* Oxford, UK: Oxford University Press, 1995.

Coward, Barry. "Disputed Inheritances: Some Difficulties of the Nobility in the Late Sixteenth and Early Seventeenth Centuries." *Bulletin of the Institute of Historical Research* 44, no. 110 (1971): 194–215.

———. *The Stanleys, Lords Stanley, and Earls of Derby, 1385–1672: The Origins, Wealth, and Power of a Landowning Family.* Manchester, UK: Manchester University Press, 1983.

Crawford, Patricia. *Blood, Bodies, and Family in Early Modern England.* London: Pearson Education, 2004.

———. *Women and Religion in England, 1500–1720.* London: Routledge, 1993.

Creaser, John. "Milton's *Comus*: The Irrelevance of the Castlehaven Scandal." *Milton Quarterly* 21, no. 4 (1987): 24–34

Cressy, David. *Birth, Marriage, and Death: Ritual, Religion, and the Life-Cycle in Tudor and Stuart England.* Oxford: Oxford University Press, 1997.

Croft, Pauline, ed. *Patronage, Culture and Power: The Early Cecils.* New Haven, CT: Yale University Press, 2002.

Cross, Claire. *The Puritan Earl: The Life of Henry Hastings, Third Earl of Huntingdon, 1536–1595.* New York: St. Martin's Press, 1966.

Curry, Patrick. *Prophecy and Power: Astrology in Early Modern England.* Cambridge, UK: Polity Press, 1989.

Cust, Richard. "Honour and Politics in Early Stuart England: The Case of Beaumont *v.* Hastings." *Past and Present* no. 149 (November 1995): 57–94.

Dabhoiwala, Fara. *The Origins of Sex: A History of the First Sexual Revolution.* Oxford, UK: Oxford University Press, 2012.

Daugherty, Leo. *The Assassination of Shakespeare's Patron: Investigating the Death of the Fifth Earl of Derby.* Amherst, NY: Cambria Press, 2013.

Davenport, Arnold, ed. *The Poems of John Marston.* Liverpool, UK: Liverpool University Press, 1961.

Daybell, James, ed. *Early Modern Women's Letter Writing, 1450–1700.* New York: Palgrave, 2001.

———, ed. *Women and Politics in Early Modern England, 1450–1700.* Aldershot, UK: Ashgate, 2004.

Detmar-Goebel, Emily. "The Need for Lavinia's Voice: Titus Andronicus and the Telling of Rape." *Shakespeare Studies* 29 (2001): 75–92.

Dickinson, J. R. *The Lordship of Man Under the Stanleys: Government and Economy in the Isle of Man, 1580–1704.* Manchester, UK: Published for the Chetham Society by Carnegie Publishing, 1996.

Dimmock, Matthew, Andrew Hadfield, and Margaret Healy, eds. *The Intellectual Culture of the English Country House, 1500–1700.* Manchester, UK: Manchester University Press, 2015.

Dolan, Francis. *Dangerous Familiars: Representations of Domestic Crime in England, 1550–1700.* Ithaca, NY: Cornell University Press, 1994.

Doolittle, Megan. "Close Relations? Bringing Together Gender and Family in English History." *Gender & History* 11, no. 3 (November 1999): 542–54.

Duffin, Ross. "Framing a Ditty for Elizabeth: Thoughts on Music for the 1602 Summer Progress." *Early Music History* 39 (2020): 115–48.

Dutton, Richard, Alison Findlay, and Richard Wilson, eds. *Theatre and Religion: Lancastrian Shakespeare.* Manchester, UK: Manchester University Press, 2003.

Eales, Jacqueline. *Women in Early Modern England, 1500–1700.* London: UCL Press, 1998.

Eckhardt, Joshua. *Religion Around John Donne.* University Park: Pennsylvania State University Press, 2019.

Edwards, Francis. *Plots and Plotters in the Reign of Elizabeth I.* Dublin: Four Courts Press, 2002.

English, Barbara. *The Great Landowners of East Yorkshire, 1530–1910.* New York: Harvester Weatsheaf, 1990.

Erickson, Amy. *Women and Property in Early Modern England.* London: Routledge, 1993.

Erler, Mary. "'Chaste Sports, Juste Prayses, & All Softe Delight': Harefield 1602 and Ashby 1607, Two Female Entertainments." In *The Elizabethan Theatre*, vol. 14, edited by A. L. Magnusson and C. E. McGee. Toronto: P. D. Meany, 1996, 1–25.

———. "Sir John Davies and the Rainbow Portrait of Queen Elizabeth." *Modern Philology* 8, no. 4 (May 1987): 359–71.

———. "Widows in Retirement: Region, Patronage, Spirituality, Reading at the Gaunts, Bristol." *Religion & Literature* 37, no. 2 (Summer 2005): 51–75.

Ewen, C. L'Estrange. *Witchcraft and Demonianism: A Concise Account Derived from Sworn Depositions and Confessions Obtained in the Courts of England and Wales.* London: Heath Cranton, 1933.

Falk, Bernard. *The Bridgewater Millions: A Candid Family History.* London: Hutchinson & Co., 1942.

Feroli, Teresa. "Sodomy and Female Authority: The Castlehaven Scandal and Eleanor Davies's *The Restitution of Prophecy* (1651)." *Women's Studies: An Interdisciplinary Journal* 24, nos. 1–2 (1994): 31–49.

Fildes, Valerie, ed. *Women as Mothers in Pre-Industrial England: Essays in Memory of Dorothy McLaren.* London: Routledge, 1990.

Finch, Mary E. *The Wealth of Five Northamptonshire Families, 1540–1640.* Oxford, UK: Oxford University Press, 1956.

Fletcher, Anthony. *Gender, Sex and Subordination in England, 1500–1800.* New Haven, CT: Yale University Press, 1995.

Fletcher, Anthony, and John Stevenson, eds. *Order and Disorder in Early Modern England.* Cambridge, UK: Cambridge University Press, 1985.

Fogle, French, and Louis Knafla, eds. *Patronage in Late Renaissance England: Papers Read at a Clark Library Seminar, 14 May 1977.* Los Angeles: William Andrews Clark Memorial Library, University of California, 1983.

Foyster, Elizabeth A. *Manhood in Early Modern England: Honour, Sex and Marriage.* London: Longman, 1999.

France, Peter, and William St. Clair, eds. *Mapping Lives: The Uses of Biography.* Oxford, UK: Oxford University Press, 2002.

Fraser, Antonia. *The Weaker Vessel: Women's Lot in Seventeenth-Century England.* London: Weidenfeld and Nicolson, 1984.

Frith, Valerie, ed. *Women & History: Voices of Early Modern England.* Toronto: Coach House, 1995.

Froide, Amy. *Never Married: Singlewomen in Early Modern England.* Oxford, UK: Oxford University Press, 2005.

Gibbons, B. J. *Gender in Mystical and Occult Thought: Behmenism and Its Development in England.* Cambridge, UK: Cambridge University Press, 1996.

Gillis, John R. *For Better, for Worse: British Marriages, 1600 to the Present.* Oxford, UK: Oxford University Press, 1985.

Girouard, Mark. *Life in the English Country House.* New Haven, CT: Yale University Press, 1978.

Gittings, Clare. *Death, Burial and the Individual in Early Modern England.* London: Croom Helm, 1984.

Goatman, Wilfrid. *Harefield and Her Church.* London: The Church, 1972.

Gowing, Laura. *Common Bodies: Women, Touch and Power in Seventeenth-Century England.* New Haven, CT: Yale University Press, 2003.

——. *Domestic Dangers: Women, Words, and Sex in Early Modern London.* Oxford, UK: Clarendon Press, 1996.

——. "Women, Status and the Popular Culture of Dishonour." *Transactions of the Royal Historical Society,* 6th series, no. 6 (1996): 225–34.

Greenberg, Lynne. *Essential Works for the Study of Early Modern Women.* Part I, vol. 1, *Legal Treatises.* Edited by Betty Travitsky and Anne Lake Prescott. Aldershot, UK: Ashgate, 2005.

Griffey, Erin, ed. *Henrietta Maria: Piety, Politics and Patronage.* Aldershot, UK: Ashgate, 2008.

Hackel, Heidi Brayman. "The Countess of Bridgewater's London Library." In *Books and Readers in Early Modern England,* edited by Jennifer Andersen and Elizabeth Sauer. Philadelphia: Pennsylvania University Press, 2002, 138–159.

Haigh, Christopher. *Reformation and Resistance in Tudor Lancashire.* Cambridge, UK: Cambridge University Press, 1975.

Hall, David. "Enclosure in Northamptonshire." *Northamptonshire Past and Present* 9 (1997): 350–67.

Hamilton, A. C. *The Spenser Encyclopedia.* Toronto: University of Toronto Press, 1997.

Hannay, Margaret Patterson, ed. *Silent but for the Word: Tudor Women as Patrons, Translators, and Writers of Religious Works.* Kent, OH: Kent State University Press, 1985.

Harbage, Alfred. *Annals of English Drama, 975-1700* (1940). Revised by Samuel Schoenbaum. Philadelphia: University of Pennsylvania Press, 1964.

Harding, Vanessa. "Choices and Changes: Death, Burial, and the English Reformation." In *The Archaeology of Reformation, 1480–1580*, edited by David Gaimster and Roberta Gilchrist. London: Routledge, 2003.

Harris, Barbara J. *English Aristocratic Women, 1450–1550: Marriage and Family, Property and Careers.* Oxford, UK: Oxford University Press, 2002.

———. "The Fabric of Piety: Aristocratic Women and Care of the Dead, 1450–1550." *Journal of British Studies* 48, no. 2 (April 2009): 308-35.

———. "Women and Politics in Early Tudor England." *Historical Journal* 33, no. 2 (June 1990): 259–81.

Heal, Felicity. *Hospitality in Early Modern England.* Oxford, UK: Clarendon Press, 1990.

———. "Reputation and Honour in Court and Country: Lady Elizabeth Russell and Sir Thomas Hoby." *Transactions of the Royal Historical Society*, 6th series, no. 6 (1996): 161–78.

Heal, Felicity, and Clive Holmes. *The Gentry in England and Wales, 1500–1700.* Stanford, CA: Stanford University Press, 1994.

Heltzel, V. B. "Sir Thomas Egerton as Patron." *Huntington Library Quarterly* 11, no. 2 (1947–48): 105–27.

Herrup, Cynthia. *A House in Gross Disorder: Sex, Law, and the 2nd Earl of Castlehaven.* Oxford, UK: Oxford University Press, 1999.

———. "The Patriarch at Home: The Trial of the 2nd Earl of Castlehaven for Rape and Sodomy." *History Workshop Journal* 41 (1996): 1–18.

———. "'To Pluck Bright Honour from the Pale-Faced Moon': Gender and Honour in the Castlehaven Story." *Transactions of the Royal Historical Society*, 6th series, no. 6 (1996): 137–59.

Heywood, Thomas. *The Earls of Derby and the Verse Writers and Poets of the Sixteenth and Seventeenth Centuries.* Manchester, UK: Robinson and Bent, 1825.

Hill, Christopher. "Science and Magic in Seventeenth-Century England." In *Culture, Ideology and Politics: Essays for Eric Hobsbawm*, edited by Raphael Samuel and Gareth Stedman Jones. London: Routledge, 1982, 176–193.

———. "Sex, Marriage, and the Family in England." *Economic History Review*, New Series 31, no. 3 (August 1978): 450–63.

Hindle, Steve. *On the Parish?: The Micro-Politics of Poor Relief in Rural England, c. 1550–1750.* Oxford, UK: Oxford University Press, 2004.

Honigmann, E. A. J. *Shakespeare: The "Lost Years."* Manchester, UK: Manchester University Press, 1985.

Houlbrooke, Ralph. *Church Courts and People During the English Reformation, 1520–1570.* Oxford, UK: Oxford University Press, 1979.

———. "Civility and Civil Observances in the Early Modern English Funeral." In *Civil Histories: Essays Presented to Sir Keith Thomas*, edited by Peter Burke, Brian Harrison, and Paul Slack. Oxford, UK: Oxford University Press, 2000, 67–85.

———. *Death, Religion, and the Family in England, 1480–1750.* Oxford, UK: Clarendon Press, 1998.

———, ed. *Death, Ritual, and Bereavement.* London: Routledge, 1989.

Hunter, William B., Jr. *Milton's* Comus: *Family Piece.* Troy, NY: Whitston Publishing Co., 1983.

Hurstfield, Joel. *The Queen's Wards: Wardship and Marriage Under Elizabeth I.* Cambridge, MA: Harvard University Press, 1958.

Ingram, Martin. *Church Courts, Sex and Marriage in England, 1570–1640.* Cambridge, UK: Cambridge University Press, 1987.

Jupp, Peter, and Clare Gittings, eds. *Death in England: An Illustrated History.* New Brunswick, NJ: Rutgers University Press, 2000.

Kawachi, Yoshiko. *Calendar of English Renaissance Drama, 1558–1642.* New York: Garland Publishing, 1986.

Klein, Joan Larsen, ed. *Daughters, Wives and Widows: Writings by Men About Women and Marriage in England, 1500–1640.* Urbana: University of Illinois Press, 1992.

Knafla, Louis. *Law and Politics in Jacobean England: The Tracts of Lord Chancellor Ellesmere.* Cambridge, UK: Cambridge University Press, 1977.

Knowles, James. "Marston, Skipwith and *The Entertainment at Ashby*." *English Manuscript Studies, 1100–1700* 3 (1992): 137–92.

———. *Politics and Political Culture in the Court Masque.* New York: Palgrave Macmillan, 2015.

Kolkovich, Elizabeth Zeman. *The Elizabethan Country House Entertainment: Print, Performance, and Gender.* Cambridge, UK: Cambridge University Press, 2016.

Laurence, Anne. *Women in England, 1500–1760: A Social History.* New York: St. Martin's Press, 1994.

———. "Women Using Building in Seventeenth-Century England: A Question of Sources?," *Transactions of the Royal Historical Society* 13 (2003): 293–303.

Lewalski, Barbara Keifer. *Writing Women in Jacobean England.* Cambridge, MA: Harvard University Press, 1993.

Lindley, David, ed. *The Court Masque.* Manchester, UK: Manchester University Press, 1984.

Llewellyn, Nigel. *The Art of Death: Visual Culture in the English Death Ritual, c. 1500–c. 1800.* London: Reaktion Books, 1991.

———. *Funeral Monuments in Post-Reformation England.* Cambridge, UK: Cambridge University Press, 2000.

Lloyd, Stephen, ed. *Art, Animals and Politics: Knowsley and the Earls of Derby.* London: Unicorn Press, 2016.

Lysons, Daniel. *An Historical Account of Those Parishes in the County of Middlesex, Which Are Not Described in the Environs of London.* London: A. Strahan, 1800.

Lytle, Guy Fitch, and Stephen Orgel, eds. *Patronage in the Renaissance.* Princeton, NJ: Princeton University Press, 1981.

Manley, Lawrence, and Sally-Beth MacLean. *Lord Strange's Men and Their Plays.* New Haven, CT: Yale University Press, 2014.

Marcus, Leah. "Justice for Margery Evans: A 'Local' Reading of *Comus.*" In *Milton and the Idea of Women,* edited by Julia Walker. Urbana: University of Illinois Press, 1988, 66–85.

———. "The Milieu of Milton's *Comus:* Judicial Reform at Ludlow and the Problem of Sexual Assault." *Criticism* 25, no. 4 (1983): 293–327.

Marshall, Peter. *Beliefs and the Dead in Reformation England.* Oxford, UK: Oxford University Press, 2002.

May, Steven. "Spenser's 'Amyntas': Three Poems by Ferdinando Stanley, Lord Strange, Fifth Earl of Derby." *Modern Philology* 70, no. 1 (August 1972): 49–52.

McClendon, Muriel C., Joseph P. Ward, and Michael MacDonald, eds. *Protestant Identities: Religion, Society, and Self-Fashioning in Post-Reformation England.* Stanford, CA: Stanford University Press, 1999.

McDonagh, Briony, and Stephen Daniels. "Enclosure Stories: Narratives from Northamptonshire." *Cultural Geographies* 19, no. 1 (January 2012): 107–21.

McLane, Paul. "Spenser's Chloris: The Countess of Derby." *Huntington Library Quarterly* 24, no. 2 (February 1961): 145–50.

McMullen, Norma. "The Education of English Gentlewomen, 1540–1640." *History of Education* 6, no. 2 (1977): 87–101.

Mendelson, Sara, and Patricia Crawford. *Women in Early Modern England, 1550–1720.* Oxford, UK: Clarendon Press, 1998.

Miles, Rosalind. *Ben Jonson: His Craft and Art.* London: Routledge, 1990.

Miller, Chanel. *Know My Name: A Memoir.* New York: Viking, 2019.

Miller, Naomi J., and Naomi Yavneh, eds. *Maternal Measures: Figurative Caregiving in the Early Modern Period.* Aldershot, UK: Ashgate, 2000.

Milton, John. *The Complete Poetry of John Milton.* Edited by John Shawcross. New York: Doubleday, 1990.

Moulton, Ian. *Before Pornography: Erotic Writing in Early Modern England.* Oxford, UK: Oxford University Press, 2000.

Neale, J. E. *Elizabeth I and Her Parliaments, 1559–1581.* London: Jonathan Cape, 1953.

O'Day, Rosemary. *The Family and Family Relationships, 1500–1900: England, France, and the United States of America.* New York: St. Martin's Press, 1994.

O'Hara, Diana. *Courtship and Constraint: Rethinking the Making of Marriage in Tudor England.* Manchester, UK: Manchester University Press, 2000.

Peck, Linda Levy, ed. *The Mental World of the Jacobean Court.* Cambridge, UK: Cambridge University Press, 1991.

Peters, Christine. *Patterns of Piety: Women, Gender and Religion in Late Medieval and Reformation England.* Cambridge, UK: Cambridge University Press, 2003.

Pevsner, Nikolaus. *The Buildings of England: Leicestershire and Rutland.* Harmondsworth, UK: Penguin, 1960.

———. *The Buildings of England: Middlesex.* Harmondsworth, UK: Penguin, 1951.

Pollock, Linda. "Honor, Gender, and Reconciliation in Elite Culture, 1570–1700." *Journal of British Studies* 46, no. 1 (January 2007): 3–29.

———. *A Lasting Relationship: Parents and Children over Three Centuries.* London: Fourth Estate, 1987.

Prior, Mary, ed. *Women in English Society, 1500–1800.* London: Methuen, 1985.

Quinlan, Daniel, and Jean Shackelford. "Economy and English Families, 1500–1850." *Journal of Interdisciplinary History* 24, no. 3 (Winter 1994): 431–63.

Raines, F. R., ed. *The Stanley Papers.* Part 2: *The Derby Household Books.* Lancashire: Chetham Society, 1853.

Ramsay, Nigel, ed. *Heralds and Heraldry in Shakespeare's England.* Donington, UK: Shaun Tyas, 2014.

Ray, Sid. "'Rape, I Fear, Was Root of Thy Annoy': The Politics of Consent in *Titus Andronicus.*" *Shakespeare Quarterly* 49, no. 1 (1998): 22–39.

Reynolds, Susan, ed. *A History of the County of Middlesex.* London: Victoria History of the Counties of England, 1962.

Ritscher, Lee. "The Semiotics of Rape in Renaissance English Literature." Ann Arbor, MI: ProQuest, 2005.

Rudolph, Julia. "Rape and Resistance: Women and Consent in Seventeenth-Century English Legal and Political Thought." *Journal of British Studies* 39 (2000): 157–84.

Sale, Carolyn. "Consented Acts: Legal Performances and Literary Authority in Early Modern England." Ann Arbor, MI: ProQuest, 2002.

———. "Representing Lavinia: The (In)significance of Women's Consent in Legal Discourses of Rape and Ravishment and Shakespeare's *Titus Andronicus.*" In *Women, Violence, and English Renaissance Literature: Essays Honoring Paul Jorgensen,* edited by Linda Woodbrige and Sharon Beehler. Tempe: Arizona Center for Medieval and Renaissance Studies, 2003.

Salter, Elisabeth. *Six Renaissance Men and Women: Innovation, Biography and Cultural Creativity in Tudor England, c. 1450–1560.* Aldershot, UK: Ashgate, 2007.

Scott, Joan Wallach, ed. *Feminism and History.* Oxford, UK: Oxford University Press, 1997.

———. *Gender and the Politics of History.* New York: Columbia University Press, 1999.

———. "Gender: A Useful Category of Historical Analysis." *American Historical Review* 91, no. 5 (December 1986): 1053–75.

Sharpe, Kevin. *Reading Revolutions: The Politics of Reading in Early Modern England.* New Haven, CT: Yale University Press, 2000.

Shaw-Taylor, Leigh. "Parliamentary Enclosure and the Emergence of an English Agricultural Proletariat." *Journal of Economic History* 61, no. 3 (2001): 640–62.

Shepard, Alexandra. *Meanings of Manhood in Early Modern England.* Oxford, UK: Oxford University Press, 2003.

Sherlock, Peter. *Monuments and Memory in Early Modern England.* Ashgate, UK: Aldershot, 2008.

Sim, Alison. *The Tudor Housewife.* Montreal: McGill–Queen's University Press, 1996.

Skeel, Caroline. "The Countess of Bridgewater's Library, 1627." *History Teacher's Miscellany* 3, no. 9 (September 1925): 129–30.

Slack, Paul. *From Reformation to Improvement: Public Welfare in Early Modern England.* Oxford, UK: Oxford University Press, 1999.

Smuts, R. Malcolm, ed. *The Stuart Court and Europe: Essays in Politics and Political Culture.* Cambridge, UK: Cambridge University Press, 1996.

Spring, Eileen. *Law, Land, and Family: Aristocratic Inheritance in England, 1300–1800.* Chapel Hill: University of North Carolina Press, 1993.

Steggle, Matthew. "John Marston's *Entertainment at Ashby* and the 1606 Fleet Conduit Eclogue." *Medieval and Renaissance Drama in England* 19 (2006): 249–55.

Stone, Lawrence. *The Crisis of the Aristocracy, 1558–1641.* Oxford, UK: Oxford University Press, 1965.

———. *The Family, Sex and Marriage in England, 1500–1800.* New York: Harper & Row, 1977.

Stretton, Tim. *Women Waging Law in Elizabethan England.* Cambridge, UK: Cambridge University Press, 1998.

Strong, Roy. *Henry, Prince of Wales, and England's Lost Renaissance.* London: Thames and Hudson, 1986.

Szőnyi, György. *John Dee's Occultism: Magical Exaltation Through Powerful Signs.* New York: State University of New York Press, 2004.

Tabor, Stephen. "The Bridgewater Library." In *Pre-Nineteenth-Century British Book Collectors and Bibliographers*, edited by William Baker and Kenneth Womack. Detroit: Gale Group, 1999, 40–50.

Thomas, Keith. *The Ends of Life: Roads to Fulfilment in Early Modern England.* Oxford, UK: Oxford University Press, 2009.

———. *Religion and the Decline of Magic: Studies in Popular Beliefs in Sixteenth- and Seventeenth-Century England.* Oxford, UK: Oxford University Press, 1971.

Thornton, Tim. *Cheshire and the Tudor State, 1480–1560.* Suffolk: Boydell Press, 2000.

Thrush, Andrew, and John Ferris, eds. *The History of Parliament: The House of Commons, 1604–1629.* Cambridge, UK: Cambridge University Press, 2010.

Tomaselli, Sylvana, and Roy Porter, eds. *Rape: An Historical and Social Enquiry.* New York: Basil Blackwell, 1986.

Travistsky, Betty S., and Adele F. Seeff, eds. *Attending to Women in Early Modern England.* Newark: University of Delaware Press, 1994.

Travistsky, Betty, ed. *The Paradise of Women: Writings by Englishwomen of the Renaissance.* London: Greenwood Press, 1981.

Vernon, W. F. "The Parish Church of Harefield, Middlesex, and the Manor of Moor Hall," *Archaeological Journal* 36, no. 1 (1879): 145–53.

Vickery, Amanda. "Golden Age to Separate Spheres? A Review of the Categories and Chronology of English Women's History." *Historical Journal* 36, no. 2 (1993): 383–414.

Walker, Garthine. "Expanding the Boundaries of Female Honour in Early Modern England." *Transactions of the Royal Historical Society,* 6th series, no. 6 (1996): 235–45.

——. "Rereading Rape and Sexual Violence in Early Modern England." *Gender and History* 10, no. 1 (April 1998): 1–25.

Walker, Katharine. "The Widowhood of Alice Spencer, Countess Dowager of Derby, 1594–1636." *Transactions of the Historic Society of Lancashire and Cheshire* 149 (2000): 1–17.

Walsh, William Shepard. *Heroes and Heroines of Fiction.* Philadelphia: J. B. Lippincott, 1914.

Warnicke, Retha. *Women of the English Renaissance and Reformation.* Westport, CT: Greenwood Press, 1983.

Weitz Miller, Nancy. "Chastity, Rape, and Ideology in the Castlehaven Testimonies and Milton's Ludlow *Mask.*" *Milton Studies* 32 (1995): 153–68.

White, Adam. "*The Booke of Monuments* Reconsidered: Maximilian Colt and William Wright." *Church Monuments: The Journal of the Church Monument Society* 9 (1994): 62–67.

——. "Maximilian Colt: Master Sculptor to King James I." *Proceedings of the Huguenot Society* 27, no. 1 (1998): 36–48.

Wiesner-Hanks, Merry. *Women and Gender in Early Modern Europe.* Cambridge, UK: Cambridge University Press, 2008.

Wilding, Michael. "Milton's 'A Masque Presented at Ludlow Castle, 1634': Theatre and Politics on the Border." *Milton Quarterly* 21, no. 4 (1987): 35–51.

Wilkie, Vanessa. "The Context for the Text: The Masque Entertainments of the Egerton-Hastings Family," *Huntington Library Quarterly* 83, no. 2 (Spring 2020): 291–304.

——. "'Here Every Dust Would Make History': The Dowager Countess of Derby and Constructing a Legacy in Reformation England." *Historical Research* 92, no. 257 (August 2019): 500–14.

Williams, Carolyn D. "'Silence, like a Lucrece Knife': Shakespeare and the Meanings of Rape." *Yearbook of English Studies* 23 (1993): 93–110.

Wilson, Richard. *Secret Shakespeare: Studies in Theatre, Religion and Resistance.* Manchester, UK: Manchester University Press, 2004.

Woodbridge, Linda. *Women and the English Renaissance: Literature and the Nature of Womankind, 1540–1620.* Urbana: University of Illinois Press, 1984.

Wordie, J. R. "The Chronology of English Enclosure, 1500–1914." *Economic History Review* 36, 2nd ser., no. 4 (1983): 483–505.

Wright, Nancy, Margaret Ferguson, and A. R. Buck, eds. *Women, Property, and the Letters of the Law in Early Modern England.* Toronto: University of Toronto Press, 2004.

Wrightson, Keith. *English Society, 1580–1680.* New Brunswick, NJ: Rutgers University Press, 1982.

Wrigley, E. A. "Small-Scale but Not Parochial: The Work of the Cambridge Group for the History of Population and Social Structure." *Family and Community History* 1 (1998): 27–36.

Yamamoto-Wilson, John. "Shakespeare and Catholicism." *Reformation and Renaissance Review* 7, nos. 2–3 (2005): 347–61.

Young, Michael. *James VI and I and the History of Homosexuality.* Basingstoke, UK: Macmillan, 1999.

UNPUBLISHED DISSERTATIONS

Wilkie, Vanessa. "'Such Daughters and Such a Mother': The Countess of Derby and her Three Daughters, 1560–1647." PhD diss., University of California—Riverside, 2009.

INDEX

Note: Please refer to the Family Trees on pages ix–xvi
for additional information.